A WORLD TRANSFORMED

Related Titles from Heyday Books

General Vallejo and the Advent of the Americans
by Alan Rosenus, 312 pages, paperback, with black & white photos
ISBN: 1-890771-21-X, $16.95

"The definitive biography of one of California's most baffling figures."—*Choice*

Gold Rush: A Literary Exploration
Edited by Michael Kowalewski, 500 pages, paperback, with black & white photos, illustrations, ISBN: 0-930588-99-1, $18.48

"A remarkable gathering of the very best writings that encompass the gold rush, before, during, and after."—Dr. J. S. Holliday, author, *The World Rushed In: The California Gold Rush Experience*

Life in a California Mission: Monterey in 1786
by Jean François de La Pérouse, Introduction and Commentary by Malcolm Margolin, 112 pages, paperback, with black & white illustrations, ISBN: 0-930588-39-8, $8.95

"A remarkable essay on the nature and character of mission life in California."—*AB Bookman's Weekly*

No Rooms of Their Own: Women Writers of Early California, 1849–1869
Edited by Ida Rae Egli, 368 pages, paperback, with black & white photos
ISBN: 1-890771-01-5, $14.95

"The journal entries, stories and poems by fifteen mid-19th-century California women offer fresh and immediate perspectives on their lives and times."—*Publishers Weekly*

A World Transformed

Firsthand Accounts of California
Before the Gold Rush

Edited with Introduction by Joshua Paddison

HEYDAY BOOKS
BERKELEY, CALIFORNIA

Library of Congress Cataloging-in-Publication Data

A world transformed : firsthand accounts of California before the Gold Rush / edited with an introduction by Joshua Paddison.
    p.   cm.
Includes bibliographical references and index.
ISBN 1-890771-13-9 (pbk.)
  1. California—History—To 1846—Sources. 2. California—History—1846–1850—Sources. 3. California—Biography. I. Paddison, Joshua, 1974– .
F864.W945 1998
979.4'03—dc21

                             98-41579
                                CIP

Front cover painting: "The Golden Gate (Looking in)," 1880, by Raymond Dabb Yelland, courtesy of Garzoli Gallery, San Rafael, CA.
Front cover map: "Plano del Puerto de San Francisco," 1776, by José de Canizares, courtesy of The Bancroft Library
Cover Design: Rebecca LeGates
Interior Design/Typesetting: Rebecca LeGates
Printing and Binding: Publishers Press, Salt Lake City, Utah

Orders, inquiries, and correspondence should be addressed to:
Heyday Books
P. O. Box 9145, Berkeley, CA 94709
510/549-3564, Fax 510/549-1889
heyday@heydaybooks.com

Printed in the United States of America

10 9 8 7 6 5 4 3 2

TABLE OF CONTENTS

———✦———

ACKNOWLEDGMENTS

This book was begun in a somewhat different form by Roger W. Olmsted in 1984, and his detailed research notes served as my starting point and an invaluable resource. In particular, the chapters on Vancouver, Chamisso, Beechey, and Simpson owe much to his fine scholarship. Peter Johnstone acted as my sounding board throughout the formation of this book; he read much of the material, offered suggestions, and, over the course of many hours of conversation, helped me develop ideas and sustained me with his encouragement. Richard J. Orsi and Marlene Smith-Baranzini read the book's introduction and provided feedback, pointing me toward new and better sources. Jeannie Bruland also read the introduction, as well as provided help with the glossary of Spanish terms and nearly a year's worth of unfailing support and encouragement. Malcolm Margolin's insight, good humor, and wise editing guided and improved this project from beginning to end. Julianna Fleming handled proofreading, production, and permissions with grace and aplomb, and compiled the book's glossary of Spanish terms. Rebecca LeGates created the interior and cover designs, as well as the maps. Kent Lightfoot provided additional information for the timeline. Alex Walker, Caroline Knapp, Cynthia Harrington, Elizabeth Campbell, and Michelle Nixon helped with scanning, proofreading, photo research,

A World Transformed

and production. Thanks also to Amy Hunter and everyone else at Heyday Books.

Thanks to the following individuals and institutions who provided photographic or literary materials: Susan Snyder, Jack Von Euw, and the entire staff of The Bancroft Library; Patricia Keats and Scott A. Shields at the California Historical Society; Sandy Taugher at the California State Museum Resource Center; Jennifer Watts and Jennifer Martinez at The Huntington Library; Henry S. Dakin and North Point Gallery; Marlene Smith-Baranzini at *California History* journal; California History Section, California State Library; The San Mateo Historical Association; Frank Stanger; Clara Grant; Donald C. Cutter; and Henry Kratz.

Finally, I would like to thank Jay Mullen, Gary Ghidinelli, and Glenn May, three historians and educators who inspired me.

Joshua Paddison

INTRODUCTION

———⟶⟶●⟵⟵———

The recent sesquicentennial (150th) anniversary of the California gold rush has focused much popular and scholarly attention on the tumultuous years 1849 and 1850. Certainly, as many have pointed out, the influx of more than 300,000 gold seekers from every continent on earth had a dramatic effect on the region's culture, economy, and environment. Ship after ship from Boston, Shanghai, Paris, and Valparaíso sailed into San Francisco Bay filled with ambitious—often voracious—young men; metropolises sprung up seemingly overnight; rivers were rerouted and mountainsides torn apart with, in the mournful words of John Muir, "a fierce and desperate energy hard to understand." About $400 million in gold (worth more than $6 billion today) was carried off by miners between 1849 and 1855, much of it spent in California at supply stores, gambling halls, saloons, and brothels built by gleeful entrepreneurs eager to make a profit from the miners' labor.[1] Half legitimate opportunity, half mass hysteria, the gold rush emphatically and irreversibly reshaped California.

However, as the title of this anthology suggests, by the time of the gold rush California was a world already transformed. Eighty years of Spanish, Russian, Mexican, and American intrusion had changed the region as significantly and pervasively as did the subsequent gold rush. In fact, many of the attitudes historians ascribe to the forty-niners—an aggressive entrepreneurial spirit, a utilitarian view of nature, violence and racism toward indigenous peoples—had already been brought to California by the missionaries, merchants, settlers, and soldiers who trickled into the region between 1769 and 1848 and settled there. A relatively gradual but inexorable Europeanization process was quickened in the 1840s when ever-increasing numbers of trappers, homesteaders, traders, and military men from the U.S. penetrated California's borders. By the time of the gold discovery in January 1848, California was already a thoroughly American terrain. The gold rush did bring profound changes to the state, mostly due to an astounding increase in population in a few short years, but the underlying attitudes, institutions, and structure of commerce were already in place. The rush for gold merely escalated the Americanization process. In short, unlike the Roman goddess Minerva who appears on the state seal, modern California was not born full formed in 1849 but traces its roots to the Europeans, Mexicans, and Americans who had colonized, converted, and conquered it in preceding decades.

California's first settlers—the remarkably diverse group of people later known as "Indians"—came into the region in successive waves beginning more than 10,000 years ago. Moving out over the state, these explorers eventually made their homes in the disparate beaches, mountains, valleys, deserts, and forests of California. Over the course of thousands of years, they evolved into more than 500 separate tribal groups, dizzying in their variety of language, custom, dress, and religion.[2] Using hunting, gathering, fishing, and agriculture, they ingeniously learned to harvest California's natural resources. Most groups dried, shelled, ground, and cooked acorns into soup and bread. Some caught trout, salmon, and ocean fish with harpoons and nets, or gathered shellfish from ocean beaches. Others hunted deer, elk, waterfowl, and rabbits with bow and obsidian-tipped arrows, a difficult endeavor that demanded cooperation, stealth, and strong nerves. Communication, trade, and intermarriage between groups was widespread, despite their speaking about 100 mutually unintelligible languages. By the time of European contact, California was the most densely populated area north of Mexico.[3]

Far from living in a "wilderness," native Californians continually tended and cultivated the land through controlled burnings, weeding, pruning, tilling, irrigation, and selective replanting. They usually altered the landscape in a manner that imitated nature itself. "When the Western Mono lit hillsides on fire to encourage the growth of young redbud shrub shoots for basketry, they simulated lightning fires. When the Washoe pruned willow, they mimicked the natural pruning caused by river flooding," note anthropologists M. Kat Anderson and co-authors. "By listening to the land's daily rhythms, scheduling activities according to its seasonal cycles, and always adjusting to California's continually changing environment, Native Americans transformed their status from newcomer to native and in doing so transformed the land and life forms as well."[4]

California remained isolated from Europe and Asia until the early sixteenth century, when Spain, having already established a colonial system in the Caribbean, sent a war expedition into Mexico led by *conquistador* Hernán Cortés. He captured and plundered the Aztec capital of Tenochtitlán (later called Mexico City) in 1521, and it became the hub of Spanish colonialism in the New World. Hoping to find a waterway from the Pacific to the Atlantic and spurred on by Indian legends of a golden city called El Dorado, Spain dispatched Juan Rodríguez Cabrillo in 1542 to explore the northwest coast of "New Spain." In September Cabrillo became the first Spaniard to glimpse Alta (or upper) California. In 1579 the notorious

British pirate and "sea dog" Francis Drake anchored his ship, the *Golden Hind,* somewhere near San Francisco Bay, most likely at present-day Drake's Bay.[5] He and subsequent ship captains would miss the narrow entrance to San Francisco due to persistent fogs and the obscuring locations of Alcatraz and Angel islands. As a result, San Francisco Bay remained unknown to European navigators for nearly two more centuries.[6]

Early descriptions of California were favorable but unenthusiastic, and Spain was unready and unwilling to invest the money, ships, supplies, and people necessary to settle such a far-flung land already inhabited by possibly warlike Indians. In the 1580s and 1590s, only the Manila galleons—annual treasure ships laden with Asian silks, spices, and gems on their way from the Philippines to Acapulco—sailed the California coast. Their grueling voyage usually took six or seven months, and their crews had to endure starvation, scurvy, and pirate attacks. Spain considered establishing a port somewhere in California to shelter and resupply its galleons, and in 1602 commissioned a merchant-adventurer named Sebastián Vizcaíno to explore and map the coastline. Fearing that he might not receive his promised recompense from Conde de Monterrey, the viceroy of New Spain, if he did not return with a glowing report, Vizcaíno exaggerated California's charms. Eager to "discover" a suitable harbor, he absurdly proclaimed rocky and exposed Monterey Bay to be "the best port that could be desired" and named it after the viceroy.[7] Ironically, he too passed by magnificent San Francisco Bay without realizing it.

Despite Vizcaíno's praise, Spain decided Alta California was too close to Mexico to warrant the establishment of a port, yet at the same time too far to colonize; in 1606 a royal order was issued prohibiting further exploration. Settlement eventually did proceed after 1697 in Baja where the Roman Catholic Society of Jesus (commonly called the Jesuits) founded twenty missions up and down the narrow peninsula. The mission system—springing equally from political, economic, and religious motivations—was Spain's centuries-old method of advancing and securing its colonial frontier by luring, Christianizing, and Hispanicizing native peoples. Lacking sufficient settlers, Spain needed Indians to colonize new lands and provide a labor force to sustain its colonies. In addition to outposts on the Baja Peninsula, by the mid-eighteenth century Spain had established a scattering of missions throughout the present-day states of Florida, Texas, New Mexico, and Arizona.

As for Alta California, Spain turned its back on it for an amazing 167 years after the Vizcaíno expedition; only competition from Great Britain and Russia in the 1760s finally prompted it to "defensively expand" up the California coast. The Jesuits had been recently expelled from the New World for plotting against the crown, so colonization was carried out by the Franciscans, who established Alta California's first mission (Mission San Diego de Alcalá) in 1769. By 1823, the Franciscans had founded twenty-one missions that extended from San Diego to Sonoma. In the course of their sixty-five years of operation, the missions of Alta California employed 142 Catholic missionaries and baptized 53,600 Indians.

A mission was at once a church, town, military fortress, school, farm, factory, and prison, typically maintained by two missionaries and a handful of armed soldiers. They were sometimes located near a *presidio* (a frontier military fort that symbolically guarded the land against foreign attacks and protected mission padres against Indian resistance) and a *pueblo* (a secular agricultural community, such as Los Angeles, San José, or San Luis Obispo). The *padres* attracted most of their Indian converts (called neophytes) through beads (i.e. money), food, and other gifts. Once baptized, however, neophytes could be held at missions against their will while *padres* attempted to regulate nearly every aspect of their lives, including sex, work, sleep, amusement, and religious practice.

Neophytes who resisted were lashed, pilloried, or chained in stocks; those who fled were apprehended by soldiers and forcibly returned. Every mission was supposedly temporary, its land to be turned over to the now "educated" Indians after ten years of mission training, but in reality the padres retained control until forced secularization in 1834.[8]

The missionaries in California were by-and-large well-meaning, devoted men. Born mostly in Spain, they were attracted to the adventure and glory of distant mission work. Attitudes toward the Indians ranged from genuine (if paternalistic) affection to wrathful disgust. They were ill-equipped—nor did most truly desire—to understand complex and radically different Native American customs. Using European standards, they condemned the Indians for living in a "wilderness," for worshipping false gods or no God at all, and for having no written laws, standing armies, forts, or churches.[9] "I might inquire what sin was committed by these Indians and their ancestors that they should grow up in these remote lands of the north with such infelicity and unhappiness, in such nakedness and misery, and above all, with such blind ignorance of everything that they do not even know the transitory conveniences of the earth in order to obtain them," wrote Father Pedro Font while traveling from Mexico to San Francisco Bay in 1776. "[Nor] do they have any knowledge of the existence of God, but live like beasts without making use of reason or discourse, and being distinguished from beasts only by possessing the bodily human form, but not from their deeds."[10] Given attitudes such as this, it was perhaps tragically inevitable that the culture clash between missionaries and Indians would be so destructive.

These missionaries, along with the soldiers, merchants, and settlers who emigrated to California before 1848, brought terrible changes to its Indian population. The biggest impact came inadvertently in the form of European germs and microbes unknown to

North American immune systems. Smallpox, influenza, dysentery, malaria, measles, and syphilis ravaged entire tribal groups, especially women and children. Although all twenty-one missions were located within thirty miles of the Pacific coastline, California's Indian population, which numbered about 310,000 before Spanish intrusion, was reduced to about 100,000 by 1848 as disease spread widely. British trapper J. J. Warner, while trekking through the San Joaquin Valley in 1833, miles from the nearest mission, reported that "the decaying [Indian] bodies compelled us nightly to pitch our tents in the open prairie."[11]

Life was especially hard at the missions, where poor sanitation, overcrowding, malnutrition, and depression produced staggering death rates. For example, a measles epidemic from 1806 to 1810 killed more than one-third of the neophytes at the San Francisco-area missions, including almost every child. After the missions were secularized by the Mexican government in 1834, those Indians who survived were forced to either flee to remote interior valleys or try to assimilate into a society of Spanish- and English-speaking strangers who did not welcome them—except as servants.[12]

The disintegration of Indian culture went hand in hand with drastic changes wrought on California's environment. Foreign germs, grasses, and animals—already intermittently introduced by such early European visitors as Cabrillo, Drake, and Vizcaíno—forever altered Californian flora and fauna after Spanish colonization in 1769. Hardy Mediterranean weeds and annuals replaced native grasses in California's extensive grasslands. Enormous herds of domesticated animals (including cattle, mules, sheep, goats, and pigs) consumed millions of acres of grasses and eroded hillsides and stream banks.[13] Horses, in particular, brought sweeping changes to Indian culture—many groups in the San Joaquin Valley and the southeast, once mounted, became more warlike; others began to rely on horse meat as a dietary staple.[14] As thousands upon thousands of Indians died from diseases, California's ecosystems spiraled out of balance. With fewer human hunters to thin their numbers, rodents, deer, antelope, and elk multiplied exponentially as they gorged on new European grasses. Grizzly bear populations also grew as they began to include domesticated animals in their diet.[15]

Many of California's European and American immigrants brought an exploitative attitude toward the natural world along with their livestock, axes, and guns. Fur trappers hunted sea and river otters, seals, beaver, and mink to near-extinction along the coast and in interior valleys. Settlers chopped down forests, exacerbating flooding. Mission *padres* and farmers often used destructive irrigation and plowing techniques that hastened soil erosion.[16]

Much of this environmental degradation came with the increased trade and commerce that rose in California, especially after Mexico gained its independence from Spain in 1821. Although California had no factories, mines, or much of a transportation system until the 1840s, it could produce plenty of raw materials like cattle hides, tallow, animal pelts, grain, and vegetables to trade with nearby Russian settlements and foreign ships. In their heyday, the missions used Indian labor to manufacture pottery, leather goods, blankets, rope, candles, wine, and simple furniture and clothing. These goods were not made for export but for trade with Spanish soldiers and settlers at local *presidios* and *pueblos.* After secularization of the missions came the rise of the great Californio *ranchos,* which grazed millions of head of cattle for the expanding hide-and-tallow trade. Whereas California's first non-Indian immigrants were soldiers and missionaries who came from a mix of political and religious motivations, by the 1820s, 1830s, and 1840s, most immigrants came for economic reasons—fur trappers from Russia, merchants from Europe and New England, farmers from the Midwest, and sailors from Boston on hide-and-tallow brigs.[17]

Decades before the gold rush, California was viewed by outsiders as a land of opportunity, possessing abundant natural resources, a warm climate, and little governmental control. A series of favorable reports from early European visitors such as Jean François de La Pérouse (1786) and George Vancouver (1792–1794) and later American ones such as Richard Henry Dana, Jr. (1835–1836) and John C. Frémont (1844–1846) increased U.S. knowledge of and interest in the region. Presidents Andrew Jackson and James Polk unsuccessfully tried to buy California from Mexico in 1835 and 1845, respectively, before Polk took it through war in 1846–1848. Americans had been steadily infiltrating California for twenty years, first as trappers, sailors, and mountain men and later as merchants, farmers, and soldiers. By the time American visitor Edwin Bryant arrived in September 1846, he heard more English spoken in San Francisco than Spanish. He described a dinner party where "it was very difficult for me to realize that I was many thousand miles from home, in a strange and foreign country. All the faces about me were American, and there was nothing in scene or sentiment to remind the guests of their remoteness from their native shores. Indeed, it seems to be a settled opinion that California is henceforth to compose a part of the United States, and every American who is now here considers himself as treading upon his own soil, as much as if he were in one of the old thirteen revolutionary states."[18] California, tended by the Indians for millennia, had gone from Spanish to Mexican to American control in one human lifetime—eighty short years.

All of the accounts that appear in this anthology were written by visitors to the San Francisco Bay Area, for the changes that occurred there are typical of those that occurred throughout the state. Once home to the Patwin, Wappo, Plains Miwok, Bay Miwok, and

Ohlone Indian language groups, the San Francisco Bay Area has always been a particularly diverse and important region.[19] It was home to five of California's twenty-one missions (San Francisco de Asís, Santa Clara de Asís, San José de Guadalupe, San Rafael Arcángel, and San Francisco Solano de Sonoma), one of its four *presidios* (San Francisco), and its first Spanish *pueblo* (San José). The town of Yerba Buena, eventually renamed San Francisco, was founded in 1835 and later became the state's largest city and chief port. Otter was hunted in San Francisco Bay; cattle grazed in its fields. It was a popular visiting place for sea captains exploring in the North Pacific and emigrants fresh from the Oregon or California trails. Its transformation from a mosaic of Indian territories in 1769 to the home of a booming American metropolis in 1848 is indicative of the unfolding of all of California.

Located on the furthest reaches of the western frontier, shielded behind miles of inhospitable desert and rugged mountain ranges, laborious to reach by ship or wagon train, pre-gold rush California attracted extreme personalities: zealous missionaries deep in a foreign land, grim sea captains on their way around the globe, adventurous mountain men seeking beaver furs, beleaguered Mormons eager to escape eastern discrimination, and restless settlers drawn by "manifest destiny" to the wide-open opportunities of the West. Mostly male, mostly young, a remarkable number of these men went mad, died prematurely, or both. Their accounts are rife with biases, both cultural and personal. Their understanding was usually limited to what they saw and heard with their own eyes and ears, often leading to incomplete, misleading, or incorrect notions. What they actually wrote down on paper and allowed to be published, often selective and self-serving, was another step removed from reality.

On the other hand, there is an unparalleled immediacy and excitement contained within these firsthand narratives. With a couple of exceptions that were written later, these are the transformers of California describing their actions in their own words, more or less as events happened.

Part I of this book contains the diaries of Spanish missionaries as they first explored California in the 1770s, encountered its often bewildering animals and people, and sized up its resources. As the explorers traveled, they engaged in the first step of colonization—giving Spanish names to the rivers, mountains, and other features of California's natural world. Part II is made up of the travel accounts of Europeans and Russians who visited San Francisco Bay between 1776 and 1816. As outsiders, they offer valuable descriptions of the isolation and harshness of life (for mission Indians and Spanish residents alike) during Spanish control. Part IV shows how trade and commerce came to be more and more prevalent in the 1820s, 1830s, and 1840s as California fell first into Mexican and then American hands. The accounts in this section increasingly reflect the interests of merchants rather than missionaries or military leaders. Their writings make it clear that, more than any other force, it was trade and commerce that transformed California.

Each account provides a snapshot in time and space. Read together, they form a tale, epic in scope, of the triumphs and excesses that went into the making of modern California.

Joshua Paddison
San Francisco
January 1999

Notes

1. Michael Kowalewski, "Introduction," *Gold Rush: A Literary Exploration* (Berkeley: Heyday Books, 1997), xv. See also J. S. Holliday, *The World Rushed In: The California Gold Rush Experience* (New York: Simon and Schuster, 1981); Malcolm Rohrbough, *Days of Gold: The California Gold Rush and the American Nation* (Berkeley: University of California Press, 1997); and Gary F. Kurutz, *The California Gold Rush: A Descriptive Bibliography* (San Francisco: The Book Club of California, 1997).

2. Malcolm Margolin, "Introduction," *The Way We Lived: California Indian Stories, Songs & Reminiscences*, Second edition (Berkeley: Heyday Books and the California Historical Society, 1993), 2–6.

3. The best sources on California Indian culture include A. L. Kroeber, *Handbook of the Indians of California* (Washington: Smithsonian Institution, 1925); Robert F. Heizer, *Handbook of North American Indians: Volume 8, California* (Washington: Smithsonian Institution, 1978); Robert F. Heizer and M. A. Whipple, *The California Indians: A Source Book,* Second edition (Berkeley: University of California Press, 1971); and Lowell J. Bean, "Indians of California: Diverse and Complex People," *California History* LXXI (Fall 1992): 302–323.

4. M. Kat Anderson, Michael G. Barbour, and Valerie Whitworth, "A World of Balance and Plenty: Land, Plants, Animals, and Humans in a Pre-European California," *Contested Eden: California Before the Gold Rush,* Edited by Ramón A. Gutiérrez and Richard J. Orsi (Berkeley: University of California Press, 1997), 14, 16. The endnotes to this essay and others in *Contested Eden* provide the most up-to-date and comprehensive bibliography available on early California.

5. Richard B. Rice, William A. Bullough, and Richard J. Orsi, *The Elusive Eden: A New History of California*, Second edition (New York: McGraw-Hill, 1996), 69–77.

6. Frank M. Stanger and Alan K. Brown, *Who Discovered the Golden Gate?* (San Mateo, CA: San Mateo Historical Society, 1969), 4.

7. James J. Rawls and Walton Bean, *California: An Interpretive History*, Sixth edition (New York: McGraw-Hill, 1993), 14–17.

8. James J. Rawls, *Indians of California: The Changing History* (Norman: University of Oklahoma Press, 1984), 14–18; Malcolm Margolin, "Introduction," *Life in a California Mission: Monterey in 1786* (Berkeley: Heyday Books, 1989), 27–30; and *California: An Interpretive History*, 17–19.

9. *Life in a California Mission*, 35–37. See also Maynard Geiger and Clement W. Meighan, editors, *As the Padres Saw Them: California Indian Life and Customs as Reported by the Franciscan Missionaries, 1813–1815* (Santa Barbara: Santa Barbara Mission Archive Library, 1976).

10. Quoted in James A. Lewis, "The Natives as Seen by the Missionaries: Preconception and Reality," *The Missions of California: A Legacy of Genocide*, Edited by Rupert Costo and Jeannette Henry Costo (San Francisco: Indian Historian Press, 1987), 82.

11. Quoted in *The Elusive Eden*, 106.

12. The best sources on the impact of colonialism on the California Indians include Sherburne F. Cook, *The Conflict Between the California Indian and White Civilization: The Indian Versus the Spanish Mission* (Berkeley: University of California Press, 1943); George Harwood Phillips, *The Enduring Struggle: Indians in California History* (San Francisco: Boyd and Fraser, 1981); Robert H. Jackson and Edward Castillo, *Indians, Franciscans, and Spanish Colonization: The Impact of the Mission System on California Indians* (Albuquerque: University of New Mexico Press, 1995); Albert L. Hurtado, *Indian Survival on the California Frontier* (New Haven: Yale University Press, 1988); and James A. Sandos, "Between Crucifix and Lance: Indian-White Relations in California, 1769–1848," *Contested Eden*, 196–229.

13. William Preston, "Serpent in the Garden: Environmental Change in Colonial California," *Contested Eden*, 267–275. See also Raymond F. Dasmann, *The Destruction of California* (New York: Collier Books, 1966); and Elna Bakker, *An Island Called California: An Ecological Introduction to its Natural Communities*, Second edition (Berkeley: University of California Press, 1984).

14. *The Elusive Eden*, 104–106.

15. William Preston, "Serpent in the Garden: Environmental Change in Colonial California," *Contested Eden*, 277–281.

16. *The Elusive Eden*, 100–101.

17. Steven W. Hackel, "Land, Labor, and Production: The Colonial Economy of Spanish and Mexican California," *Contested Eden*, 111–146; and *The Elusive Eden*, 96–97. See also Robert Archibald, *The Economic Aspects of the California Missions* (Washington, D.C.: Academy of American Franciscan History, 1978).

18. Edwin Bryant, *What I Saw in California: Being a Journal of a Tour, by the Emigrant Route and South Pass of the Rocky Mountains, Across the Continent of North America, the Great Desert Basin, and Through California, in the Years 1846–1847* (New York: D. Appleton & Company, 1848), 327.

19. Randall Milliken, *A Time of Little Choice: The Disintegration of Tribal Culture in the San Francisco Bay Area, 1769–1810* (Menlo Park, CA: Ballena Press, 1995), 13.

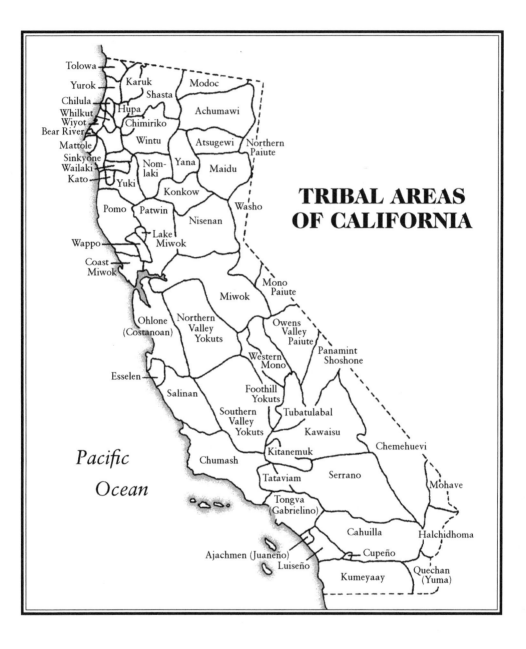

TRIBAL AREAS
OF CALIFORNIA

Tolowa
Yurok
Chilula
Whilkut
Wiyot
Bear River
Mattole
Sinkyone
Wailaki
Kato
Karuk
Shasta
Hupa
Chimiriko
Wintu
Nomlaki
Yuki
Konkow
Pomo
Patwin
Wappo
Lake Miwok
Coast Miwok
Ohlone (Costanoan)
Esselen
Salinan
Modoc
Achumawi
Atsugewi
Northern Paiute
Yana
Maidu
Nisenan
Washo
Northern Valley Yokuts
Miwok
Mono Paiute
Owens Valley Paiute
Panamint Shoshone
Western Mono
Foothill Yokuts
Southern Valley Yokuts
Tubatulabal
Kawaisu
Chemehuevi
Chumash
Kitanemuk
Tataviam
Serrano
Mohave
Tongva (Gabrielino)
Ajachmen (Juaneño)
Luiseño
Cahuilla
Cupeño
Kumeyaay
Halchidhoma
Quechan (Yuma)

Pacific Ocean

CALIFORNIA 1769–1848

- ■ Missions
- ▲ PRESIDIOS
- ◆ Pueblos and Other Settlements

Fort Ross (1812) ◆   ◆ Sutter's Fort (1839)
■ San Francisco Solano de Sonoma (1823)
San Rafael Arcángel (1817) ■   Sonoma (1835)
SAN FRANCISCO ▲   Yerba Buena/San Francisco (1835)
San Francisco de Asís (1776) ■   ■ San José de Guadalupe (1797)
Santa Clara de Asís (1777) ■   ■ San José (1777)
Santa Cruz (1791) ■   ◆ Branciforte (1797)
■ San Juan Bautista (1797)
MONTEREY ▲
San Carlos Borromeo (1770) ■   ■ Nuestra Señora de la Soledad (1791)
San Antonio de Padua (1771) ■   ■ San Miguel Arcángel (1797)
■ San Luis Obispo de Tolosa (1772)
Santa Ines (1804) ■   ■ La Purísima Concepción (1787)
SANTA BARBARA ▲   ■ ▲ Santa Barbara (1782)
San Buenaventura (1782) ■
◆ ▲ San Fernando Rey de España (1797)
■ San Gabriel Arcángel (1771)
Los Angeles (1781) ◆
■ San Juan Capistrano (1776)
■ San Luis Rey de Francia (1798)

**Pacific
Ocean**

■ San Diego de Alcala (1769)
▲ SAN DIEGO

PART I:

EARLY EXPLORATIONS

"The Indians who came on this occasion were nine in number....They were by no means filthy, and the best favored were models of perfection; among them was a boy whose exceeding beauty stole my heart. One alone of the young men had several dark blue lines painted from the lower lip to the waist and from the left shoulder to the right, in such a way as to form a perfect cross. God grant that we may see them worshipping so sovereign an emblem."

—Father Vicente Santa María, 1775

JUAN CRESPÍ
1769

After neglecting California for nearly 170 years, Spain was finally compelled in 1765 to turn its attention once again to the region, as it suddenly had two foreign competitors with which to contend. Great Britain, victorious two years earlier in the Seven Years' War, had seized Florida from Spain and now controlled the entire east coast of North America. Rumors began circulating that Britain—expanding everywhere—was exploring as widely as the North Pole. And word spread through Europe that Russia, already hunting sea otters in Alaska, was looking to extend its fur-trading business down the Pacific coast toward Monterey Bay. Alta California, claimed by Spain but never colonized, seemed ripe for the taking by one of these foreign powers.

The job of "defensively expanding" into Alta California fell to José de Gálvez, an accomplished but mentally unstable Spanish-born diplomat. Under the title *visitador-general,* * Gálvez established a new port at San Blas, Mexico, specifically to serve as a supply depot for his proposed California settlements. He then arranged to send a "sacred expedition" (three ships and two overland parties) up the Pacific coast to construct missions and *presidios* at California's two

---

* See glossary, p. 337, for definition and translation of Spanish terms.

3

known harbors, San Diego and Monterey. This daunting task, considered hopeless by many in New Spain, might never have been attempted without Gálvez's brilliance, zeal, and near-obsession. Convinced he could speak directly to God and from time to time overtaken by bouts of temporary insanity, Gálvez once toyed with the idea of training 600 Guatemalan apes as soldiers against rebellious Indians. Some thought the idea of colonizing remote Alta California was equally outlandish.

Gálvez's plan for the "sacred expedition" was five-pronged. Three hastily constructed ships (the *San Carlos*, the *San Antonio*, and the *San José*), carrying supplies and more than 100 experienced sailors, would sail independently from the Baja Peninsula in early 1769. Meanwhile, two more parties, outfitted with priests, furniture, vestments, and livestock from the Baja missions, would make their way overland. If all went according to plan, all five parts of the expedition—including more than 300 soldiers, sailors, carpenters, cooks, Christianized Indians, and priests, along with a huge herd of horses, cattle, and mules—were to converge on San Diego Bay by early summer.

The "sacred expedition" was led by Captain Gaspar de Portolá and Franciscan Father Junípero Serra. Portolá, the fifty-year-old governor of Baja, was loyal and aristocratic; unfortunately, he was not an experienced explorer nor particularly comfortable in the wilderness. Serra, himself age fifty-five, possessed a remarkable intelligence (he was once a professor of philosophy in his native Majorca) and a fiery religious fervor (he longed to one day die a martyr), but also a swollen and ulcerated foot that required a slow pace and frequent rides in a stretcher. Portolá brought along a group of Baja mission Indians in the misguided hope that they would act as interpreters or even fledgling missionaries.

As an omen of things to come, the *San Carlos*, the *San Antonio*, and the *San José* all reached Baja from San Blas in wretched condition and had to be repaired before the longer journey could begin. The three ships sailed separately for San Diego in early 1769, and the two overland parties followed. The first land party, led by Captain Fernando Rivera, was immediately reminded why earlier administrations had hesitated at expanding north. In their fifty-one-day journey, they struggled through inhospitable desert terrain and weathered several Indian attacks. Portolá's contingent, following Rivera's path, arrived in San Diego on July 1 only to find that the *San José* had never arrived and the crews of the other two ships were decimated from scurvy and dysentery. All told, in this first, supposedly easy leg of the journey, the "sacred expedition" had already lost half of its members (including most of the Christianized Indians, who died or deserted because the soldiers refused to share food with them).

Behind schedule and low on supplies, Portolá sent a few surviving sailors back on the *San Antonio* to San Blas for provisions. The remaining men buried their dead and foraged for food as Portolá planned his next move. He decided to lead a party north to find Monterey, leaving Serra behind to begin building Mission San Diego de Alcalá. He took along the sixty heartiest men, including Rivera, military engineer Miguel Costansó, and Father Juan Crespí.

Portolá undoubtedly had fixed in his mind explorer Sebastián Vizcaíno's exaggerated, glowing 1602 description of Monterey Bay as "the best port that could be desired, for besides being sheltered from all the winds, it has many pines for masts and yards, and live oaks and white oaks, and water in great quantity, all near the shore." So when Portolá and his men arrived at Monterey on October 1 after four months of rigorous hiking along California's rugged coast, they looked at the sparse, rocky, windy beach, decided there had been a mistake in the latitude calculations, and pressed on. These confused, half-starved conquistadors had no idea, of course, that they were a few days from the sheltered, abundant bay now known as San Francisco. Buoyed by their faith in God and occasional trade with "affable" Indians, they persevered.

Father Juan Crespí, who faithfully kept a diary of the harrowing trip, was born in Majorca in 1721. He followed his teacher Junípero Serra to Mexico in 1749, and like his teacher, he was driven to be a missionary not from any knowledge of real Indians but from an idealized vision of a missionary's life of adventure, significance, and perhaps eventual martyrdom. His diary reveals him to be perceptive, level-headed, and devout. Although the party was lost and weary, he insisted on saying Mass and giving the sacraments. He was much impressed by the abundance and diversity of California's forests, wildlife, and human inhabitants. Even in October, well into the region's dry season, Crespí found the San Francisco Bay Area to be well-watered with streams and lakes, wooded with redwoods and oaks, and inhabited by a people who were "friendly," "well-featured," and "stout." His diary provides a unique mile-by-mile view of the clearly prosperous Bay Area and its peoples just prior to Spanish colonization.

After surviving the Portolá expedition, Crespí accompanied two more exploration campaigns (another to the San Francisco Bay Area in 1772 and one to Alaska in 1774) before returning to serve with Serra at Mission San Carlos in Monterey Bay. He died there in 1782. This excerpt from his journal of the "sacred expedition" begins Sunday, October 8, 1769, near the Pajaro River (near present-day Watsonville), the confused party doggedly heading north.

Juan Crespí

Account of the "Sacred Expedition"

October 8 [1769]. After both of us[1] saying Mass and administering the viaticum [Eucharist given to a dying person] and holy oils to two buffcoat soldiers who had turned dangerously ill from scurvy, we set out about eight o'clock in the morning on a northerly course from here at the Santa Brígida pool, going through higher hills lying out from the mountains and through hollows, in order to be able to get around a throng of lakes that they said lay close to the shore and were very miry. At times we went in view of the shore, though very far away from it. We went five hours and must have made four leagues, upon which we came to the edge of a fine little river with a fair-sized bed and a great many willow trees, sycamores, and other timber. This river was not carrying much flow of water, but it has a very large bed with a great many sandbanks, which show how much it must rise at flood. The bed is not very deep, and to one side and the other of the river is a great deal of flat land of half-whitish sod, but all of it well overgrown with a great deal of tall grasses and other very lush plants, so that the soil is plainly very good despite its color, since it is clothed so. I named this place the River of Santa Ana [present-day Pajaro River, near Watsonville], a very fine place for a very large mission, with a great deal of soil and water for irrigating it, and a great amount of timber. For besides the many good-sized cottonwoods on the river, there begins here a large mountain range covered with a tree very like the pine in its leaf,

---

[1] Crespí was accompanied on the "sacred expedition" by Franciscan Father Francisco Gómez.

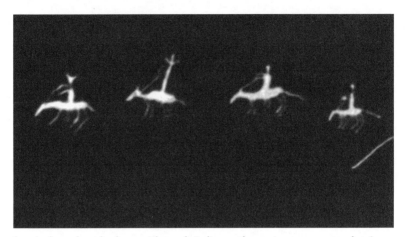

Spaniards on horseback at a Chumash Indian rock art site near present-day Santa Barbara. *Photograph from* Rock Paintings of the Chumash *(University of California Press, 1965) by Campbell Grant.*

save that this is not over two fingers long. The heartwood is red, very handsome wood, handsomer than cedar. No one knew what kind of wood it might be; it may be spruce, we cannot tell. Many said savin, and savin 'twas called, though I have never seen them red. There are great numbers of this tree here, of all sizes of thickness, most of them exceedingly high and straight like so many candles. What a pleasure to see this blessing of timber.[2]

Here at the Santa Ana River is where the scouts, when they came to explore here, found a very large heathen village at the same place where we stopped. They said there must have been over 500 souls, all of them so ill-mannered that it took them a great deal of trouble to pacify them and give them to understand that we came in peace and not to harm them. They made peace, throwing down all their weapons, but now that we have come here, the village where they were is found burned and abandoned, not a heathen in sight anywhere. The thing is a great surprise and wonder to us, for

---

[2] This is the first known European description of a redwood.

in all the way up to here we have met great numbers of heathens, all of whom were very friendly and tractable, as will appear from this, my journal. After burning and abandoning the village, they left the whole place surrounded with upright poles, which we found surrounded with arrows, and great quantities of their seeds scattered on the ground at the foot of them. Hanging on one of these poles we found half the body of a black bird with the two wings fastened together—spread out these measured thirteen *cuartas* [nine feet] from tip to tip—and because of this bird, this place of Santa Ana is known among the soldiers as the Río del Pájaro, Bird River. What I spoke of above concerning the poles, arrows, and seeds was not observed by the scouts when they came here exploring; instead, it must all have been left when the place was abandoned, a thing that has caused no small wonder among the soldiers. A soldier left behind, at a lake here, a lame, starving mule which could go no further; on our return at the end of November, he found it whole and well, and very fat from the good grass and better water it had had. Not one heathen has appeared of the many the scouts saw here. The latitude has been impossible to observe ever since we crossed the mountains because of the heavy fog overcast, with a chilliness by day and night of which there is no call to speak. It is only what is to be expected when living in the open.

October 9. We lay by at this place while they went out to explore for the following days' marches. We had been in the belief this second river must be the Carmelo, as there was a range of hills with many pine trees on it in sight nearby, which seems to run out to sea. The scouts went off to explore down the river toward the shore to see whether there were any signs of a harbor; the report they brought back was that this river empties into a large inlet, and none of the trees are to be seen down there that are spoken of in the history. They returned to explore toward the point of pine trees and still had no report of a harbor to bring back. It may be that we still have not passed the Santa Lucia Mountains and that none of the ranges behind us are they.

October 10. At about eight o'clock in the morning, we set out from here at the Santa Ana River, flat lands and savins, course northwest. The day was very overcast; the sun has hardly been seen at all for days past. We set out over flats of very good soil all covered with grass, and beyond went through very low hill ranges lying out from the mountains. The mountains are not very high or steep. We have passed a great many of the trees I spoke of—like the pine in its leaf—named savins. There are trees so extremely thick, tall, and very straight that they are a pleasure to see. We were not able to make the whole march intended because of the sick men, some six or seven of whom are turning very ill so that they cannot stay on horseback. On going about two leagues we had to stop within a hollow with a great deal of grass and good water, and much tall, thick growth of the savin trees aforesaid. We set up camp upon a little tableland next to a very good-sized spring-fed lake, and there were two good-sized springs of fine, fresh, delicious water running down from a hill.

October 11. The two of us said Mass, with special intention to St. Joseph as patron of this expedition, for the alleviation of these poor, sick men and the well-being of everyone. In my Mass I gave the sacrament to two more buffcoat soldiers, and Father Gómez, in his, gave the sacrament to another. Along the way on the last day's march they showed me various tracks that looked like cattle, and we suppose they are buffalo. I did not see any of the beasts myself, but the scouts reported that along the shore hereabouts they saw as many as twenty-one beasts together, of all colors, with calves at their feet like cows; also, that they had seen deer or stags, very big-bodied and with very large spreading antlers, like two such which I saw lying cast-off in the open beside the way on this march, and the soldiers brought along. Tracks and droppings of a mule-like creature have been seen, and at the place where we made camp here, there was a dried-up pile which I looked at a great while; the droppings are less than a horse's. The soldiers say they have seen bands of these beasts, that they are long-eared like mules, with a short, wide tail. I myself saw none of these beasts [undoubtedly elk], only the droppings mentioned.

At this place there are six quite large lakes, one after another, some amount of soil, a great deal of good grass, and many trees of the sort aforesaid, with the very handsome red heartwood, very tall and straight. Some of them are extremely thick; the soldiers measured one that was three musket-lengths in diameter. While here at this place, they have reported that there are many hills covered with hazelnut thickets throughout this vicinity, some of which they have found bearing nuts. They say it had been burned off by the heathens, and plainly when the trees were in flower. All the signs are that the harbor of Monte Rey cannot be very far; may Divine Providence grant we come upon it quickly. A soldier gave me six hazelnuts; three of the six had meat that we shared among four of us, tasted, and found good. They grow on thickets, the highest of which are a yard-and-a-half or a yard-and-three-fourths tall. As we could see, the heathens burn them [probably for basketry materials], for it was plainly not long since they had been burnt. The hazelnuts are the same as in Spain. I named this fine place the lakes and hazelnuts of Nuestra Señora del Pilar.

October 14. October 11, 12, 13, and 14 we spent lying by here while the scouts were out exploring; and since Monte Rey had not been found, theories passed freely around that the Santa Lucia Mountains would be found ahead of us. And so they came back in

11

the evening of the 14th, reporting that…they had come across two rivers and seventeen running creeks with good-sized flows, and that a high white mountain range had been seen. With this, we again took up our way.

October 23. Monday, at a half past eight o'clock in the morning, we set out from here at the San Luís Beltrán—or La Salud—Creek [Waddell Creek]; following the shore, where there was a way through; going along the shore at the foot of a white mountain range, pretty high and all standing very, very precipitous above the sea. Along all of these mountains, between the creek we set out from and Point Año Nuevo about half a league distant, there is very good fresh water springing from their cliffs and skirts; in two or three places we saw good-sized streams of water dropping from the heights through these same mountains and flowing over the sands of the shore into the sea. On traveling about half an hour on a northwesterly course, going about half a league, we reached a cliff close to a point of low land going far out to sea, close to which a creek with a good flow of running water empties into the sea and has a great deal of live-oak wood in its bed….

Three hours' march and we must have made two leagues, at which we came to a little valley in among very grassy hills and all surrounded by them. Here we stopped close to a large village of very well-behaved good heathens, who greeted us with loud cheers and rejoiced greatly at our coming. At this village there was a very large grass-roofed house, round like a half-orange, which, by what we saw of it inside, could hold everyone in the whole village. Around the big house they had many little houses of split sticks set upright. The village lay within the little valley, all surrounded by grassy hills (nothing but soil and tall grass), a place well-sheltered from all quarters, and near the shore. There is good soil in the valley, though there is not much of it, which could support some crops irrigated from a good-sized creek with a good flow of fine delicious water, running through this valley. They have a very dense little grove of nut-bearing pine trees dropping down some hills from the mountains running in back, which are grown over with these pines. These heathens presented us with a great many large black- and white-colored *tamales*; the white *tamales* were made of acorns, and they said the black-colored ones were very good, too. They brought two or three bags of the wild tobacco they use, and our people took all they wanted of it. One old heathen man came up smoking upon a very large and well-carved Indian pipe made of hard stone. The Indians almost all carry tall, red-colored staffs, some with many feathers; they presented four of these staffs to Sergeant Don Francisco Ortega, who was the one they knew best because he had been the one who had explored this place with other soldiers. They made us a long address, and by their signs we could tell they were offering us their lands so that we would stay here. The officers distributed beads to them all, and they were well pleased. After we had reached here, eight or ten heathens came from another village they say is not far off, all of them carrying their tall, red staffs and wearing a sort of wreath made of green leaves on their heads. They all go naked and bare-headed, and all of them are well-featured, stout, and bearded. We have gathered from these heathens that in three days' journey, between sunrise and sunset, one comes to two harbors where there are many pine trees, and that the ship is there.[3] May Divine Providence grant it may be so, and that we reach there as soon as may be. I named this place the little valley of San Juan Nepomuceno.

---

[3] The Indians were probably referring to the *San Carlos*, anchored at Monterey; Crespí and the Spaniards mistakenly thought they meant the *San José*, which in reality capsized at sea on its way to San Diego.

October 24 to October 26. At a quarter before nine o'clock in the morning, we set out from here at the little San Juan de Nepomuceno Valley on a due north course in company with four heathens of this place, who came with us to show us the watering places and villages beyond. We went in view of the shore, over high, big hills all covered with good soil and grass—though almost all the grasses had been burned—and all very bare of trees. It was only through gaps between the hills that we caught sight of the white mountains in back, still grown over with pine woods. On going something near half a league from the place, we crossed two creeks with a good flow in each. On going about two leagues we crossed two hollows with very good, dark, friable soil in no small amount, and all of it very lush, as much as was not burnt. The two hollows adjoin, and there is a large stream of water running in each; the one creek must carry a *buey* of water [about 2,600 gallons per minute], and the other, it seemed, more. A grand place for a very large mission, with plenty of water and soil, which in passing I named San Pedro Regalado. We came across empty villages, and the heathens with us said the people were living farther up. We saw some hazelnut trees upon the creeks here—in their beds. In one of the hollows is a good-sized lake. The day's march was seven hours-and-a-quarter, all through the mountains and the hills here I spoke of. We must have made five long leagues, on which we came to a small valley having a great deal of good soil and, in its midst, a good-sized creek [San Gregorio Creek] with a large flow of very fine, delicious running water; it must carry as much water as the one at La Puríssima [Mission in Baja California]. A good deal of land could be put under irrigation with this water; outside the valley all the hills are good dry-farming land. There are many willows in the creek bed, and here at this place there is a large village with many grass-roofed houses, where they are living on the very edge of the creek near the shore where the creek empties out. They have a village near the shore—

about half a league from where we stopped, where they have many grass houses at the place this valley opens onto the beach—but are now living in the valley. It is perfectly astonishing to see the quantity of brambles all through these places; they are a great hindrance to travel. There is no wood in the valley, but the mountains close by have a good stand of savins. A good place for a good-sized mission, I named it Santo Domingo.

As soon as we had reached this place named for our father St. Dominic, the whole of the big village here came over, all of them very well-behaved, fair, and well-bearded heathens, who received us with much kindness and pleasure. The men all wore from neck to waist a kind of white tippet made of carded plants, from a distance looking like nothing so much as white tippets open at the sides, with a hole for putting the head through. This was the whole of the clothes they wore, for the rest of their body was bare; indeed, all the men hereabouts go wholly naked, with whatever nature endowed them with in plain view. Many of them carried staffs painted in all colors with a great many feathers. They brought us large shares of big, dark-colored *tamales* they make from their grass-seeds, and the soldiers said they were very good and rich when used in *atole* mush. They were with us during almost all the time we spent here, very happy and friendly, bringing a new lot of *tamales* again at every mealtime.

November 3. About eight o'clock at night, the scouts who had been sent out came back from their exploring, firing off their guns as they arrived; and on reaching camp reported that they had come upon a great estuary or very broad arm of the sea [San Francisco Bay] extending many leagues inland, and had arrived near one end of its length, and at it had found some seven villages within a short distance; that there are great plains, many lakes with countless geese, ducks, cranes and other fowl, and large groves of tall live-oaks there;

and that the heathens say there are two harbors very close together, and a ship is at the second one.[4] They were willing to bring them to it, but they did not go as their term for exploring was nearly over. We are all very joyful, though in the midst of this we all feel considerable misgiving and apprehension that Monte Rey may lie behind us; the more so since we have seen the six or seven *farallones* that the histories place nowhere but at the harbor of San Francisco;[5] and are here in the latitude I spoke of, which Don Miguel Constanzó with his instruments made out to be 37°24´. May Providence grant us full comfort as soon as may be, for they say the provisions are now running out.

November 4. About one o'clock in the afternoon, we set out from the two creeks here at the gorge at the side of this bight, went down to the shore of the bight because of the two small creeks and inlet being miry, traveled for a while along the shore on a northwest course, and went over some pretty high hills with nothing but soil and grass, but the grass all burnt off by the heathens. Beyond, through hollows between hills, we once more came to climb an extremely high hill [Sweeney Ridge] and shortly descried from the height a large arm of the sea or an extremely large estuary, which they assert may be four or five leagues in width in some places, in others two, and at narrowest it may be a league wide or more. We stopped a while to look at it, although pretty far away and unable to see it plainly. About a league-and-a-half or two leagues from where we were, some mountains [Mount Tamalpais and the San Bruno Mountains] were made out that seemed to make an opening, and it seemed to us the estuary must go in by there, and as if there

---

[4] Again, the Indians probably meant the *San Carlos* at Monterey.

[5] Crespí refers here to present-day Drake's Bay, which was confusingly sometimes called San Francisco Bay.

were a sort of harbor there within the mountains. We could not see clearly, as the mountains, which were high, stood in the way. The estuary, or arm of the sea, runs far along into the land, eight or ten leagues it may easily be; its course seemed to me to lie northeast and southwest. We traveled three hours and must have gone two leagues, and had changed course to the south on descending, from the hill we were on, into a hollow running among high, grassy hills on this side of the estuary, while alongside us to the right ran mountains, very green with low woods. At two leagues we set up camp at the foot of these mountains, close to a lake [San Andreas Reservoir] where there were countless ducks, cranes, geese, and others.

November 6. From here we went up over a hill and down upon a large plain, five or six leagues in extent, all grown over with white-oaks—large and small—and some live-oaks. From the hill we once again saw the arm of the sea about a league away from us, still drawing down to the foot of some mountains in the south. We saw three or four smokes within these woods from heathen villages, of which the scouts say there are many. It was all flat land to appearance for many leagues, the whole plain being good, black, very grassy soil, though most of the tall grasses had been burned and the whole plain grown over with a great many white- and live-oaks. Four-and-a-quarter hours' march, in which we must have made three leagues, and camped in this same plain of white-oaks, about a league away from the estuary and two or three leagues from where it ended to the southeast. We stopped at the edge of a good-sized creek [San Francisquito Creek, east of El Camino Real] with a good flow of very fine, delicious running water (almost as much it may be as the one at La Puríssima), which runs through this plain and they say goes to empty into the estuary. The soldiers report that down next to the large estuary there are many lakes and little inlets with countless fowl, ducks, geese, cranes, and others, and that these lakes and little inlets being miry are very hard to get through. So that seemingly there is now beginning to be some show of Monte Rey's being not far off, though the fact is that we have been encountering the same sort of thing for many days past. On our reaching here, the governor ordered Sergeant Ortega with some soldiers to explore four days; wherefore during November 7, 8, 9, and 10, we lay by here until they returned from scouting to see what report they were bringing back.

November 7 to November 9. This is the furthest point reached by this expedition in search of the harbor of Monte Rey, having got almost to the end of the large estuary here, which all, or most of us, hold to be that of the San Francisco harbor. A grand place this for a very large plenteous mission, with great amounts of good soil and trees of the sorts mentioned, and great numbers of heathens, the finest and best-mannered that have been met in the whole journey; and this, one of the most excellent places for a large mission. At once upon our reaching here, several very well-behaved heathens, most of them well-bearded, came to the camp, giving us to understand they were from three different villages, and I do not doubt there must be many of these, from the many smokes seen in different directions. Very large bears have been seen, and here where the camp was set up I saw two fresh droppings of these beasts, full of acorns; they must eat plentifully of the great quantities of large ones yielded by the white-oak trees here. Under some of these oaks there were so many large, ripe acorns lying fallen as to hide the ground; our soldiers and Indians gathered large amounts, as we are now in considerable want of provisions, and the soldiers have been getting by on only one *tortilla* for days past. After reaching this place, we noted the weather to be always very clear, with none of the fogs we had had most days on the coast. Here we had sunshine so hot it could not be borne; yet as soon as the sun went down, one commenced to shiver with cold. To the south, the sea arm or estuary turns into great numbers of other inlets, and I suppose lakes as well. I had a clear view of it from the height, and it looks like a maze.

November 10. At night the scouts returned from their exploration, bringing back no report of any harbors; what exploring they did was done with immense toil, they reported, because of the many inlets, lakes, and mires they were faced with, and the country all rough and burnt besides. At about five leagues from where we had stopped, at the end of the estuary, they had come upon a full-flowing river [Guadalupe River], having a great many trees in its bed: very tall, thick cottonwoods, sycamores, willows, and other trees they could not recognize. The river's course lay through a very large plain with very good soil, emptying its waters into the estuary. It cost them a great deal of trouble to cross the river, as it ran very swift and deep; indeed, the only way they could cross was atop a fallen tree lying across it which served them for a bridge. Their mules, where the water was not calm, went in up to their bellies; where it was calm, they had to swim. About some five or six leagues past the river, on the other side of the estuary, they had come across another large creek with a large flow of running water and a great many trees on its bed; its course was through another large plain with very good soil. The lakes and little inlets surrounding the big estuary were many and very hard going because [they were] very miry. They had met many heathens, but they seemed wild and rude upon the other side of the estuary and would pay no attention to anything. They had spent about an hour stopping with one heathen in order to pacify him, and if they gave any of them anything either they would not take it, or if they did, it was only to throw it away at once. They had not reached even halfway down the estuary's length. Having gone up to the height of a hill [site of present-day San Leandro], they had seen the country very far along, and there was no mountain range at all to be seen in that immediate vicinity. The remaining part of the estuary extended so far along to the north that it seemed to them it would take them a whole week to be able to get around it from where they then were. There were no indications of any harbor, save what was formed by the estuary in among some high mountain ranges, which was still very far off, and it could not be told whether there might indeed be a harbor there; they had descried no pine woods anywhere. The grass on the other side was all burnt, and it was hard going for their mounts. At the last, it is seen that this shows no signs of being anything but the harbor of San Francisco, as I explained above.

VICENTE SANTA MARÍA
1775

⟨⟩

Portolá and his men limped back into San Diego on January 24, 1770. In their six month absence, not much had improved: Serra had built some crude stick-and-mud huts (which he grandly christened Mission San Diego de Alcalá), but the *San Antonio* and *San José* were nowhere in sight, and the surviving men were sick, starving, and wounded from Indian attacks. Portolá announced they would wait until March 20; if no help arrived, they would abandon the plan and march back to Mexico. Rather than leave the newly founded mission, Serra and Crespí arranged to have themselves left behind in the *San Carlos*, still deserted on the beach, should the ship not arrive in time. On the afternoon of March 19, one day before they were set to return, the *San Antonio* appeared on the horizon, laden with food and other supplies.

Now rested and well-fed, Portolá grimly turned his attention back toward Monterey. Leaving eight soldiers to continue working at San Diego, Portolá marched north once again, sending half the expedition with Serra on the *San Antonio*. They converged on the latitude where Monterey should have been and this time took a closer look, determining that the barren beach was Vizcaíno's "best port that could be desired" after all. They began construction on Mission San Carlos Borromeo and a nearby *presidio*, formally founding both on

21

June 3, 1770. Exhausted, Portolá ceded command to Lieutenant Pedro Fages and sailed back to Mexico a few weeks later.

Pedro Fages, born in Catalonia in eastern Spain in 1730, had come to Mexico as an infantry lieutenant at the age of thirty-seven. He had served under Colonel Domingo Elizondo on the Sonora frontier before he was sent along on the "sacred expedition." An adept soldier, Fages—at first not accustomed to riding in a saddle—had quickly become one of Portolá's surest horsemen. Now appointed *gobernador* of Alta California, Fages scrambled to establish a permanent settlement at Monterey before the onset of winter rains. He and his soldiers planted fields of corn, grain, and vegetables and erected a compound of barracks and warehouses protected by a palisade. A harsh disciplinarian, Fages was hated by his men for making them work when sick, beating them with a cudgel, and reducing their rations, then offering to sell them raisins and figs at hugely inflated prices.

Fages had been present when Portolá and Crespí first sighted the splendid San Francisco Bay, and by November 1770, he was eager to explore the area again. He and a few soldiers trekked northwestward through Santa Clara Valley, past the point where the "sacred expedition" had turned around, and up San Francisco's east bay. On November 28, they climbed a hill near present-day El Cerrito and glimpsed the "large mouth of the estuary"—the Golden Gate.

News of the newfound bay excited and confused the administration of New Spain. Spanish sea captains had long been aware of Point Reyes and the cove presently known as Drake's Bay, but Portolá's and Fages's descriptions did not match what they knew of the region's geography. If their accounts were to be believed, a potentially invaluable port—secluded, lined with trees, fed by plenty of freshwater streams—existed just eighty miles north of Monterey. Perhaps this "great estuary" was in fact the fabled Straight of Anián linking the Pacific and Atlantic oceans. On behalf of the viceroy of New Spain, Fages and Crespí (personifying the sword and cross of Spain) made a second exploration of San Francisco Bay in the spring of 1772. The pair again returned with a report praising the Bay's numerous creeks, "very good grass-covered soil," and "great many antelope, deer, geese, cranes, and no few tracks of the buffalo [sic] or mule-deer."

In the years Fages was busy supervising the building of Monterey's *presidio* and exploring San Francisco Bay, Junípero Serra oversaw the creation of three new missions along the coast between San Diego and Monterey (missions San Antonio de Padua, San Gabriel Arcángel, and San Luis Obispo de Tolosa). He also relocated Mission San Carlos Borromeo to the bank of the Carmel River, away from the *presidio* and Fages, with whom he had developed a feud. Fages, a lifelong soldier, viewed the Spanish settlements in California as military institutions first and religious second. Proud and inflexible, he refused to finance any more missions until he had the soldiers to protect them—after all, Spanish residents of Alta California still numbered fewer than 100 as late as 1773. Serra, on the other hand, was an insatiable proselytizer, baptizing Indians by the dozen and struggling to learn their languages. Fages's delays and excuses infuriated him.

The growing rift between Serra and Fages marked the beginning of a power struggle between church and state that would grow increasingly heated in ensuing decades. Dependent on each other for survival, mission *padres* and military leaders nevertheless disputed over the allocation of supplies from San Blas, rights to desirous land, protection of the missions, and especially control over Indian neophytes. The missions needed Indian labor to support themselves and, later, to produce food, clothing, and tallow for trade with nearby settlements and Yankee ships. They tried to shield their neophytes from soldiers and civilians, who exposed them to alcohol, gambling, venereal diseases, and notions of private property. But the *padres* also relied on soldiers to buy the missions' wares, round up deserted neophytes, and quash occasional uprisings. This uneasy relationship persisted for more than sixty years.

In the spring of 1773, Serra paid a visit to Mexico City and obtained an audience with Antonio de Bucareli, New Spain's newest viceroy. Serra submitted a thirty-two-point legal brief outlining his problems with Fages and the miserable conditions his missionaries endured. Bucareli recalled later, "Father Fray Junípero Serra, almost in a dying condition, [came] into this capital to present his requests and to inform me personally, a thing which rarely can be presented with such persuasion in writing. On his arrival I listened to him with the greatest pleasure, and I realized the apostolic zeal that animated him, while I accepted from his ideas those measures which appeared proper to me to carry out." In fact, Bucareli accepted most of Serra's thirty-two points, which included demoting Fages (replaced by Fernando Rivera) and promising doctors, blacksmiths, and carpenters for the new missions, along with bells, vestments, and other goods.

In addition, the mission president's personal appearance refocused Bucareli's attention on strategic San Francisco Bay—Serra had been packing supplies and even branding cattle for a proposed mission there since 1771. Bucareli ordered Rivera, California's new *gobernador*, to re-explore the area "for the purpose of establishing a mission there." He also adopted a proposal from Captain Juan Bautista de Anza, who wanted to open a land route from Sonora to Monterey. These two decisions underscore the extent to which Spain, once possessors of a world-famous sailing armada, had become almost exclusively a land-based power by the 1770s (unlike Great Britain, whose Captain James Cook was exploring the Pacific Northwest during those same years).

The few ships Bucareli did have at his disposal were lightweight vessels like the *San Carlos* and the *San Antonio*, commanded by *prácticos* with crews of destitute Mexican fishermen and petty criminals. But a royal order in 1773 provided New Spain with six regular naval officers trained in navigation, chart making, and coastal surveying. In early 1775, Bucareli sent one of these officers, Captain Juan de Ayala, along with Ship-Lieutenant Miguel Manrique on a mission to sail the packet-boat *San Carlos* and larger frigate *Santiago* into San Francisco Bay to survey its waters.

On March 18, the ships lay at anchor a few miles north of San Blas when Manrique, suffering violent delusions of persecution, carried ten loaded pistols onto the afterdeck of the *San Carlos* and ordered his pilots at gunpoint to turn the ship around. He then got into a longboat, pistols in hand, and rowed to shore without explanation. Captain Ayala took command of the *San Carlos* but accidentally shot himself in the foot with a loaded pistol Manrique had left behind. The voyage continued, but Ayala could not climb out of his bunk until the middle of May.

They reached the entrance to San Francisco Bay on the morning of August 5, but swirling eddies and a strong current pushed them back out to sea. Using a tailwind, they managed to make slow, excruciating progress against the tide, but night fell before they could reach the safety of the sheltered bay. Despite the dangers of sailing into uncharted waters and with only a half moon to light the way, Ayala decided to press on, and the *San Carlos* slipped through the Golden Gate at 10:30 p.m.

The *San Carlos* dropped anchor behind Angel Island, and over the next forty-four days, its pilots used the longboat to chart the various arms of the bay. Unfortunately, Ayala's injury prevented him from directly supervising the survey and the resulting map was crude and distorted. Still, it remained the best guide for subsequent navigators until the arrival of Captain Frederick William Beechey in 1826. Ayala, impressed by the bay, later reported: "It is true that this port is good, not only for the beautiful harmony that offers to the view, but because it does not lack very good fresh water, wood, and ballast in abundance. Its climate, though cold, is healthful and free from those troublesome fogs which we had daily in Monterey...."

While the pilots charted the bay as best they could, the chaplain of the *San Carlos*, Father Vicente Santa María, kept a journal of his fascinating encounters with local Huimen and Huchiun Indians. Inquisitive and cordial, the Indians he encountered clearly considered themselves the Spaniards' equals. Echoing Crespí, Santa María could not help but be impressed by their "good presence and fine stature," "beauty," and "comely elegance of figure and quite faultless countenance." Sympathetic as he was, Santa María still paternalistically labeled them "heathens" and "unfortunates."

Born in the tiny Spanish village of Haras in 1742, Vicente Santa María joined the Franciscans at age seventeen and attended seminary at the Colegio de San Fernando in Mexico City in 1769. He represented a second, younger generation of Franciscans sent to labor in the mission fields of Alta California. Unlike level-headed Crespí and fervent Serra, Santa María was youthful and impetuous. When later serving at Mission San Francisco de Asís, his independent spirit rankled Serra, who wrote of him, "Up here, the only supernumerary is Father Santa María, who is in San Francisco, and I find him superfluous for a fact, because he is not exactly one for being kept in hand." When Mission San Buenaventura was founded in 1782, Santa María was transferred there, where he lived until his death in 1806. His journal of his time among the amicable Indians of San Francisco Bay begins August 6, 1775.

Vicente Santa María

Journal of the first Spanish ship to enter San Francisco Bay

The longboat returned to the ship, and the captain and the first sailing master set out in it to make the first excursion in the reconnoitering of this new harbor. In a short time they came to a very large bay [San Francisco Bay proper] to which they gave the name of San Carlos.

Shortly before the longboat, returning from this venture, reached the ship, we saw on the slope of a hill that was in front of us a number of Indians coming down unhurriedly and in a quiet manner, making their way gradually to the edge of the shore. From aboard the ship we made signs to them to wait, and though they did not stop calling us over to where they were, all of them obeyed our signs immediately and sat down.

The captain came aboard and with his permission I went in the longboat with the two sailing masters and the surgeon to communicate at close quarters with those poor unfortunates who so persistently desired us to do so, and by easy steps to bring them into close terms with us and make them the readier when the time should come for attracting them to our holy faith.

As we came near the shore, we wondered much to see Indians, lords of these coasts, quite weaponless and obedient to our least sign to them to sit down, doing just as they were bid. There remained standing only one of the eldest, who mutely made clear to us with what entire confidence we should come ashore to receive a new offering, which they had prepared for us at the shore's edge.

"Indian Woman and Men of Monterey," 1791, by José Cardero. The Ohlone woman in the foreground wears a buckskin apron, tule skirt, and otter-skin robe. *Courtesy of The Bancroft Library.*

Keeping watch all 'round to see if among the hills any treachery were afoot, we came in slowly, and when we thought ourselves safe we went ashore, the first sailing master in the lead. There came forward to greet him the oldest Indian, offering him at the end of a stick a string of beads like a rosary, made up of white shells interspersed with black knots in the thread on which they were strung.[1] Then the rest of us who went in the longboat landed, and at once the Indian mentioned above (who came as leader among them) showed us the way to the place where they had made ready for us a number of baskets, some filled with *pinole* and others with loaves made with a distinctly sulfurous material that seemed to have been kneaded with some sort of oil, though its odor was so slight that we could not decide what it might be. The sailing master accepted everything and at once returned the favor with earrings, glass beads, and other trinkets. The Indians who came on this occasion were nine in number, three being old men, two of them with sight impaired by cataracts of some sort. The six others were young men of good presence and fine stature. Their coloring was not so weak as we have seen in Indians at Carmel. They were by no means filthy, and the best favored were models of perfection; among them was a boy whose exceeding beauty stole my heart. One alone of the young men had several dark blue lines painted from the lower lip to the waist and from the left shoulder to the right, in such a way as to form a perfect cross. God grant that we may see them worshipping so sovereign an emblem.

Besides comely elegance of figure and quite faultless countenance there was also—as their chief adornment—the way they did up their long hair: after smoothing it well, they stuck in it a four-toothed wooden comb and bound up the end in a net of cord and very small feathers that were dyed a deep red; and in the middle of

---

[1] The knots in the string may have indicated the number of days until the beginning of an upcoming festival.

the coiffure was tied a sort of ribbon, sometimes black, sometimes blue. Those Indians who did not arrange their hair in this fashion did it up in a club so as to keep it in a closely-woven, small net that seemed to be of hemp-like fibers dyed a dark blue.

It would have seemed natural that these Indians, in their astonishment at our clothes, should have expressed a particular surprise and no less curiosity—but they gave no sign of it. Only one of the older Indians showed himself a little unmannerly toward me; seeing that I was a thick-bearded man, he began touching the whiskers as if in surprise that I had not shaved long since. We noticed an unusual thing about the young men: none of them ventured to speak and only their elders replied to us. They were so obedient that, notwithstanding we pressed them to do so, they dared not stir a step unless one of the old men told them to; so meek that, even though curiosity prompted them, they did not raise their eyes from the ground; so docile that when my companions did me reverence by touching their lips to my sleeve and then by signs told them to do the same thing, they at once and with good grace did as they were bid.

The time we were with them seemed to us short, but it was enjoyable, all the more when, upon my pronouncing the most sweet names of Jesus and Mary Most Holy, they repeated them clearly, a great satisfaction and pleasure to me and to my companions. We observed a singular thing about the gift of glass trinkets that we had presented to them: not knowing what to do with them, or what not to do, they had put them aside until we should demonstrate how they should be used; so they brought in their hands the earrings and glass beads we had given them and, reaching them out to us, made gestures with them as if asking us what they were for and how to use them. Then all of us began putting the earrings in their ears, at which they were much pleased, as they showed with faces full of joy. We urged them to come on board the ship, but with long speeches they avoided doing so, and by signs they invited us to come with them, pointing out the way to their *rancherías*. We took leave of them, however, setting out in the longboat for the ship, and they went home.

Rash, seemingly, was what I did with five sailors and the surgeon on the afternoon of the 9th of August: we decided to go as far as an Indian *ranchería* that was about a league from the shore and with a poor approach. We were sustained only by our Catholic faith and were impelled by godly zeal lest our gains be lost. It so happened that the Indians had assembled with their usual daily present, but we could not go over to get it because the dugout, inadequate though it was as a conveyance, was not available, being in immediate need of repair. About midday, twelve Indians appeared with the new supply. Though they called repeatedly to us, it was not feasible for us to respond to them; we lacked the means, since the longboat had not yet returned from its first expedition. Tired, at last, of pressing us and seeing that we did not comply with their requests, they all began putting on a dance. When they were done, they returned to calling us over to where they were waiting for us; and then, as we could not give them that pleasure for want of a boat, they went away as if with hurt feelings, showing by the speed of their departure that they had begun to feel worried at so decided a change in our behavior.

When we had about given up hope of satisfying our Indians, the longboat returned to the ship with the sailing master, José Cañizares. Day and night he had gone exploring what parts of the harbor he could....This would have been about a quarter past six o'clock in the evening, and the captain, as a mark of kindness, asked if I should like to take a walk along the shore. The surgeon and I accepted the favor, and setting out in the longboat, we went ashore without delay. We were mindful that the Indians might have gone away offended; so, like the hunter fearless of dangers, who leaps over the rough places and forces his way through obstacles until he meets his quarry, we went up the slopes, taking chances, hunting for our Indians until we should find them. In pursuing this venture we did not share our intentions with the captain because, if we had, from that moment he would have had nothing to do with it in view of the risks involved in our desire to visit the *ranchería* at so unseasonable a time and in so remote a place. Notwithstanding all this, and even though we had no notion of how soon we might reach the Indians, we were nevertheless making our way by their very path. As night was now approaching, we were considering a return to the ship, and were of two minds about it, when we caught sight of the Indians. At the same time seeing us, they began inviting us with repeated gestures and loud cries to their *ranchería*, which was at the shore of a rather large, round cove.[2]

Although we might on that occasion have succumbed to dread, we summoned our courage because we had to, lest fear make cowards of us. We thought that if we turned back and for a second time did not heed the call of the Indians, this might confirm them in their resentment or make them believe that we were very timid— not an agreeable idea, for many reasons. As none of those who came along declined to follow me, ignoring our weariness we went on toward the *ranchería*. As soon as the Indians saw that we were near their huts, all the men stood forward as if in defense of their women and children, whom undoubtedly they regard as their treasure and their heart's core. They may have thought, though not expressing this openly to us, that we might do their dear ones harm; if so, their action was most praiseworthy.

We were now almost at the *ranchería*. As we were going to be there a while, an Indian hustled up some clean herbage for us to sit

---

[2] This village was located somewhere on the northern coast of the San Francisco Peninsula, opposite Angel Island.

on, made with it a modest carpet, and had us sit on it. The Indians sat on the bare ground, thus giving us to understand in some degree how guests should be received. They then made quite clear to us how astonished they had been that we had not joined them at the shore, but we succeeded in giving them some reassurances. When I saw there was so large a gathering, I began to speak to them for a short time, though I knew they could not understand me unless God should work a miracle. All the time that I was speaking, these Indians, silent and attentive, were as if actually comprehending, showing by their faces much satisfaction and joy. When I had finished speaking, I said to those who had come with me that we should sing the "Alabado."[3] When we had got as far as the words *"Pura Concepción,"* there was a great hubbub among the Indians, for some of them had come with two kinds of hot *atole* and some *pinoles*, and they gave all their attention to urging our participation in the feast. So our chorus stopped singing, and we gave the Indians the pleasure they wished, which was that we should eat. After the sailors had finished with the supper that our hosts had brought, I called to the Indian who seemed to me the head man of the *ranchería* and, taking his hand, began to move it in the sign of the cross, and he, without resisting, began repeating my words with so great clearness that I stood amazed and so did those who were with me.

One of the sailors had brought a piece of chocolate. He gave some of it to an Indian who, finding it sweet, made signs that he would go get something of similar flavor. He did so, bringing back to him a small *tamale* that has a fairly sweet taste and is made from a seed resembling *polilla*. We gave the Indians, as usual, some glass beads and received their thanks; and as they saw that the moon was rising they made signs to us to withdraw, which we then did.

---

[3] A Catholic hymn praising the Blessed Sacrament.

Because there was not much daylight when we got to the *ranchería*, we couldn't take note of the appearance and the features of the Indian women, who were at some distance from us, but it was clear that they wore the pelts of otters and deer, which are plentiful in this region. There were a number of small children about. Many of the Indian men we had seen at other times, including some of the leaders, were not present. We headed back for the ship, and as we reached the shore, we came upon the usual present, which the disquieted Indians had left in the morning. After having made them this visit, we were without sight of the Indians for four days, that is, until the 13th of August.

On that day the captain, the second sailing master, the surgeon, and I, with some sailors, went ashore. Three Indians who had been sitting for some time at the top of a slope that came down to the shore, as soon as they saw us landed, fled from our presence to the crest of the ridge without pausing in their flight to heed our friendly and repeated calls.

Accompanied by a sailor, I tried to follow them in order to pacify them with the usual gifts and to find out what it was that troubled them. With some effort we got to the top of the ridge and found there three other Indians, making six in all. Three of them were armed with bows and very sharp-tipped flint arrows. Although at first they refused to join us, nevertheless, when we had called to them and made signs of good will and friendly regard, they gradually came near. I desired them to sit down, that I might have the brief pleasure of handing out to them the glass beads and other little gifts I had had the foresight to carry in my sleeves. Throughout this interval they were in a happy frame of mind and made me hang in their ears, which they had pierced, the strings of glass beads that I had divided among them. When I had given them this pleasure, I took it into my head to pull out my snuffbox and take a pinch; but the moment the eldest of the Indians saw me open the box, he took

34

fright and showed that he was upset. In spite of all my efforts, I couldn't calm him.[4] He fled along the trail and so did all his companions, leaving us alone on the ridge; for which reason we went back to the shore. As the place where we were anchored would not in any case be a good one for the ship, on account of the strong currents, today the captain decided to go to an island that we called Santa María de los Angeles. This was done, and when the ship was anchored again, we went ashore to reconnoiter the island terrain.

With one sailor along, I was foremost in making a diversion of this duty, in hopes of coming upon Indians. All afternoon of the 14th I wore myself out at it. On the pitch of a hill slope I discovered two huts, certainly Indian lodgings, though deserted. I went near them, and seeing them unoccupied, I was minded to take the path to a spring of fresh water to quench a burning thirst brought on as much by the great seasonal heat as by the hard work of climbing up and down such rugged high hills. In a short while I came to a large rock with a cleft in the middle of it, in which rested three remarkable, amusing objects, and I was led to wonder if they were likenesses of some idol that the Indians reverenced.

These were slim round shafts about a yard-and-a-half high, ornamented at the top with bunches of white feathers, and ending, to finish them off, in an arrangement of black- and red-dyed feathers imitating the appearance of a sun. They even had, as their drollest adornment, pieces of the little nets with which we had seen the Indians cover their hair.

At the foot of this niche were many arrows with their tips stuck in the ground as if symbolizing abasement. This last exhibit gave me the unhappy suspicion that those bunches of feathers representing the image of the sun (which in their language they call *gismen)* must be objects of the Indians' heathenish veneration; and if this was

---

[4] Anthropologist Randall Milliken has suggested that the Indians probably believed the snuffbox contained poisons such as those stored by shamans in bone tubes.

true—as was a not unreasonable conjecture—these objects suffered
a merited penalty in being thrown on the fire. After spending several days in going over other parts of this island, I came upon two
rancherías with no one in them. I inferred that they served as shel-
ters to Indians when they came there to hunt deer, which are the
most numerous animals on the island.

On the 15th of August the longboat set out on a reconnaissance of
the northern arm [of the Bay] with provisions for eight days. On
returning from this expedition, which went to have a look at the rivers, José Cañizares said that in the entranceway by which the arm
connects with them [Carquinez Strait] there showed themselves
fifty-seven Indians of fine stature who as soon as they saw the
longboat began making signs for it to come to the shore, offering
with friendly gestures assurances of good will and safety. There was
in authority over all these Indians one whose kingly presence
marked his eminence above the rest. Our men made a landing, and
when they had done so the Indian chief addressed a long speech to
them. He would not permit them to sit on the bare earth; some Indians were at once sent by the *themi* (which in our language means
"head man") to bring some mats—cleanly and carefully woven—
from rushes, simple ground coverings on which the Spaniards might
lie at ease. Meanwhile, a supper was brought them; right away came
atoles, *pinoles*, and cooked fishes, refreshment that quieted their
pangs of hunger and tickled their palates too. The *pinoles* were
made from a seed that left me with a taste like that of toasted hazelnuts. Two kinds of *atole* were supplied at this meal, one
lead-colored and the other very white, which one might think to
have been made from acorns. Both were well flavored and in no way
disagreeable to a palate little accustomed to *atoles*. The fishes were
of a kind so special that besides having not one bone they were most
deliciously tasty; of very considerable size, and ornamented all the

way round them by six strips of little shells [likely sturgeon]. The Indians did not content themselves with feasting our men, on that day when they met together, but, when the longboat left, gave more of those fishes, and we had the enjoyment of them for several days.

After the feast, and while they were having a pleasant time with the Indians, our men saw a large number of heathen approaching, all armed with bows and arrows. It was a frightening sight to those of the longboat, the Indian's advantage for an attack was so great and the resistance so slight that could be made by no more than ten men, which was all there were in the longboat's party, with barely weapons enough for defending themselves if there should be a fight. This fear obliged the sailing master to make known by signs to the Indian chieftain the misgivings they had in the presence of so many armed tribesmen. The *themi,* understanding what was meant, at once directed the Indians to loosen their bows and put up all their arrows, and they were prompt to obey. The number of Indians who had gathered together was itself alarming enough. There were more than 400 of them, and all, or most of them, were of good height and well built. All were naked. Their hair was well done up; some wore it on top of the head, and others confined it in a small woven net such as I have already mentioned.

On this occasion, also, the Indians gave the visitors a feather rope, some bunches of feathers such as they use in headdresses, a large quantity of *pinoles,* and some loaves made from the same substance. Our side made a return of favors, not only giving them many glass beads, but also handing over some handkerchiefs they were wearing.

The Indians of this *ranchería,* unlike those of the one earlier visited, did not keep their women out of view. No sooner were signs made to the women to approach than many of them ran up, and a large number of their small children, conducting themselves toward all with the diffidence the occasion demanded. Our men stayed longer with the little Indians than with the women, feeling great commiseration for these innocents whom they could not readily help under the many difficulties that would come with the carrying out of a new and far-reaching extension of Spanish authority.

It seems that to this *ranchería* the sight of Spaniards was no marvel, for they explained by signs that on another occasion they had seen similar men, even on horseback, and a not unjustified inference was that it was the expedition of Pedro Fages, which Father Crespí, who was with him, gave much information about.[5] The Indians didn't want our party to go away, but rather, staying with them, to become dwellers in their *rancherías*. That was a fine idea for a better occasion, and some way might have been found to satisfy their wishes if the longboat had not been needed for as long as the exploring of this harbor should require. As it was, allowing them some hopes, our party left without delay to get on with the purposes of the expedition.

Once our ship had been removed from neighborly contact with the Indians we had first dealt with, we thought our absence might lose us that new friendship. And so it seemed, for several days passed without our seeing them again, hardly even on the hills, where on other occasions they usually appeared. We didn't think their non-appearance very important, for we supposed that the distance to the ship and the Indians' apprehensions about coming on board explained why they did not care to waste time on visits that would not gain them the object of their desires; and furthermore, this was in any case an advantage to us because, the longboat being engaged in its explorations, we were spared the distress of not being able to make visits in return for theirs.

However, their great liking for us from the time of the first visit made them forego their fears and come to see us on board at a time

---

[5] Fages and Crespí explored the East Bay as far north as the Carquinez Strait in 1772.

when we were least expecting them. It would be about ten o'clock in the forenoon of the 23rd of August when, towards the point of the Isla de Santa María de los Angeles near which we stayed, two reed boats were seen approaching, in which were five Indians. As soon as the captain was informed of this, he directed that signs be made inviting them aboard, to which they promptly responded by coming, which was what they wanted to do. Leaving their boats, they climbed aboard quite fearlessly. They were in great delight, marveling at the structure of the ship, their eyes fixed most of all on the rigging. They wondered no less at the lambs, hens, and pigeons that were providently kept to meet our needs if someone on board should fall sick. But what most captivated and pleased them was the sound of the ship's bell, which was purposely ordered to be struck so we could see what effect it had on ears that had never heard it. It pleased the Indians so much that while they were on board they went up to it from time to time to sound it themselves. They brought us, as on other occasions, gifts of *pinoles*, and they even remembered men's names that we had made known to them earlier. They brought among their party an Indian we had not seen before. Soon after receiving our greetings, he went away alone in his boat, leaving in another direction than the one they had taken. We thought he had been sent by the others to bring us back a present; but when he did not return even after the others had gone away we dismissed this unworthy thought from our minds.

Throughout the time the Indians were on board, we tried to attract them to Christian practices, now having them cross themselves or getting them to repeat the "Pater Noster" and "Ave Maria," now chanting the "Alabado," which they followed so distinctly that it was astonishing with what facility they pronounced the Spanish.

The Indian chieftain, less reserved than the others, showed how much pleased he was at our warmth of feeling; more than once he took to dancing and singing on the roundhouse. I paid close attention to their utterances that corresponded with their actions, and found that their language went like this: *piré* means, in our language, "Sit down"; *intomene,* "What is your name?"; *sumite,* "Give me"; and this last is used with respect to various things, as, a man on the ship having given an Indian a cigar, the Indian said, *sumite sot sintonau,* which means, "Give me a light to start it with." They call the sun *gismen,* the sky, *carac.* And so on. Close on midday they took to their boats again, bidding farewell to us all and promising to be back on the morrow, and they made good their promise so effectually that at seven o'clock the next morning they were already aboard. They had no sooner arrived than I went to meet and welcome these guests, although I did not stay with them as long as they wanted me to because I was about to say Matins and to prepare myself for celebrating the holy sacrament of the Mass. I made signs to them to wait for me until I should be through and those who occupied the cabin should get up; but they couldn't hold their expectations in suspense so long. For while I was at my prayers in the roundhouse, the Indian chieftain, seeing that I was putting them off, began calling the surgeon by his name and saying to me, "Santa María, Vicente, Father, *ilac,*" which means "Come here." Seeing that the surgeon did not leave his bunk and that I did not come down, he came up to where I was reciting my prayers and, placing himself at my side on his kneecaps, began to imitate me in my manner of praying, so that I could not keep from laughing; and seeing that if the Indian should continue I would not be getting on with my duty, I made signs to him to go back down and wait for me there. He obeyed at once, but it was to set out in his boat with a chieftain, not known to us before, whom he had brought to the ship, and as if offended, he left behind the daily offering of *pinoles.*

Word of the kindliness with which those on the ship dealt with these heathen was spread so quickly from *ranchería* to *ranchería* that it served to dispel the fears of a number of Indians not hitherto seen by us, so that they hastened to come aboard. They came, at the same time, to offer us (perhaps depriving themselves) the food of their daily sustenance. This event, which set before our eyes a new spectacle, took place that same day, the 24th of August, two-and-a-half hours after those Indians I have just told about had gone away. These others came in two *balsas* [lightweight reed canoes] and numbered about eight in all. When they were in sight close by, and we made signs to them to come to the ship, one of them, who doubtless came to the bow of his boat for the purpose, began to make a long speech, giving us to understand that it was the head man of the *ranchería* who came, and that he was at our service. This visit was not a casual one, for all of them appeared to have got themselves up, each as best he could, for a festive occasion. Some had adorned their heads with a tuft of red-dyed feathers, and others with a garland of them mixed with black ones. Their chests were covered with a sort of woven jacket made with ash-colored feathers; and the rest of their bodies, though bare, was all worked over with various designs in charcoal and red ochre, presenting a peculiar sight.

As soon as they left their boats, it was made clear to them who it was that commanded the ship, and they endeavored to point out their leader to us. The chieftain of the *ranchería* had all his men, one after another, in the order of their importance, salute our captain; and when this ceremony was completed he begged us all to sit down, as the Indians also did, for distribution among us of their offering, which they brought to us in all tidiness. All being in their places in due order, the second chieftain, who was among the company, asked of another Indian a container made of reeds that he carried with him, in which were many pats or small cakes of *pinole*. It was given him, and having placed it beside him, he indicated that he was to be listened to. With no lack of self composure he spoke for quite a while, and then, opening the container, handed the *pinole* cakes to the first chieftain, who as soon as he received them handed them to our captain, making signs to him to distribute them among all the men of the ship, insisting moreover, that he be the first to taste the *pinole*. The second chieftain was now very watchful to see if by chance anyone of the ship's company had missed partaking of the bread of hospitality. He went up to the roundhouse and several times stuck his head in the after hold; there was no limit to his painstaking inspection. After this our captain directed the steward to bring some pieces of pilot bread and gave them to the Indian head man, who distributed them with all formality among his party.

We gave them glass beads and other little gifts, which they put in their reed container. This done, I brought out a representation of our holy father St. Francis, most edifying, and upon my presenting it to the Indians to kiss they did so with so much veneration, to all appearances, and willingness, that they stole my heart and the hearts of all others who observed them. Then I had them make the sign of the cross and repeat the "Pater Noster," which they did very clearly and showing in their faces that they took pleasure in such things, although lacking comprehension because the Spanish language was beyond them.

They left us about one o'clock in the afternoon, taking to their boats and heading toward the island contiguous to us. On it were some casks with which our supply of water aboard was in part replenished, and a board and some tools that had been taken off the ship for making certain repairs to the dugout. The Indians went ashore, and our captain, on seeing them do so, prudently entertained doubts of their trustworthiness, thinking that, if not through self-interest—at any rate from greed—they might take some of the things we had on the island. The Indians, however, were of quite another mind: as soon as they saw the dugout approach land, they all headed for it, bent on catching up with it and helping our men to run it ashore. Next, after seeing that it was intended to take aboard ship the things that were on shore, the Indians, supposing that the sailors were going after wood, went to a tree that was lying at the waterside and exerted their strength prodigiously to put it aboard the dugout. Then our men came loaded down with the water casks on their shoulders, and going to meet them two of the Indians took the casks on their own backs, carried them to the dugout, and stowed them in it. They all helped to get the dugout afloat again to return to the ship.

I watched all this from the ship, and as the Indians remained seated on the shore, I could not bear to lose the rest of the afternoon when I might be communicating with them; so, setting out in the dugout, I landed and remained alone with the eight Indians, so that I might communicate with them in greater peace. The dugout went back to the ship and at the same time they all crowded around me and, sitting by me, began to sing, with an accompaniment of two rattles that they had brought with them. As they finished the song all of them were shedding tears, which I wondered at for not knowing the reason. When they were through singing they handed me the rattles and by signs asked me also to sing. I took the rattles and, to please them, began to sing to them the "Alabado" (although they would not understand it), to which they were most attentive and indicated that it pleased them. I gave them some glass beads that I had had the forethought to bring with me, and they made me with my own hands hang them in their ears, which most of them had pierced. Thus I had a very pleasant afternoon until, as nightfall neared, our captain sent the dugout for my return to the ship.

I came back well-pleased, reflecting on how quick-witted the Indians were and how easy the acquisition of their language—as we all put to the test when, early next morning, the Indians came back to the ship. We designedly put before them several objects, asking what these were called in their language, to which they answered with great care; seeing that what they said was put down on paper,

43

they came near and repeated the word as if anxious not to give occasion for any blunders in the writing. With this good opportunity we improved the occasion to acquaint ourselves with some words that tallied with what was presented to their attention. Thus, their manner of counting is as follows: *imen,* one; *utin,* two; *capan,* three; *catauas,* four; *misur,* five; *saquen,* six; *quenetis,* seven; *osatis,* eight; *tulau,* nine; *iguesizu,* ten; *imeniluen,* eleven; *capanuya,* twelve; *imenaye,* thirteen; *catsuya,* fourteen; etc. We learned other words, but, lest I grow tiresome I do not put them down. I shall record only some names that, like baptismal names, distinguish them one from another. Thus, the eight Indians who came to us on this occasion were named as follows: their chieftain was called *Sumu;* the second chieftain, *Jausos;* the others, *Supitacse* (1); *Tilacse* (2); *Mutuc* (3); *Logeacse* (4); *Guecpostole* (5); *Xacacse* (6).[6] To give an example of Jausos' liveliness: on being taught to say "*piloto Cañizares,*" he made signs that Sumu be taught to say the same thing. When Sumu mistakenly said "pinoto" instead of "piloto," Jausos corrected him, laughing so hard as to astonish all of us. They are very fond of trading. All of them hanker for our clothes, our cloaks most of all, and so as to move us to make them warm they show us with sad gestures how they suffer from the cold and even say the words *coroec cata,* "I am cold," and the like.

Soon after these Indians came to the ship there came eight others of our new friends, and at first it appeared that those of the one and the other *ranchería* did not look on each other with much friendliness, but our treating them all as equals made them friends and on speaking terms with one another.

We taught all of them how to cross themselves; and although those who came under Sumu's command were better disposed toward these pious observances, the Indians who came under the com-

---

[6] Mission records indicate that at least six of these men were later baptized at Bay Area missions.

mand of the other *ranchería*'s head man became compliant, and all of them came to me to be instructed. Among all these Indians, Mutuc is noticeably clever, so perceptive that he not only grasped at once what we said to him in Spanish and repeated it exactly, but also, as if well versed in our language, he showed how the Spanish terms we asked about were expressed in his. On this day it came off colder than usual, and of the poor unfortunates on board, those who could do so took refuge under my cloak, showing with piteous looks how keenly—being stark naked—they felt the chill. Luck, it seems, offered a sailor's long coat to Supitacse, the oldest and least forward of them all, as soon as he came on board, and he took it at once and kept himself warm in it, huddling in corners. When it was time to leave, he most considerately put the garment back where he had taken possession of it. True, the first day that Sumu's party came aboard, most of his Indians, especially Jausos and one other, were somewhat troublesome because they had a fancy for everything. Everything looked good to them, and they all wanted to barter with their feathers and little nets. But once we had given them to understand that this was doing wrong, they behaved quite differently thereafter, so that two who had been wandering all over the ship did not now leave my side unless they were called. This was a striking example of how tractable they were.

On the 7th of September we hoisted sail to leave this harbor, but were unable to succeed because, when we were near the mouth, a very strong head wind supervened so that we had to put into a cove that was very near the outlet. Our rudder hit some rocks near the cove's entrance, and this kept us in a state of anxiety because the rudder and two of its pivots were damaged. Consequently, we had to stay in harbor until repairs were completed, which took until the feast of the Stigmata of St. Francis [September 17th].

In these days Indians came from another *ranchería*, to which on the 11th I went, accompanied by a number of heathen and a sailor and the surgeon. Our reception was such that on our approach all the Indian men and women living there came out and the *themi*, or head man, putting his arms over my shoulders, steered me to a councilhouse in the middle of the *ranchería*. As soon as we reached the entrance, he made signs for me to go in first, then the surgeon and the sailor who had come with me. On going in by the small entranceway, I said, "Ave Maria," whereupon five old Indians who were there said *"Piré, piré,"* which means "Sit down, sit down." We sat down, and then all the Indians came in. After making the customary speech, I began handing out glass beads to all of them, which they received with much pleasure. While I was making this distribution there came in three old women (who among them would sum up 350 years),[7] each with her little basket of *pinole* for us to eat; later they brought us water, which we drank. After this social affair, I set to inquiring their names and writing them down on paper. This gave them great amusement; for when I had finished, a number of them kept coming up and asking me how the names were spoken, and as I answered according to the paper they gave way to bursts of laughter. Thus we enjoyed ourselves that afternoon until we took our leave. The head man of this *ranchería* comported himself so politely that he came out with one arm around me and the other around the surgeon and went with us a part of the way until, taking leave of us, he went back to his *ranchería*, and we returned to the ship, which was more than half a league distant. This is the manner in which these unfortunates have behaved toward us. What is certain is that they themselves seem to be asking a start at entering within the fold of our Catholic religion. Not to avail of this opportunity would be a lamentable misfortune. To succeed as planned would be the best fortune for all.

---

[7] 250 years is more creditable; regardless, it is noteworthy that the village was home to both the very old and very young.

Francisco Palóu
1776

⸻⊰⊹⊱⸻

About the same time Father Santa María was inviting San Francisco Bay Indians onboard the *San Carlos*, Captain Juan Bautista de Anza was beginning his second overland expedition from Sonora to California. Born in Mexico of Spanish parents, Anza had dreamt since boyhood of exploring Alta California, that mysterious region to the north. Whereas his earlier expedition of 1774 had been exploratory, the expedition of 1776 was colonizing; this time Anza's party consisted of thirty-four families (including the first non-Indian women and children to see Alta California) and more than a thousand mules, horses, and cattle. Their goal, set forth by Viceroy Bucareli, was to establish and populate two new missions and a *presidio* at San Francisco Bay. Alta California had such an unsavory reputation that Bucareli had to promise to pay for the colonists' clothing, food, and supplies for years to come, and still only Sonora's poorest families had volunteered. Bucareli sent married soldiers because he hoped it would decrease the troublingly high number of rapes at the missions.

Their 500-mile route followed the Gila River through present-day Arizona, forded the Colorado River, and crossed the desert to Mission San Gabriel Arcángel (nine miles from where the *pueblo* of Los Angeles would be founded in 1781). As was customary on such expeditions, the colonists made do with the plainest of rations while Captain Anza dined on sausage, wine, cheese, and chocolate. Despite the length and danger of the trip, the 240-member party arrived at San Gabriel in January 1776 numbering 244, as several women had given birth on the trail. Anza's route, clearly more feasible than Portolá's coastal one, would be used by subsequent caravans in the 1820s.

While resting at Mission San Gabriel, they received news of an Indian attack on Mission San Diego two months earlier that had left a *padre* and two soldiers dead. The violence at San Diego was one example of a dozen similar rebellions that sooner or later arose at almost every mission in California. Due to superior Spanish weapons and the inability of dissimilar tribes to unite, the uprisings tended to be localized and short-lived. (One exception came in 1781 when members of the Yuma tribe destroyed two missions along the Colorado River and killed thirty-four Spaniards, effectively closing Anza's trail for forty years.) Indian resistance more commonly came in the form of desertion, raids on mission livestock, and noncooperation.

Gobernador Rivera was marching to San Diego to reclaim the mission, and Anza agreed to accompany him, bringing along twenty of his San Francisco-bound colonists. On the way, Rivera—sixty-five-years old, bitterly jealous of young Anza, and unconvinced of the need for new missions—tried to dissuade him from continuing on to San Francisco Bay, pleading, "Why do you want to go there and tire yourselves out, when I have already told you that I have carefully examined all that region, and have reported to the viceroy that there is nothing there for the purpose in mind?" They arrived in San Diego along with two supply ships from San Blas and another battalion of soldiers from Mexico. Together they overwhelmed the insurgent Ipai and Tipai Indians.

Shrugging off Rivera's warnings, Anza proceeded up the coast, reaching Monterey in March 1776. Word had spread of the expedition's arrival, and a large group of *padres*, soldiers, and Indians gathered to watch Anza's colorful menagerie (men, women, children, and animals) troop in. The colonists overflowed the *presidio* and had to erect tents in the *plaza*. Although Mission San Carlos was hardly prosperous, Serra managed to feed and outfit the expedition, delighted that his proposed missions on San Francisco Bay were finally materializing. He also sent along two *padres*—including Father Francisco Palóu—to man the first mission. It was not Palóu's first visit to the Bay Area; he had traveled there with Rivera in 1774 and decided San Francisquito Creek (near present-day Palo Alto) would be an ideal site for a mission.

On June 27, 1776, the expedition reached the sandy, northernmost tip of the San Francisco peninsula where Anza, scouting ahead, had selected a site for the new *presidio*. About three miles to the southeast, they started building Mission San Francisco de Asís near a small creek they named Laguna de Nuestra Señora de los Dolores, soon spawning the nickname Mission Dolores. (In later years, the area's fog and cold weather would cause Palóu to regret they had not chosen his earlier suggested site near sunny San Francisquito Creek.) Formal establishment was delayed for several months due to the tardiness of the supply ship *San Carlos* and Rivera's refusal to issue the proper orders. By the autumn of 1776, while on the other side of the continent American revolutionaries warred with Great Britain for independence, Spain finally secured a military and religious presence (feeble, to be sure) in San Francisco Bay. The colonists split up—some remained in Monterey, others settled at the San Francisco *presidio*, and a few moved to San José, Alta California's first Spanish *pueblo*, founded a year later.

Palóu's description of the founding of San Francisco's mission and *presidio* appeared in his 1787 biography of Junípero Serra. Like Crespí, Palóu had fallen under Serra's spell while a young philosophy student in Majorca. It marked the beginning of an intense friendship that would last nearly forty-five years and span two continents. "From the year 1740 when [Serra] received me as one of his students, until the year 1784 when death separated us, I was the object of his very special affection, an affection we always mutually shared, more than if we had been brothers in the flesh," wrote Palóu. In fact, he spent most of his adult life following Serra from place to place and chronicling his exploits. Palóu headed Mission San Francisco de Asís for its first eight years and took over as president-general of the Alta California missions for a short time after Serra's death in 1784. Three years later, Palóu wrote California's first published biography, *Relación Histórica de la Vida y Apostólicas Tareas del Venerable Padre Fray Junípero Serra*. Written expressly to help procure Serra's beatification, it contains anecdote after gushing anecdote demonstrating Serra's courage, kindness, and saintliness (including several miracles attributed to him). Much of Serra's subsequent fame stemmed from Palóu's loving, detailed biography. Palóu died soon after the book's publication, having spent nearly forty years of his life in the New World. The following selection from Palou's *Relación Histórica* recounts the founding of Mission Dolores in the summer and autumn of 1776.

FRANCISCO PALÓU

Account of the founding of Mission Dolores

*J*une 23, 1776. Four days before we reached the port, in the great plain called San Bernardino [the Santa Clara Valley], while the expedition was strung out at length, we descried in the distance a herd of large animals that looked like cattle, but we could not imagine where they belonged or from whence they had come. Some soldiers then went out to round them up, so that they should not stampede our tame cattle, but as the soldiers approached, they perceived that this was not a herd of cattle, but deer, or a species of deer, as large as the largest ox or bull, with horns similar in shape to those of the deer, but so large that they measured sixteen palms from tip to tip. The soldiers succeeded in killing three of them, which they carried on mules to the next watering place— a half league or so away. They wanted to bring one in whole, but it was too much for a single mule to carry all the way, and it was only by shifting it from one mule to another that they managed to arrive with it and to give us the pleasure of seeing that monstrous animal with its great horns. I had the curiosity to measure them and found that their width was indeed the four varas [11 feet] aforesaid. I noticed that beneath each eye there was an orifice, so that it seemed to have four eyes, but the two lower ones were empty and apparently served as tearducts. The soldiers who had pursued them told me that they always run in the direction of the wind. Doubtless this is because the great weight of their enormous horns and the way in which they spread out fanlike with their many points would either

Francisco Palóu (ca. 1722–1789). *Courtesy of The Bancroft Library.*

upset them or slow them down if they were to run against the wind. As it was, their speed was so great that of fifteen that were sighted, the soldiers with their good horses were able to catch only three. The meat was dried and furnished food for the people for several days, and lasted many of them to the port. The meat is very savory and healthful and so fat that a sack-and-a-half of lard and suet was obtained from the one that was brought in whole. These animals [elk] are called *ciervos* in order to differentiate them from the ordinary Spanish variety of deer—here called *venados*, which also exist in abundance and of large size in the vicinity of this port—and the color of some of them approaches yellow or sorrel.

In the said plains of San Bernardino, about halfway between the ports of Monterey and San Francisco, as also in the plains nearer to Monterey, there is another species of deer about the size of a three-year-old sheep. They are similar in appearance to the deer, except that they have short horns and also short legs like the sheep. They live in the plains where they go in herds of 100, 200, or more. They run all together over the plains so fast that they seem to fly. Whenever they see travelers, the herds always cross in front of them. The hunters manage to secure some by the plan of dividing the best mounted men and stationing them along the course, where they wait while others start the herd, and they frighten and drive them by turns, thus wearing them down without tiring the horses. As soon as they see one of them lagging behind, which is a sign of fatigue, they ride out, and when they succeed in cutting him off from the herd, they are able to secure him. This they can do also when they get them into the hills, for unlike the deer, they are swift only in the level country. These animals [antelope] are called *berrendos,* and there are many of them also in the southern missions wherever the country is level; but the great *ciervos* have only been found from Monterey upward. This [fine hunting] greatly pleased the soldiers and the colonists of the expedition. Having rested for a day at the stopping place named for the Wounds of our Father St. Francis [Llagas Creek between Morgan Hill and San Martin], the expedition went on toward this port.

On the 27th day of June we arrived in the vicinity of this port [San Francisco Bay], and a camp was made composed of fifteen bell-shaped tents on the shore of a large lagoon that empties into the arm of the bay, which extends fifteen leagues to the southeast. The purpose was to await here the arrival of the ship so that the site for the *presidio* might be selected with reference to the best anchorage.

As soon as the expedition halted, many peaceful Indians approached. They expressed pleasure at our arrival, and especially after they had experienced the friendliness with which we treated them and the little presents of glass beads and food that we gave to attract them. They visited us frequently, bringing such little presents as their poverty afforded—nothing more than mussels and wild grass-seeds.

The day after the arrival, a shelter of branches *(enramada)* was built and an altar set up in it, and there I said the first Mass on the day of the Holy Apostles SS. Peter and Paul. My fellow priest immediately said another, and we continued saying Mass every day of the whole month that we remained at that place. During that time, as the ship did not appear, we occupied ourselves in exploring the country and visiting the villages *(rancherías)* of the Indians, who all received us peacefully and expressed themselves glad of our arrival in their country. They conducted themselves politely, returning our visit—entire villages coming with their little presents for which we took occasion to compensate them with better things, of which they afterward became very fond.

By the survey that we made, we found that we were on a peninsula, with no way to go in or out except between the south and the southeast, for on all other sides we were bounded by the sea. To the east of us is the arm of the sea that extends to the southeast, but as this is only three leagues wide, the land and mountain range on the other side can be seen very clearly. To the north is the other arm of the sea, and to the west and somewhat to the south the Great or Pacific Ocean and the roadstead of the Farallones, where the mouth and entrance of this port is.

In view of the ship's delay, it was decided to begin cutting wood for the construction of the *presidio* near the entrance of the port, and for the mission buildings in this same site of the lagoon on the level ground that lies to the westward. As we had been here

"The Indian Manner of Combat," 1791, by José Cardero, an artist who visited California with a Spanish scientific expedition led by Alejandro Malaspina. *Courtesy of The Bancroft Library.*

a month and neither the ship nor the soldiers that Commander [Fernando] Rivera was to send with orders had arrived, the lieutenant decided to leave us six soldiers as guard for this chosen mission site, and he moved with all the rest of the people near to the entrance of the port, so that they might work while awaiting the arrival of the ship.

It entered the port on the 18th of August, its delay having been due to contrary winds, which had forced it down to 32° [north] latitude. With the aid of the sailors whom the master of the ship divided between the *presidio* and the mission, two structures were built at the *presidio*, one for a chapel and another for a storeroom for provisions, and at the mission one likewise for a chapel and another divided into living quarters for the fathers. The soldiers made their own houses at the *presidio* and at the mission as well, all of wood with roofs of tule thatch.

Formal possession of the *presidio* was taken on the 17th of September, the day of the Impression of the Wounds of our Holy Father St. Francis, patron of the *presidio* and of the port. I sang the first Mass that day, after blessing, venerating, and raising the Holy Cross. When the service ended with the Te Deum, the *señores* went through the ceremony of taking possession in the name of our Sovereign, amid much firing of cannon from ship and shore, and shooting of muskets by the troops.

Formal taking possession of the mission was put off, waiting for the arrival of Commander Rivera's order, and meanwhile the commanders of the new *presidio* and of the ship decided to send an expedition by sea to explore the large arm of water that extends northward from the entrance of the port, and another [expedition] by land to explore the great river of Our Father St. Francis [the Sacramento and San Joaquin rivers], which empties into the roadstead of the Farallones through the mouth of the port. They set out then for the exploration, agreed as to the place where they might meet and from which the ship's launch might go up the great river, while the land expedition should follow it along the bank....

After completing the survey, the launch returned to the port, and the two commanders exchanged their reports of all that they had seen and observed, so that an account might be given to His Excellency. As it was then time for the ship to return to San Blas, and the orders of Commander Rivera for the founding of the mission of Our Father St. Francis had not arrived, they resolved nevertheless that formal possession should be taken and the mission started, which was done on the 9th of October.

The site was first blessed, the Holy Cross was raised, and the image of Our Father St. Francis was carried in procession on a platform and afterward placed on an altar. I then sang the first Mass and preached on Our Holy Father as the patron of the mission, the founding of which all the people of the *presidio*, the ship, and the mission attended, firing a salute at each stage of the service.

The Indians saw none of the services, for toward the middle of August they had left this peninsula and gone on tule rafts, some to the uninhabited islands in the port, others to the other side of the strait. This sudden move was caused by a surprise attack made upon them by their greatest enemies, the Salson nation. These latter live some six leagues to the southeast near the arm of the sea. Setting fire to the villages, they killed and wounded many,[1] and we could not help them for we knew nothing about it until they left for the other shore; and though we did all that we could to hold them, we were unable to succeed.

This departure of the natives delayed the work of conversion, for they did not put in an appearance again until the last of March of the year '77, as little by little they began to lose the fear of their enemies and to gain confidence in us. Thus they began to frequent the mission, attracted by trinkets and presents of food, and the first baptisms were performed on St. John the Baptist's day of that year '77, and gradually they were converted and the number of Christians increased so that the Venerable Father President [Junípero Serra] before he died saw 394 baptized [at Mission San Francisco], and the teaching of the catechism still goes on.

---

[1] The Salson Indians, an Ohlone-speaking people who lived near present-day San Mateo, in fact attacked and burned several neighboring villages in August 1776; their violence may have been an attempt to secure Spanish favors for themselves or simply part of a local feud.

PART II:

LIFE UNDER SPANISH CONTROL

"Instead of finding a country tolerably well-inhabited and far advanced in cultivation—if we except its
natural pastures, the flocks of sheep, and herds of
cattle—there is not an object [in California] to indicate the most remote connection with any European
or other civilized nation."

—George Vancouver, 1792

GEORGE VANCOUVER
1792

———⟐———

Father-president Junípero Serra died in 1784 after baptizing about 6,000 Indians and founding nine missions (including two in the San Francisco Bay Area). He was succeeded the following year by Fermín Francisco de Lasuén, an urbane and diplomatic administrator more inclined than Serra to work with California's military and civilian leaders rather than against them. In his eighteen years as father-president, Lasuén doubled the number of missions in Alta California and quadrupled their neophytes from 5,800 to about 20,000. He replaced Serra's ramshackle stick-and-mud mission buildings with elegant tile-roofed stone and *adobe* churches, arcades, and courtyards—creating what is today considered "mission architecture." He envisioned the missions as equal parts church, school, and factory, employing neophytes as carpenters, masons, and *vaqueros,* and processing raw materials into clothing, pottery, candles, soap, and furniture.

While the missions grew, they hardly prospered. Despite Lasuén's attempts at economic diversification, late-eighteenth century California missions relied heavily on cattle raising, which furnished not only meat but horns, hides, and tallow. Mission agriculture utilized a mix of Spanish and New World crops but struggled with soil depletion, inefficient fertilization, and frequent droughts. Indian workers tended to be malnourished, depressed, and often sick (almost 60 percent of mission Indians died during the 1890s). Spanish settlement was confined to a swath of coastal land 500 miles long but only thirty miles wide.

Spain, conscious of its tenuous grasp on California and the New World, officially closed the entire coast north of Chile to all foreign vessels, hoping its once-fearsome reputation as a colonial and naval power would hide its vulnerability. But in 1784 English explorer James Cook's journal stirred European imaginations with its descriptions of abundant Pacific Northwest furs (Cook sold his modest cargo in Hong Kong for 2,000 pounds); five or six private fur traders a year began to make the difficult journey from China. None of these ships stopped at California, but Spain, alarmed by the potential threat, attacked and captured several English ships near Nootka, Alaska, in 1789. War between the two nations was averted only by Spain's realization that it had no vessels with which to fight the armada that England was rapidly assembling. In 1790 the two governments agreed on the Nootka Sound Convention, wherein Spain relinquished exclusive sovereignty of the northern Pacific coast, opening it to entrepreneurs of both nations. By pressing its claims to the entire coastline, Spain had revealed how little power stood behind them.

George Vancouver, a British naval captain who had sailed as a midshipman on Cook's second and third voyages, was commissioned in 1791 to repossess the property seized from the English traders and to survey the coast and visit California settlements in the process. Born in Norfolk, England, in 1757 to an upper-class deputy customs collector, Vancouver dropped out of school at age fifteen to join the navy. After sailing to virtually every point in the Pacific during his eight years with Cook, Vancouver spent most of the 1780s exploring in the West Indies. His unique knowledge of the Pacific and meticulous cartographic skills made him a natural choice to command the *Discovery*'s voyage to California.

Vancouver first stopped at Nootka to discuss points of repossession with Spain's representative, Juan Francisco de la Bódega y Cuadro. While regaling the officers of the *Discovery* with lavish dinner parties, Bódega y Cuadro attempted to renegotiate a more favorable northern California boundary for Spain. Although impressed with Spanish hospitality, Vancouver had no authority to reopen negotiations and so departed with the northern limit of California left undefined. Sailing south, the *Discovery* stopped often to chart the coastline, dispatching boats up navigable rivers and fjords (proving once and for all that there was no Northwest Passage to the Atlantic among the channels of Puget Sound). The problem of exactly locating the ship's position was solved through the use of chronometers set to Greenwich time, supplemented through tedious astronomical observations—no less than eighty-five observations of the moon were taken off Cape Mendocino.

It took a month to reach San Francisco Bay from Nootka. The trip was harrowing at times—heavy rains and turbulent waves buffeted the ship, washing one sailor overboard. Some of the seamen began showing signs of scurvy, a condition that could have been alleviated had fresh fruit been found onshore, but despite their fastidious surveying, they had encountered no harbor safe enough to enter. The *Discovery* anchored in San Francisco Bay on November 14, 1792. Vancouver surely had in mind an image of Spanish colonial life founded on three centuries of Spanish dominance of the western hemisphere, an image reinforced by Bódega y Cuadro's court at Nootka. But instead of a proud military *presidio* he found a collection of impoverished mud huts protected by two antiquated cannons. Clearly, the defense of California rested not on these guns but on the ignorance of the rest of the world.

The *Discovery* was the first non-Spanish ship to sail into San Francisco Bay but not the first to visit Spanish settlements in Alta California. For ten days in 1786, French navigator Jean François de La Pérouse and his team of engineers, artists, and scientists sojourned at Monterey, gathering information on the region's geography, natural resources, and government. In his widely read journal, La Pérouse sang California's praises, calling the soil "inexpressibly fertile," adding that "no country is more abundant in fish and game of every description." Five years later, Italian naval officer Alejandro

Malaspina, leader of a Spanish round-the-world scientific expedition, likewise stopped at Monterey. His naturalists and artists completed surveys of Monterey Bay Area birds, sea life, and trees (including the first scientific description of a redwood).

The military leaders of California had received La Pérouse and Malaspina with much fanfare but argued over how to treat Vancouver. On one hand, the *Discovery* offered exotic gifts and news of the outside world to isolated California, but on the other, it reported back to England, Spain's greatest rival for the Pacific. José Darío Argüello and Hermenegildo Sal (temporary commanders of Monterey and San Francisco while Gobernador José Arrillaga was visiting Baja) extended Vancouver every hospitality during his initial two-month visit to California, providing free supplies, entertainment, and tours. But when Vancouver revisited California in 1793 after sailing to the Hawaiian Islands, Arrillaga had returned, and he was barely permitted to leave his ship.

Vancouver's life after his voyage on the *Discovery* was marked by scandal and ill health. He most likely suffered from a hyperthyroid condition (probably Graves' disease) that accounted for his bouts of irritability, loss of temper, and fatigue. In 1796 a young midshipman named Thomas Pitt, who had sailed with Vancouver, accused him of mistreatment. Although a dozen lashes with the cat-o'-nine-tails was a common naval punishment, Pitt alleged that Vancouver brutally flogged and shackled his men for the slightest offense. Ship records indicate Vancouver administered a total of ninety-five floggings during the four-and-a-half-year trip (ranging from twelve to seventy-two lashes each), a record similar to other long voyages of the time. But because Pitt hailed from an influential family, he managed to launch a formal investigation into Vancouver's conduct. Controversy continued to swirl around Vancouver until his death two years later at age forty-one.

The popularity of *A Voyage of Discovery*, published in 1798, suffered from Vancouver's reputation as cruel and tyrannical. But his portrayal of California's enticing landscape and the Spaniards' pitiful defenses did increase interest in the region and further encouraged European ships to defy Spanish policy. Today, *A Voyage of Discovery*'s greatest value lies in Vancouver's descriptions of early life in the missions. However, it should be noted that Vancouver's disgust at California's poverty and the mistreatment of the Indians was, at least in part, influenced by Spain's status as a rival power. Modern defenders of the mission system have also suggested that his misgivings were likely bolstered by "the Black Legend," a two-centuries-old tradition of gruesome stories by French, Dutch, and English propagandists that detailed Spanish cruelties toward indigenous peoples of the New World. Nevertheless, one cannot help but notice the profound differences between early descriptions of native peoples (from Crespí, Santa María, and other observers) given before the missions were established and Vancouver's depiction of Indians under the mission system as miserable, dispirited, and degraded. That Vancouver held little sympathy for the depressed Indians he observed illustrates his failure to perceive that they had not always been so.

In fact, the San Francisco Bay Area had been radically altered between 1776 and 1792. The traditional, communal life the region's various Indian groups had known for millennia had been increasingly replaced by forced assimilation, oppression, and death. Indians, first attracted to the missions out of curiosity or self-interest, discovered they were not allowed to leave. Massive environmental changes were triggered by the prohibition of controlled burnings and the overgrazing of mission livestock. And a host of diseases, most notably dysentery and syphilis, devastated entire Bay Area tribal groups, especially infants. By the time of Vancouver's visit in 1792, the Indians of San Francisco Bay had been rendered, in the words of anthropologist Randall Milliken, "a culturally shocked and broken people living in a bewildering foreign environment." This account of Vancouver's visit begins Thursday, November 15, 1792, on the *Discovery*'s first morning in San Francisco Bay.

Portrait believed to be of George Vancouver (1757–1798). The goiter-like appearance of his neck supports historians' belief that he suffered from a hyperthyroid condition (probably Graves' disease). *Courtesy of The Bancroft Library.*

GEORGE VANCOUVER

from *A Voyage of Discovery to the North Pacific Ocean*

Thursday morning, November 15, we discovered our anchorage to be in a most excellent small bay, within three-fourths of a mile of the nearest shore, bearing by a compass south; one point of the bay bearing N 56 W, the other S 73 E; the former at the distance of two-and-a-half, the latter about three miles. The herds of cattle and flocks of sheep grazing on the surrounding hills were a sight we had long been strangers to and brought to our minds many pleasing reflections. These indicated that the residence of their proprietors could not be far remote, though we could perceive neither habitations nor inhabitants. On hoisting the colors at sunrise, a gun was fired, and in a little time afterwards several people were seen on horseback coming from behind the hills down to the beach, who waved their hats and made other signals for a boat, which was immediately sent to the shore. On its return, I was favored with the good company of a priest of the order of San Francisco and a sergeant in the Spanish army to breakfast. The reverend father expressed, and seemingly with great sincerity, the pleasure he felt at our arrival and assured me that every refreshment and service in the power of himself or mission to bestow, I might unreservedly command since it would be conferring on them all a peculiar obligation to allow them to be serviceable. The sergeant expressed himself in the most friendly manner and informed me that in the absence of the commandant, he was directed on our arrival to render us every accommodation the settlement could afford.

We attended them on shore after breakfast, where they embraced the earliest opportunity of proving that their friendly expressions were not empty professions by presenting me with a very fine ox, a sheep, and some excellent vegetables. The good friar, after pointing out the most convenient spot for procuring wood and water, and repeating the hospitable offers he had before made in the name of the fathers of the Franciscan order, returned to the mission of San Francisco, which we understood was at no great distance, and to which he gave us the most pressing invitation.

From these gentlemen, we learned that the station we had taken was far within the general anchoring place of the Spanish vessels, which they said was off that part of the shore where the light was shone and guns fired the preceding night on the beach, near the entrance into the port. Our situation was, however, perfectly commodious and suitable to all our purposes, and with permission of the sergeant, I directed a tent to be pitched for the accommodation of the party employed in procuring wood and water, whilst the rest of the crew were engaged on board in repairing the damages sustained in our sails, rigging, etc., during the tempestuous weather with which we had lately contended.

We amused ourselves with shooting a few quails on the adjacent hills and, in the afternoon, returned on board to partake of the excellent repast, which had been supplied by our hospitable friends. Whilst we were thus pleasantly engaged, our boat brought off Father Antonio Danti,[1] the principal of the mission of San Francisco, and Señor Don Hermenegildo Sal,[2] an ensign in the Spanish army and commandant of the port. This gentleman, like those who visited us in the morning, met us with such warm expressions of friend-

---

[1] Father Antonio Danti oversaw Mission San Francisco from 1790 to 1796.

[2] Hermenegildo Sal, born in Spain, had accompanied Anza to San Francisco in 1776. He served as *comandante* of the San Francisco *presidio* from 1791 to 1794. Vancouver, impressed by Sal's hospitality, later named Point Sal on the Santa Barbara County coast after him.

ship and goodwill, as were not less deserving our highest commendations than our most grateful acknowledgments....

The little we had seen of Port San Francisco enabled us to decide that it was very extensive in two directions; one spacious branch took its course east and southward to a great distance from the station we had quitted in the morning, the other apparently of equal magnitude led to the northward. In this were several islands. Although I had been informed by Señor Quadra[3] that the boundaries of this inlet had been defined, I was anxious to be more particularly acquainted with its extent, having since been given to understand that Señor Quadra's was by no means correct.

Near the branch leading to the east and southeastward above mentioned is situated the mission of Santa Clara.[4] These gentlemen informed me that this branch had been thoroughly examined, but that the branch leading to the north never had. I was, however, obliged to remain contented under the uncertainty of such contradictory information; for the port having been established by Spain, I did not consider it prudent authority for so doing; nor was the weather favorable for such an undertaking, though it did not prevent the exercise of those friendly dispositions in the Spanish *comandante*, which he had before professed. He had been sometime on the beach in the rain before we anchored, for the purpose of instantly affording us any assistance in his power to supply.

A message to this effect was brought by three of the native Indians who spoke Spanish and who came on board in a canoe of the country; which with another, (though perhaps the same) seen crossing the harbor the evening we entered it, were the only Indian vessels we had met with, and were without exception the most rude and

---

[3] Juan Francisco de la Bódega y Cuadro, the Spanish lieutenant Vancouver negotiated with at Nootka.

[4] Mission Santa Clara de Asís was established in 1777 on the bank of the Guadalupe River in the present-day town of Santa Clara.

sorry contrivances for embarkation I had ever beheld. The length of them was about ten feet, the breadth about three or four. They were constructed of rushes and dried grass of a long broad leaf, made up into rolls the length of the canoe, the thickest in the middle, and regularly tapering to a point at each end. These are so disposed that on their ends being secured and lashed together, the vessel is formed, which being broadest in the middle, and coming to a point at each extremity, goes with either end foremost. These rolls are laid and fastened so close to each other that in calm weather and smooth water I believe them to be tolerably dry, but they appeared to be very ill-calculated to contend with wind and waves. The wind now blew strong with heavy squalls from the SW, and in the middle of this spacious inlet, the sea broke with much force; notwithstanding which, as soon as these people had delivered their message, they crossed the inlet for the purpose of catching fish, without seeming to entertain the least apprehension for their safety. They conducted their canoe or vessel by long, double-bladed paddles, like those used by the Esquimaux [Eskimo].

The SW wind, attended by much rain, blew very hard until Saturday morning the 17th; when the weather became more moderate, I visited the shore. I was greatly mortified to find that neither wood nor water could be procured with such convenience, nor of so good a quality, as at the station we had quitted a league-and-a-half within the entrance of the port on the southern shore. But as our Spanish friends had informed us that the water here was far superior in its quality to that at Monterey, there was now no alternative but that of taking what the country afforded. A tent was immediately pitched on the shore, wells were dug for obtaining water, and a party was employed in procuring fuel from small, bushy, holly-leaved oaks, the only trees fit for our purpose. A lagoon of sea water was between the beach and the spot on which these trees grew, which rendered the conveying the wood when cut a very laborious operation.

Whilst engaged in allotting to the people their different employments, some saddle horses arrived from the commandant with
a very cordial invitation to his habitation, which was accepted by
myself and some of the officers. We rode up to the *presidio*, an appellation given to their military establishments in this country and
signifying a safeguard. The residence of the friars is called a mission.
We soon arrived at the *presidio*, which was not more than a mile
from our landing place. Its wall, which fronted the harbor, was visible from the ships; but instead of the city or town, whose lights we
had so anxiously looked for on the night of our arrival, we were
conducted into a spacious verdant plain, surrounded by hills on every side, excepting that which fronted the port. The only object of
human industry that presented itself was a square area, whose sides
were about 200 yards in length, enclosed by a mud wall and resembling a pound for cattle. Above this wall, the thatched roofs of their
low, small houses just made their appearance. On entering the
presidio, we found one of its sides still unenclosed by the wall and
very indifferently fenced in by a few bushes here and there, fastened
to stakes in the ground. The unfinished state of this part afforded
us an opportunity of seeing the strength of the wall and the manner in which it was constructed. It is about fourteen feet high and
five feet in breadth, and was first formed by uprights and horizon-
tal rafters of large timber, between which dried sods and moistened
earth were pressed as close and as hard as possible; after which the
whole was cased with the earth made into a sort of mud plaster,
which gave it the appearance of durability and of being sufficiently
strong to protect them, with the assistance of their firearms, against
all the force which the natives of the country might be able to collect.

The Spanish soldiers composing the garrison amounted, I understood, to thirty-five; who, with their wives, families, and a few
Indian servants, composed the whole of the inhabitants. Their houses
were along the wall within the square, and their fronts uniformly

"Soldier of Monterey," 1791, by José Cardero, an artist with the Malaspina expedition. Gabriel Moraga, the twenty-six-year-old soldier depicted, came to California with his mother in 1781 and later became the leading explorer of the Central Valley. *Courtesy of The Bancroft Library.*

extended the same distance into the area, which is a clear open space, without buildings or other interruptions. The only entrance into it is by a large gateway; facing which, and against the center of the opposite wall or side, is the church, which, though small, was neat in comparison to the rest of the buildings. This projects further into the square than the houses and is distinguishable from the other edifices by being whitewashed with lime made from seashells (limestone or calcareous earth not having yet been discovered in the neighborhood). On the left of the church is the commandant's house, consisting, I believe, of two rooms and a closet only, which are divided by massy walls, similar to that which encloses the square and communicating with each other by very small doors. Between these apartments and the outward wall was an excellent poultry house and yard, which seemed pretty well-stocked. Between the roof and ceilings of the rooms was a kind of lumber garret; those were all the conveniences the habitation seemed calculated to afford. The rest of the houses, though smaller, were fashioned exactly after the same manner; and in the winter, or rainy seasons, must at the best be very uncomfortable dwellings. For though the walls are a sufficient security against the inclemency of the weather, yet the windows, which are cut in the front wall, and look into the square, are destitute of glass, or any other defense that does not at the same time exclude the light.

The apartment in the commandant's house, into which we were ushered, was about thirty feet long, fourteen feet broad, and twelve feet high; and the other room, or chamber, I judged to be of the same dimensions, excepting in its length, which appeared to be somewhat less. The floor was of the native soil raised about three feet from its original level, without being boarded, paved, or even reduced to an even surface. The roof was covered in with flags and rushes; the walls on the inside had once been whitewashed; the furniture consisted of a very sparing assortment of the most indispensable articles, of the rudest fashion and of the meanest kind; and ill-accorded with the ideas we had conceived of the sumptuous manner in which the Spaniards live on this side of the globe.

It would, however, be the highest injustice, notwithstanding that elegancies were wanting, not to acknowledge the very cordial reception and hearty welcome we experienced from our worthy host, who had provided a refreshing repast, and such a one as he thought likely to be most acceptable at that time of the day; nor was his lady less assiduous, nor did she seem less happy than himself in entertaining her new guests.

On approaching the house we found this good lady—who, like her spouse, had passed the middle age of life—decently dressed, seated cross-legged on a mat, placed on a small, square wooden platform raised three or four inches from the ground, nearly in front of the door, with two daughters and a son, clean and decently dressed, sitting by her; this being the mode observed by these ladies when they receive visitors. The decorous and pleasing behavior of the children was really admirable and exceeded anything that could have been expected from them under the circumstances of their situation, without any other advantages than the education and example of their parents; which however seemed to have been studiously attended to and did them great credit. This pleasing sight, added to the friendly reception of our host and hostess, rendered their lowly residence no longer an object of our attention. Having partaken of the refreshments they had provided, we remounted our horses in order to take a view of the surrounding country before we returned on board to dinner, where Señor Sal and his family had promised to favor me with their good company, and who had requested my permission to increase their party by the addition of some other ladies in the garrison.

Our excursion did not extend far from the *presidio*, which is situated as before described in a plain surrounded by hills. This plain

"The Wife of a Monterey Soldier," 1791, by José Cardero. She likely came to California from Sonora with Juan Bautista de Anza in 1775. *Courtesy of The Bancroft Library.*

is by no means a dead flat, but of unequal surface; the sod is of a sandy nature and was wholly under pasture, on which were grazing several flocks of sheep and herds of cattle. The sides of the surrounding hills, though but moderately elevated, seemed barren, or nearly so; and their summits were composed of naked, uneven rocks. Two small spaces in the plain, very insecurely enclosed, were appropriated to kitchen gardens. Much labor did not appear to have been bestowed either in the improvement of the soil, in selecting the quality of the vegetables, or in augmenting their produce; the several seeds once placed in the ground, nature was left to do the rest without receiving any assistance from manual labor.

Señor Sal, having been made acquainted with the difficulties we had to encounter in removing our wood to the sea side, politely offered us the carts he had for the use of the *presidio*; but on their being produced, I was greatly disappointed, as they were by no means so well-calculated as the miserable straw canoes for the service they were intended to perform.

Thus, at the expense of very little examination, though not without much disappointment, was our curiosity satisfied concerning the Spanish town and settlement of San Francisco. Instead of finding a country tolerably well-inhabited and far advanced in cultivation—if we except its natural pastures, the flocks of sheep, and herds of cattle—there is not an object to indicate the most remote connection with any European or other civilized nation.

This sketch will be sufficient, without further comment, to convey some idea of the inactive spirit of the people and the unprotected state of the establishment at this port, which I should conceive ought to be a principal object of the Spanish crown, as a key and barrier to their more southern and valuable settlements on the borders of the north Pacific. Should my idea of its importance be overrated, certain it is, that considered solely as an establishment, which must have been formed at considerable expense, it possesses no other means for its protection than such as have been already described; with a brass three-pounder mounted on a rotten carriage before the *presidio*, and a similar piece of ordnance which (I was told) was at the SE point of entrance lashed to a log instead of a carriage; and was the gun whose report we heard the evening of our arrival. Before the *presidio* there had formerly been two pieces of ordnance, but one of them had lately burst to pieces.

The examination of these few objects, and the consequent observations upon them, occupied our leisure until dinnertime, when we returned on board, accompanied by Señor Sal, his wife, and party, and one of the fathers of the mission of San Francisco, Martín de Landaeta, who brought me a pressing and polite invitation from his brethren, and who proved to be a very pleasing and entertaining acquisition to our society.

The next day, Sunday the 18th, was appointed for my visiting the mission [San Francisco]. Accompanied by Mr. Menzies and some of the officers, and our friendly Señor Sal, I rode thither to dinner. Its distance from the *presidio* is about a league in an easterly direction. Our ride was rendered unpleasant by the soil being very loose and sandy, and by the road being much incommoded with low, groveling bushes.

Its situation and external appearance in a great measure resembled that of the *presidio*; and, like its neighborhood, the country was pleasingly diversified with hill and dale. The hills were at a greater distance from each other and gave more extent to the plain, which is composed of a soil infinitely richer than that of the *presidio*, being a mixture of sand and a black vegetable mold. The pastures bore a more luxuriant herbage and fed a greater number of sheep and cattle. The barren sandy country through which we had passed seemed to make a natural division between the lands of the mission and those of the *presidio*, and extends from the shores of the port to the foot of a ridge of mountains, which border on the exterior coast, and appear to stretch in a line parallel to it. The verdure of the plain continued to a considerable height up the sides of these hills; the summits of which, though still composed of rugged rocks, produced a few trees.

The buildings of the mission formed two sides of a square only and did not appear as if intended, at any future time, to form a perfect quadrangle like the *presidio*. The architecture and materials, however, seemed nearly to correspond.

On our arrival, we were received by the reverend fathers with every demonstration of cordiality, friendship, and the most genuine hospitality. We were instantly conducted to their mansion, which was situated near, and communicated with the church. The houses formed a small, oblong square; the side of the church composed one end, near which were the apartments allotted to the fathers. These were constructed neatly after the manner of those at the *presidio*, but appeared to be more finished, better contrived, were larger, and much more cleanly. Along the walls of this interior square were also many other apartments adapted to various purposes.

Whilst dinner was preparing, our attention was engaged in seeing the several houses within the square. Some we found appropriated to the reception of grain, of which, however, they had not a very abundant stock; nor was the place of its growth within sight of the mission, though the richness of the contiguous soil seemed equal to all the purposes of husbandry. One large room was occupied by manufacturers of a coarse sort of blanketing, made from the wool produced in the neighborhood. The looms, though rudely wrought, were tolerably well-contrived and had been made by the Indians, under the immediate direction and superintendence of the fathers, who, by the same assiduity, had carried the manufacture thus far into effect. The produce resulting from their manufactory is wholly applied to the clothing of the converted Indians. I saw some of the cloth, which was by no means despicable, and, had it received the advantage of fulling, would have been a very decent sort of clothing.

The preparation of the wool, as also the spinning and weaving of it, was, I understood, performed by unmarried women and female children, who were all resident within the square and were in a state of conversion to the Roman Catholic persuasion. Besides manufacturing the wool, they are also instructed in a variety of necessary, useful, and beneficial employments until they marry—which is greatly encouraged—when they retire from the tuition of the fathers to the hut of their husband. By these means it is expected that their doctrines will be firmly established and rapidly propagated, and the trouble they now have with their present untaught flock will be hereafter recompensed, by having fewer prejudices to combat in the rising generation. They likewise consider their plan as essentially necessary, in a political point of view, for ensuring their own safety. The women and girls being the dearest objects of affection amongst these Indians, the Spaniards deem it expedient to retain constantly a certain number of females immediately within their power, as a pledge for the fidelity of the men, and as a check on any improper designs the natives might attempt to carry into execution, either against the missionaries or the establishment in general.

By various encouragements and allurements to the children or their parents, they can depend upon having as many to bring up in this way as they require. Here they are well fed, better clothed than the Indians in the neighborhood, are kept clean, instructed, and have every necessary care taken of them. In return for these advantages they must submit to certain regulations; amongst which, they are not suffered to go out of the interior square in the daytime without permission, are never to sleep out of it at night, and to prevent elopements, this square has no communication with the country but by one common door, which the fathers themselves take care of, and see that it is well secured every evening, and also the apartments of the women, who generally retire immediately after supper.

If I am correctly informed by the different Spanish gentlemen with whom I conversed on this subject, the uniform, mild, and kind-hearted disposition of this religious order has never failed to attach to their interest the affections of the natives, wherever they sat down amongst them. This is a very happy circumstance, for their situation otherwise would be excessively precarious, as they are protected only by five soldiers who reside under the directions of a corporal in the buildings of the mission at some distance on the other side of the church.

The establishment must certainly be considered as liable to some danger. Should these children of nature be ever induced to act an ungrateful and treacherous part, they might easily conceal sufficient weapons to effect any evil purpose. There are only three fathers[5]—these live by themselves—and should any attempt be made upon them at night, the very means they have adopted for security might deprive them of any assistance from the guard until it might be too late; individually, they could make but little resistance. Should a conspiracy for their destruction take place, the mission would soon fall, and there would be little doubt of the conspirators being joined by the Indians of the village, which is in the vicinity of the mission and was said to contain 600 persons, but on visiting it, I considered their number greatly overrated. The major part of them, I understood, were converted to the Roman Catholic persuasion; but I was astonished to observe how few advantages had attended their conversion.

They seemed to have treated with the most perfect indifference the precepts and laborious example of their truly worthy and benevolent pastors, whose object has been to allure them from their

---

[5] Actually two: Fathers Danti and Landaeta. Vancouver likely thought Father Diego Noboa, who often visited Mission San Francisco, lived there.

life of indolence and raise in them a spirit of emulous industry; which, by securing to them plenty of food and the common conveniences of life, would necessarily augment their comforts and encourage them to seek and embrace the blessings of civilized society. Deaf to the important lessons and insensible of the promised advantages, they still remained in the most abject state of uncivilization; and if we except the inhabitants of Tierra del Fuego and those of Van Dieman's land [Tasmania], they are certainly a race of the most miserable beings—possessing the faculty of human reason—I ever saw. Their persons, generally speaking, were under the middle size and very ill made; their faces ugly, presenting a dull, heavy, and stupid countenance, devoid of sensibility or the least expression. One of their greatest aversions is cleanliness, both in their persons and habitations; which, after the fashion of their forefathers, were still without the most trivial improvement. Their houses were of a conical form, about six or seven feet in diameter at their base (which is the ground) and are constructed by a number of stakes, chiefly of the willow tribe, which are driven erect into the earth in a circular manner, the upper ends of which being small and pliable are brought nearly to join at the top, in the center of the circle; and these, being securely fastened, give the upper part or roof somewhat of a flattish appearance. Thinner twigs of the like species are horizontally interwoven between the uprights, forming a piece of basket work about ten or twelve feet high. At the top, a small aperture is left, which allows the smoke of the fire made in the center of the hut to escape and admits most of the light they receive. The entrance is by a small hole close to the ground, through which with difficulty one person at a time can gain admittance. The whole is covered over with a thick thatch of dried grass and rushes.

These miserable habitations, each of which was allotted for the residence of a whole family, were erected with some degree of uniformity, about three or four feet asunder, in straight rows, leaving lanes or passages at right angles between them; but these were so abominably infested with every kind of filth and nastiness as to be rendered not less offensive than degrading to the human species.

Close by stood the church, which for its magnitude, architecture and internal decorations, did great credit to the constructors of it, and presented a striking contrast between the exertions of genius and such as bare necessity is capable of suggesting. The raising and decorating this edifice appeared to have greatly attracted the attention of the fathers; the comforts they might have provided in their own humble habitations seemed to have been totally sacrificed to the accomplishment of this favorite object. Even their garden, an object of such material importance, had not yet acquired any great degree of cultivations, though its soil was a rich black mold and promised an ample return for any labor that might be bestowed upon it. The whole contained about four acres, was tolerably well fenced-in, and produced some fig, peach, apple, and other fruit trees, but afforded a very scanty supply of useful vegetables—the principal part lying waste and overrun with weeds.

On our return to the convent, we found a most excellent and abundant repast provided of beef, mutton, fish, fowls, and such vegetables as their garden afforded. The attentive and hospitable behavior of our new friends amply compensated for the homely manner in which the dinner was served and would certainly have precluded my noticing the distressing inconvenience these valuable people labor under, in the want of almost all the common and most necessary utensils of life, had I not been taught to expect that this colony was in a very different stage of improvement, and that its inhabitants were infinitely more comfortably circumstanced.

After dinner we were engaged in an entertaining conversation, in which, by the assistance of Mr. Dobson, our interpreter, we were each able to bear a part. Amongst other things, I understood that this mission was established in the year 1775, and the *presidio* of

San Francisco in 1778,[6] and that they were the northernmost settlements, of any description, formed by the court of Spain on the continental shore of northwest America, or the islands adjacent, exclusive of Nootka, which I did not consider as coming under that description any more than the temporary establishment which, in the preceding spring, had formed by Señor Quadra near Cape Flattery, at the entrance of the Straits of Juan De Fuca [in northwest Washington State]; and which has been already stated to be entirely evacuated. The excursions of the Spaniards seemed to be confined to the neighborhood of their immediate place of residence and the direct line of country between one station and another, as they have no vessels for embarkation excepting the native canoe—and an old rotten wooden one—which was lying near our landing place. Had they proper boats on this spacious sheet of water, their journeys would not only be much facilitated, but it would afford a very agreeable variety in their manner of life and help to pass away many of the solitary and wearisome hours which they must unavoidably experience.

I understood that the opposite side of the port had been visited by some soldiers on horseback who obtained but little information. Some converted Indians were found living amongst the natives of the northern and western parts of the port who were esteemed by the Spaniards to be a docile and in general a well-disposed people, though little communication took place between them and the inhabitants of this side. The missionaries found no difficulty in subjecting these people to their authority. It is mild and charitable, teaches them the cultivation of the soil, and introduces amongst them such of the useful arts as are most essential to the comforts of human nature and social life. It is much to be wished that these benevolent exertions may succeed, though there is every

---

[6] Both were established in 1776.

appearance that their progress will be very slow; yet they will probably lay a foundation on which the posterity of the present race may secure to themselves the enjoyment of civil society.

The next establishment of this nature, and the only one within our reach from our present station, was that of Santa Clara, lying to the southeastward at the distance of about eighteen leagues and considered as one day's journey. As there was no probability of our wood and water being completely on board in less than three or four days, I accepted the offer of Señor Sal and the reverend fathers, who undertook to provide us horses for an expedition to Santa Clara the following morning. At the decline of day we took our leave and concluded a visit that had been highly interesting and entertaining to us, and had appeared to be equally grateful to our hospitable friends....

During the night, the wind from the SW blew a strong gale and continued with much rain until Tuesday morning the 20th, when the weather being serene and pleasant, we undertook our journey to Santa Clara. We called on our way on our friends at the *presidio* and mission, with whose company we were to have been favored; but in consequence of some dispatches received by Señor Sal that required his immediate attention and of the indisposition of one of the fathers, they begged leave to decline the engagement. We therefore, agreeably with the fashion of the country, set out, attended by a drove of spare horses—more than double the number of our party—under the guidance of the sergeant of the *presidio*, who was accompanied by six stout, active soldiers, fully accoutered for our protection and for affording us such assistance as we might require.[7]

We considered our route to be parallel with the sea coast, between which and our path, the ridge of mountains before-mentioned

---

[7] The guard of soldiers was also sent to prevent Vancouver from spying, and Sal was reprimanded sharply by Gobernador Arrillaga for allowing the Englishman to see the interior of the country at all.

"A Remarkable Mountain near the River of Monterrey [sic]," 1794, by John Sykes, a British naval officer who visited California with Vancouver aboard the *Discovery*. *Courtesy of the California Historical Society, FN-30521*.

extended to the south-eastward; and as we advanced, their sides and summits exhibited a high degree of luxuriant fertility, interspersed with copses of various forms and magnitude, verdant open spaces, and enriched with stately forest trees of different descriptions. The plain on which we rode stretched from the base of these mountains to the shores of the port, and gradually improved as we proceeded. The holly-leaved oak, maple horse-chestnut, and willow were increased from dwarf shrubs to trees of tolerable size, having some of the common English dwarf oak scattered amongst them.

Our journey was estimated at eighteen leagues, in which distance the country afforded no house, hut, nor any place of shelter excepting such as the spreading trees presented. About noon, having then advanced about twenty-three miles, we arrived at a very pleasant and enchanting lawn, situated amidst a grove of trees at the foot of a small hill, by which flowed a very fine stream of excellent water. This delightful pasture was nearly enclosed on every side and afforded sufficient space for resting ourselves and baiting our cavalry. The bank, which overhung the murmuring brook, was well adapted for taking the refreshment that our provident friends had supplied; and with some grog we had brought from the ship (spirits and wine being scarce articles in this country), we all made a most excellent meal; but it required some resolution to quit so lively a scene, the beauty of which was greatly heightened by the delightful serenity of the weather. To this, however, after resting about an hour, we were obliged to submit, when a fresh supply of cavalry being selected from the drove of horses, we mounted and pursued our journey.[8]

We had not proceeded far from this delightful spot, when we entered a country I little expected to find in these regions. For about twenty miles it could only be compared to a park, which had originally been closely planted with the true old English oak. The underwood that had probably attended its early growth had the appearance of having been cleared away and had left the stately lords of the forest in complete possession of the soil, which was covered with luxuriant herbage and beautifully diversified with pleasing eminencies and valleys; which, with the range of softly rugged mountains that bounded the prospect, required only to be adorned with the neat habitations of an industrious people to produce a scene not inferior to the most studied effect of taste in the disposal of grounds.[9] Especially when seen from the port or its confines, the waters of which extend some distance by the side of this country; and though they were not visible to us, I was inclined to believe they approached within about a league of the road we pursued. Our

---

[8] Through a mix-up in communication, a number of Vancouver's men had understood the distance to Mission Santa Clara to be eighteen miles rather than eighteen leagues (about fifty-four miles); the sailors, unaccustomed to riding for such a long distance, soon required a slow pace. When they finally reached the mission, several men went straight to bed.

[9] In fact, an "industrious people"—the Indians—had helped create this "park" through controlled burnings and land management.

riding was attended with some inconvenience on account of the fox earths and burrows of rabbits, squirrels, rats, and other animals, but our sure-footed horses avoided every danger; notwithstanding, we rode at a brisk rate.

Having passed through this imaginary park, we advanced a few miles in an open, clear meadow and arrived in a low, swampy country, through which our progress was very slow, the horses being nearly knee-deep in mud and water for about six miles. The badness of our road rendered this part of our journey somewhat unpleasant. About dark we reached better ground, and soon after the night closed in, we arrived at the mission of Santa Clara, which according to my estimation is about forty geographical miles from San Francisco. Our journey, excepting that part of it through the morass, had been very pleasant and entertaining, and our reception at Santa Clara by the hospitable fathers of the mission was such as excited in every breast the most lively sensations of gratitude and regard. Father Tomás de la Peña appeared to be the principal of the missionaries. The anxious solicitude of this gentleman and that of his colleague, Father José Sanchez,[10] to anticipate all our wishes, unequivocally manifested the principles by which their conduct was regulated. Our evening passed very pleasantly, and after a most excellent breakfast the next morning (the 21st), on tea and chocolate, we took a view of the establishment and the adjacent country.

The buildings and offices of this mission, like those of San Francisco, form a square, but not an entire enclosure. It is situated in an extensive fertile plain, the soil of which, as also that of the surrounding country, is a rich black productive mold, superior to any I had before seen in America. The particular spot, which had been selected by the reverend fathers for their establishment, did not appear so suitable to their purpose as many other parts of the

---

[10] Father José Bernardo Sánchez (1778–1831) later served as father-president of the Californian missions from 1827 to 1831.

plain within a little distance of their present buildings, which are erected in a low, marshy situation for the sake of being near a run of fine water; notwithstanding that within a few hundred yards they might have built their houses on dry and comfortable eminencies.

The stream of water passes close by the walls of the fathers' apartments, which are upon the same plan with those at San Francisco: built near, and communicating with the church, but appearing to be more extensive and to possess in some degree more comforts, or rather less inconveniences, than those already described. The church was long and lofty, as well built as the rude materials of which it is composed would allow, and when compared with the unimproved state of the country, infinitely more decorated than might have been reasonably expected.

Apartments within the square in which the priests resided were appropriated to a number of young female Indians—and the like reasons were given as at San Francisco for their being so selected and educated. Their occupations were the same, though some of their woolen manufactures surpassed those we had before seen and wanted only the operation of fulling, with which the fathers were unacquainted, to make them very decent blankets. The upper story of their interior oblong square, which might be about 170 feet long and 100 feet broad, were made use of as granaries, as were some of the lower rooms—all of which were well stored with corn and pulse of different sorts. Besides these, in case of fire, there were two spacious warehouses for the reception of grain detached from each other and the rest of the buildings, erected at a convenient distance from the mission. These had been recently finished, contained some stores, and were to be kept constantly full as a reserve in the event of such a misfortune.

They cultivate wheat, maize, peas, and beans; the latter are produced in great variety, and the whole in greater abundance than their necessities require. Of these several sorts they had many thousand bushels in store, of very excellent quality, which had been obtained with little labor and without manure. By the help of a very mean and ill-contrived plow drawn by oxen, the earth is once slightly turned over and smoothed down by a harrow. In the month of November or December, the wheat is sown in drills, or broadcast on the even surface, and scratched in with the harrow; this is the whole of their system of husbandry, which uniformly produces them in July or August an abundant harvest. The maize, peas, and beans are produced with as little labor; these are sown in the spring months and succeed extremely well, as do hemp and flax, or linseed. The wheat affords in general from twenty-five to thirty for one according to the seasons, twenty-five for one being the least return they have ever yet deposited in their granaries from the field; notwithstanding the enormous waste occasioned by their rude method of threshing, which is always performed in the open air by the treading of cattle. The product of the other grains and pulse bears a similar proportion to that of the wheat. I was much surprised to find that neither barley nor oats were cultivated; on inquiry I was given to understand that as the superior kinds of grain could be plentifully obtained with the same labor that the inferior ones would require, they had some time ago declined the cultivation of them. The labors of the field are performed—under the immediate inspection of the fathers—by the natives who are instructed in the Roman Catholic faith and taught the art of husbandry. The annual produce is taken under the care of these worthy pastors, who distribute it in such quantities to the several persons as completely answers all the useful and necessary purposes.

Besides a few acres of arable land, which we saw under cultivation near the mission, was a small spot of garden ground producing several sorts of vegetables in great perfection and abundance. The extent of it, however, like the garden at San Francisco, appeared unequal to the consumption of the European residents: the priests and their guard, consisting of a corporal and six soldiers. Here were planted peaches, apricots, apples, pears, figs, and vines, all of which excepting the latter promised to succeed very well. The failure of the vines here, as well as at San Francisco, is ascribed to a want of knowledge in their culture; the soil and climate being well adapted to most sorts of fruit. Of this we had many evidences in the excellence of its natural unassisted productions. In this country the oak, as timber, appears to take the lead. A tree of this description near the establishment measured fifteen feet in girth and was high in proportion, but was not considered by the fathers as of an extraordinary size; and I am convinced that on our journey we passed several oaks of greater magnitude. The timber of these trees is reputed to be equal in quality to any produced in Europe. The elm, ash, beech, birch, and some variety of pines grew in the interior and more elevated parts of the country in the greatest luxuriance and abundance.

Our attention was next called to the village of the Indians near the mission. The habitations were not so regularly disposed, nor did it contain so many as the village at San Francisco; yet the same horrid state of uncleanliness and laziness seemed to pervade the whole. A sentiment of compassion involuntarily obtruded on the mind in contemplating the natural or habitual apathy to all kind of exertion in this humble race. There was scarcely any sign in their general deportment of their being at all benefited or of having added one single ray of comfort to their own wretched condition by the precepts and laborious exertions of their religious instructors, whose lives are sacrificed to their welfare, and who seem entirely devoted to the benevolent office of rendering them a better and a happier people. They appeared totally insensible to the benefits with which they were provided, excepting in the article of food; this they now find ready at hand, without the labor of procuring it, or being first reduced by cold and hunger nearly to a state of famine, and then being obliged to expose themselves to great inconvenience in quest of a precarious and often scanty means of subsistence. Not only grain, but the domestic animals have been introduced with success amongst them; many of the natives have, by the unremitted labor of the fathers, been taught to manufacture very useful and comfortable garments from the wool of their sheep. For the introduction of this animal they ought to be highly grateful, since by the mildness of the climate and the fertility of the soil, they are easily propagated and reared; and while they provided them with comfortable clothing, afford them also nourishing and delicate food.

These advantages however seemed to have operated as yet to little purpose on the minds of these untaught children of nature, who appeared to be a compound of stupidity and innocence, their passions are calm; and regardless of reputation as men or renown as a people, they are stimulated neither to the obtaining of consequence amongst themselves by any peaceful arts nor superiority over their neighbors by warlike achievements, so common amongst the generality of the Indian tribes. All the operations and functions, both of body and mind, appeared to be carried on with a mechanical, lifeless, careless indifference; and as the Spaniards assert they found them in the same state of inactivity and ignorance on their earliest visits, this disposition is probably inherited from their forefathers.

Further efforts are now making at this mission to break through the gloomy cloud of insensibility in which at present these people are enveloped by giving them new habitations; an indulgence that will most probably be followed by others, as their minds appear capable of receiving them. A certain number of the most intelligent, tractable, and industrious persons were selected from the group and were employed in a pleasant and well-adapted spot of land facing the mission, under the direction and instruction of the fathers, in building for themselves a range of small, but comparatively speaking, comfortable and convenient habitations. The walls, though not so thick, are constructed in the same manner with those described in the square at San Francisco, and the houses are formed after the European fashion, each consisting of two commodious rooms below with garrets over them. At the back of each house a space of ground is enclosed, sufficient for cultivating a large quantity of vegetables, for rearing poultry, and for other useful and domestic purposes. The buildings were in a state of forwardness, and when finished, each house was designed to accommodate one distinct family only; and it is greatly to be wished, for the credit of the rational part of the creation, that this supine race of our fellow creatures may not long remain insensible to, and unconvinced of, the superior advantages they may derive, or the new comforts they may possess, by this alteration in their mode of living.

It is by no means improbable that by this circumstance alone they may be roused from their natural lethargic indifference and be induced to keep themselves clean, and to exert themselves in obtaining other blessings consequent on civilized society. This once effected, the laborious talk of their worthy and charitable benefactors will wear the appearance of being accomplished; and should it be hereafter attended with a grateful sense of the obligations conferred, it is not possible to conceive how much these excellent men will feel rewarded in having been the cause of meliorating the comfortless condition of these wretched humble creatures.

Our conversation admitted of no pause with these seemingly happy and benevolent priests; whilst we acquired much information we were highly entertained, and the day was far advanced by the time our curiosity was thus far gratified.

In compliment to our visit, the fathers ordered a feast for the Indians of the village. The principal part of the entertainment was beef, furnished from a certain number of black cattle, which were presented on the occasion to the villagers. These animals propagate very fast, and being suffered to live in large herds on the fertile plains of Santa Clara—in a sort of wild state—some skill and adroitness is required to take them. This office was at first intended to have been performed by the natives, but it was overruled by Señor Paries, an ensign in the Spanish army, who, with one of the priests of Señor Quadra's vessel, had joined our party from a mission at some little distance called Santa Cruz. This gentlemen conceived the business of taking the cattle would be better performed by the soldiers, who are occasionally cavalry and are undoubtedly very good horsemen. We mounted and accompanied them to the field to be spectators of their exploits. Each of the soldiers was provided with a strong line made of horsehair or of thongs of leather, or rather hide, with a long running noose. This is thrown with great dexterity whilst at full speed, and nearly with a certainty, over the horns of the animals by two men, one on each side of the ox, at the same instant of time; and having a strong highpeaked pummel to their saddles, each takes a turn round it with the end of the line, and by that means the animal is kept completely at bay and effectually prevented from doing either the men or horses any injury, which they would be very liable to, from the wildness and ferocity of the cattle. In this situation the beast is led to the place of slaughter, where a third person, with equal dexterity, whilst the animal is kicking and plunging between the horses, entangles its hind legs by a rope and throws it down, on which its throat is immediately cut.

Twenty-two bullocks, each weighing from four to six hundred weight, were killed on this occasion; eighteen were given to the inhabitants of the village, and the rest were appropriated to the use of the soldiers and the mission, in addition to their regular weekly allowance of twenty-four oxen, which are killed for their service every Saturday. Hence it is evident, as the whole of their stock has sprung from fifteen head of breeding cattle, which were distributed between this and two other missions, established about the year 1778, that these animals must be very prolific to allow of such an abundant supply. Their great increase in so short a time is to be ascribed to the rigid economy of the fathers, who would not allow any to be killed until they had so multiplied as to render their extirpation not easy to be effected. The same wise management has been observed with their sheep, and their horses have increased nearly at the same rate.

Although this village did not appear so populous as that at San Francisco, I was given to understand that there were nearly double the number of inhabitants belonging to it; and that in consequence of the many unconverted natives in the neighborhood of Santa Clara, several of the Christian Indians of good character were dispersed amongst their countrymen for the purpose of inducing them to partake of the advantages held out to them, in which they had not been altogether unsuccessful. All who have offered themselves as converts have been admitted and adopted, notwithstanding the artifices of several, who have remained in and about the mission until they have acquired a stock of food and clothing, with which they have decamped. This improper conduct has, however, had no sort of effect on the benevolent minds of the fathers, who have not only uniformly supplied their wants on a second visit, but also those of many wandering tribes that would be at the trouble of asking their assistance.

Thus concluded our morning's entertainment, and we retired to dinner. In the convent, a most excellent and abundant repast of the productions of the country was provided, which were in the greatest perfection. The day passed to the mutual satisfaction of all parties, and we found ourselves under some difficulty the next morning, Thursday 22nd, to excuse ourselves from accepting the pressing solicitations of these good people to prolong our stay at Santa Clara; however, necessity and not inclination obliged us to decline. We took our leave at an early hour, highly gratified by our reception and entertainment, which had amply compensated for the fatigue or inconvenience attending so long a journey, performed in a way to which we were so little accustomed.

Nikolai Petrovich Rezanov and Georg von Langsdorff

1806

————◦◦◦————

From the time of Vancouver's visit to the American conquest more than fifty years later, California's successive governors were never free from the fear of foreign invasion. San Francisco's *presidio* might appear to protect the Golden Gate, but Spain had no money to maintain such a costly edifice, let alone expand it. Even the most patriotic Spaniard recognized that there was little hope of defending such a long and empty coastline—for that settlers were needed, and California had few immigrants (its non-Indian population numbered only 1,800 at the turn of the century). Plans were developed to evacuate the coast in the event of an invasion, moving people and cattle to hidden interior valleys. Whenever a crisis appeared imminent, a watch was set for foreign ships, and mission *padres* were ordered to pray for a Spanish victory. But despite Spain's weakness, California's isolation was sufficient to hide its military frailty.

The few strange ships that did sail its coast in the first decade of the nineteenth century were New England smugglers bound for China and fur traders from England, France, Portugal, and, increasingly, Russia. Russian traders had been collecting sea otter pelts in

Alaska as early as the 1740s, and in 1799 such commerce fell under the control of a single monopoly, the Russian-American Company. That same year they established a permanent capital called Novo-Arkhangelsk (later Sitka) on Baranof Island in southeast Alaska. In 1803, Boston sea captain Joseph O'Cain and Russian governor Aleksandr Baranov agreed on a multinational, cooperative venture: local Alaskan Aleut Indians, converted by Russian Orthodox missionaries, used canoes and bone spears to hunt California beavers and otters; then Yankee ships transported the furs to China. Using the Aleuts and working from a series of bases down the coast, the joint company could send expeditions to systematically slaughter all the animals in a particular region. The first such trip brought Sitka $80,000.

Trade soon flourished between these ships and California's missions, *pueblos*, and *presidios*. Officially, Spanish trade with foreign vessels was outlawed, and any ship caught trafficking could be impounded and its captain and crew imprisoned. But Californians encouraged the illicit commerce, as they were desperate for everyday necessities and exotic luxuries from New England, Europe, and China not available from the annual supply ship from San Blas. As for the Russians, they needed California's fruit, vegetables, and meat, which were in short supply at their northern settlements.

Nikolai Petrovich Rezanov, one of the founders of the Russian-American Company, launched the first Russian circumnavigation of the globe in 1803. Commanded by Captain Adam Johann Krusenstern, the expedition's goals included improving trade relations with Japan and investigating the quality of life at the Alaskan colonies. Joining Rezanov onboard was a German naturalist, Georg Heinrich von Langsdorff. The two men could not have been more different. Rezanov was born into a noble family in St. Petersburg in 1764 and spent his youth working as a diplomat in Siberia for Empress Catherine II. Affluent and haughty, Rezanov dreamt of annexing western North America and populating it with Russians. Ten years younger, less worldly and more scholarly, Langsdorff was an enthusiastic scientist with a doctoral degree in medicine and surgery from the University of Göttingen. He was so eager to see the world that, when not initially chosen for the Krusenstern expedition, he sailed to Copenhagen, checked into the same hotel as the officers, and pleaded with the captain. Kursenstern admired "the enthusiasm of this philosopher.... So great was his ardor to join in the voyage that he was not to be deterred." In contrast, Krusenstern and Rezanov quarreled constantly, especially after a disastrous stop at Japan where Rezanov, laden with gifts for the *mikado*, was humiliatingly imprisoned.

The expedition finally reached Sitka in August 1805 only to discover a terrible scene of famine and disease caused by the delay of supply ships (not unlike similar scenes in California thirty years earlier). To make matters worse, cold rains drizzled for weeks. The 200 men of the colony were reduced to eating whatever they could catch on their desolate island, including eagles, crows, and manta rays. Their Aleutian converts were in even worse condition: "It is revolting to a mind of any feeling to see these poor creatures half-starved and almost naked," wrote Langsdorff. He also recorded that the Aleuts were routinely "put to death in the most horrible manner" by the Russians. Rezanov was instructed to remain there and act as plenipotentiary while the expedition continued on to warmer lands. He talked Langsdorff into staying with him.

They managed to survive the cruel Alaskan winter, but Sitka had no food, medicine, or supplies. Luckily, the American trading ship *Juno* put in at Sitka, and Rezanov bought the entire ship and cargo for 8,000 dollars. The ship's supplies offered temporary relief, but Rezanov and Langsdorff soon were forced to sail for the only colony on the Pacific that offered any hope of providing the food the Russians needed—California. With nearly every man onboard wracked with scurvy, the *Juno* limped through the Golden Gate on April 8, 1806. California seemed a paradise, its abundance of game and lush fields a stark contrast to Alaska. For several days the Russians did little but eat.

Gobernador Arrillaga, always a stickler for regulations, gladly fed the Russians but refused to furnish supplies for Sitka. In despair, Rezanov seized upon a plan to improve his bartering position—he proposed marriage to Doña Concepción, the fifteen-year-old daughter of José Argüello, commander of the San Francisco presido. She agreed, undoubtedly awed by the well-traveled nobleman and his tales of courtly life in St. Petersburg. But she was Roman Catholic and he Eastern Orthodox, so Rezanov explained that he would first have to speak with Russian religious authorities, promising to return soon for a wedding. The *Juno* was then loaded with bread, dried meat, and supplies from the missions.

Meanwhile, Langsdorff was permitted to visit missions San Francisco and San José and to make drawings of local residents, plants, and animals. His unflattering descriptions of the mission Indians—he called them "filthy," "badly proportioned," and "dull, heavy, and neglectful"—reveal the stultifying effects of mission life, not to mention his cultural biases. His visit came at the beginning of the single worst epidemic of the Spanish era—between 1806 and 1810, measles killed more than one-third of all neophytes in the San Francisco Bay Area but left the Spaniards untouched. "Measles have wreaked havoc upon the Indians of this province, but none at all upon the *gente de razón* [Spaniards]," noted Father Martín de Landaeta at Mission San Francisco on April 28, 1806. "We missionaries here find ourselves with about 400 sick." About 150 neophytes at Mission San Francisco alone perished from measles during the Russians' visit, a tragedy Langsdorff only mentioned once in passing.

The *Juno* sailed back to Sitka on May 21. Langsdorff was by this time quite disenchanted with Rezanov. "Though at Kamschatka large promises were made me, both in writing and orally, as to what should be done for the promotion of scientific undertakings, no alacrity has been shown in fulfilling these promises," he complained in his journal. He secured permission to leave Rezanov at Sitka on June 19, 1806, trekking overland through Siberia. It took him almost two years to reach St. Petersburg. He went on to be elected a full member of the Russian Academy of Sciences and appointed Russian consul-general at Rio de Janeiro. His diary of the Krusenstern expedition was published as *Voyages and Travels in Various Parts of the World* in 1813. Eight years later he caught a fever (probably malaria) and went mad while leading an expedition into the interior of Brazil. He spent the last thirty years of his life being cared for by a friend in Freiburg.

In June 1806, Rezanov wrote his account of, in his words, "the first step of a Russian on the soil of Nueva California." Addressed to Russian Minister of Commerce Nikolai Petrovich Rumiantsev, his report was not published until 1863 in *Historical Review of the Organization of the Russian-American Company.* Three months after finishing it, Rezanov followed Langsdorff's frigid overland path but died of fever and exhaustion in Krasnoiarsk, Siberia, on March 8, 1807. His true intentions regarding young Doña Concepción died with him. In what would become California's most famous love story, the fifteen-year-old bride-to-be reportedly languished for thirty-five years before learning of his death. The following narrative of Rezanov and Langsdorff's visit to San Francisco Bay, drawn from their accounts, begins on April 8, 1806.

Nikolai Petrovich Rezanov (1764–1807). *Courtesy of The Bancroft Library.*

NIKOLAI PETROVICH REZANOV AND
GEORG VON LANGSDORFF

The Rezanov Voyage

*R*EZANOV: Embracing at once the opportunity offered by a favoring wind and tide to enter the *puerto* on the following morning [April 8, 1806], and the suspicious nature of the Spanish government being known to me, I thought it best to go straight through the gate and by the fort, in view of our desperate situation. I deemed it useless to send in and ask for permission to enter, since, in the event of refusal, we should necessarily perish at sea, and decided that two or three cannonballs would make less difference to us than refusal.

With all sails full, we ran for the *puerto*. As we neared the fort a great commotion was observed among the soldiers, and when abreast of it one of them asked, through a speaking-trumpet, "What ship is that?" "Russian," we replied. They shouted to us several times to anchor, but we merely replied, *"Sí, señor; sí, señor,"* and simulated an active effort to comply with their demand, but in the meantime we had passed the fort and were running up the *puerto*, and at a cannon-shot's distance complied.

Some twenty horsemen—among whom were the *comandante* and one *misionero*—soon after this demanded the surrender of the ship, but we were not alarmed, as their cavalry was within range of our grape-shot. I dispatched Lieutenant Davidov to inform them that I was the Russian officer of whose coming I hoped they had been notified by their government; that I should have proceeded to

Monterey had not my ship been damaged by storms, which compelled me to seek shelter in the first port; that I should leave as soon as the repairs were made.

The answer brought back was that orders had already been received from the Spanish sovereign to render us all necessary assistance, and that the *comandante* invited me to dine with him at the *presidio*, at the same time assuring me that all my requests should be promptly attended to. Inspired by gratitude, I thereupon went ashore and was met by Don Luís Antonio Argüello,[1] a son of the *comandante*, temporarily in command during the absence of his father. We were proffered saddlehorses, but as the *presidio* is not more than a verst [about two-thirds of a mile] from the shore, we went on foot, with the *comandante* and the *misionero padre* José Antonio Uría.

The cordial reception by the hospitable family of the *comandante* overwhelmed us. An invitation to dinner followed. We remained until evening, and then returned to the ship.

Don Luís informed me with marked courtesy and tactfulness that he must send a courier to the *gobernador* at Monterey, the capital, to advise him of my arrival, and that he therefore found himself compelled to ask where our ships, the *Nadeschda* and the *Neva*, were, of which they had previously been notified.

I replied that I had ordered them back to Russia; that I had been entrusted by the emperor with the command over all his American territories, and had visited them during the past year, having wintered at Norfolk Sound; that I had finally decided to visit the *gobernador* of Nueva California to confer with him, as the chief of a neighboring territory, as to our mutual interests.

---

[1] Luís Antonio Argüello (1784–1830), son of José Dario Argüello and brother of Concepción Argüello, was twenty-two years old at the time of Rezanov's visit in 1806. In 1817, he succeeded his father as *comandante* of the San Francisco *presidio* and went on to become California's first native-born *gobernador* (1822–1825).

Be pleased, gracious sire,[2] not to consider that it was from empty pride, but merely to impress the Spaniards with the importance of our possessions in the north and to further our interests with them, that I thus proclaimed myself *comandante*. The welfare, the interests of our country required it. In any case, even here I transgressed but very little, as I really have the chief command, and that by our emperor's order, and also by the power of attorney given me by the [Russian-American Company's] shareholders. I made no improper use of these, but, on the contrary, sacrificed myself every hour for the benefit of those whom I represented.

By the courier sent by Don Luís Argüello to the *gobernador*, I also sent a letter in which I thanked him for his gracious manifestations of hospitality and informed him that as soon as the vessel was repaired, I should leave for Monterey.

On the following day, the *misionero padres* of the Misión San Francisco de Asís extended to us an invitation to dinner. This *misión* is about an hour's ride from the *presidio*, and with my officers I went there in compliance with the invitation. In our conversation with the *misioneros* there, we touched upon the subject of trade, and it was very perceptible to us that they were strongly inclined thereto.

Later, in a more fitting connection, I shall have the honor of setting out for the consideration of your excellency the condition of all the *misiones* and *presidios*, the trade, surplus, and requirements of this territory; but now, gracious sire, be kind enough to permit me to invite your attention to what are perhaps but trifling matters, that I may show you how, imperceptibly to those of whom I shall speak, I accomplished my purpose, despite the desperate straits we were then in, and also the means I employed.

Upon our return from the *misión*—not only as a vehicle for the reciprocation of the dinners given by the *comandante* and the

---

[2] Rezanov addressed his account to Russian Minister of Commerce Nikolai Petrovich Rumiantsev.

misioneros, but also in order to hide from the Spaniards our distress and needfulness, of which the Boston vessels had told them to our disadvantage—I distributed fitting and valuable presents, thus displaying every evidence of wealth and demonstrating our generosity. My efforts were crowned with success. There was not one, either male or female, who did not receive something especially desired, and the hearts of the people were won for us by the general satisfaction following. Not only this, but their reports of the generosity of the Russians allured the *padres* from distant *misiones,* while those nearby voluntarily offered to supply us with a cargo of breadstuffs.

Perceiving the possibility of obtaining a cargo of breadstuffs at this *puerto* in a short time, I decided to go overland to Monterey and sent by courier a letter to the *gobernador,* stating that as the repairs to my ship would perhaps detain me a considerable time at San Francisco, I would respectfully ask him to permit me to visit him. His reply was framed in the most courteous terms. He would not permit me to go to so much trouble; he would undertake the journey, himself, the following day; and stated that he had sent orders that I should be assisted in everything. At the same time, he sent me, through the *comandante* temporal, official congratulations on my arrival.

Thereupon I recognized the suspicious nature of the Spanish government, which at every point prevents foreign visitors from gaining a knowledge of the interior of the country and from observing the weakness of their military defenses.

In the meantime, the excellent climate of Nueva California, the abundance of breadstuffs there, and the comparison of the resources of the country with our destitution were hourly subjects of conversation among the members of our crew. We noticed their inclination and desire to remain here permanently, and thereupon we took the necessary precautions against their desertion.

The third day after we arrived, three Bostonians and a Prussian, who, when we purchased the *Juno,* entered the company's service as sailors, expressed to me their desire to stay. I told them that I would consult the *comandante,* but he, when conferred with, refused to consent, whereupon I ordered their removal to a barren island, where they were held until the day of our departure.

In the meantime, we placed pickets on shore and established rounds, and a mounted patrol was given us by the Spaniards; but, in spite of every precaution, two of our most esteemed men, Mikhail Kalianin and Peter Polkanov, seized the opportunity to escape when at the creek washing their clothes, vanishing without a trace.

Subsequently I obtained the word of honor of the Spanish authorities that the deserters, if found, would be deported to Russia by way of Vera Cruz; but I ask your excellency that they be punished and returned to America to remain forever. Without severe punishment as an example, it will be hard to control the others.

While awaiting the arrival of the *gobernador* we made visits daily to the residence of the hospitable Argüellos and soon became on intimate terms with them. Loveliest of the lovely sisters of Don Luís, the *comandante* temporal, the Doña Concepción is the universally recognized beauty of Nueva California, and your excellency will concur with me when I say that our past sufferings were thus delightfully requited, for our time was passed very joyously.

LANGSDORFF: The Misión Santa Clara de Asís, lying between San Francisco and Monterey is—with regard to its fine situation, fertility of soil, population, and extent of buildings and grounds—considered the largest and richest *misión.* All the *misiones* have cattle in great numbers and an abundance of other productions necessary to the support of man; and the *padres,* in general, conduct themselves with such prudence, kindness, paternal care, and justice, in their at-

Georg Heinrich von Langsdorff (ca. 1774–1852). *Courtesy of The Bancroft Library.*

titude towards the *neófitos*, that tranquillity, happiness, obedience, and unanimity are the natural results of their methods. Corporal punishment commonly follows disobedience. The *padres* have recourse to the *presidios* only on very extraordinary occasions, as, for instance, when expeditions are sent out in pursuit of prospective converts, or when couriers carrying communications require protection, or as a precaution against sudden attacks.

The number of soldiers being so small and their services so slight, it does not seem worthwhile to maintain an establishment for them. The Presidio de San Francisco has not more than forty, and it has three *misiones* under its protection. These are San Francisco (same name as the *presidio*), Santa Clara, and San José, the last named being established but a few years ago [1797]. There are seldom more than from three to five soldiers at any time at any *misión*, but this seemingly small number has hitherto been always found sufficient to keep the Indians under proper restraint. I was assured by a person worthy of credit that the Spanish *cortes* [representative assembly] does not spend less than a million *piastres* annually for the support of the *misiones* and their military establishments in the two Californias; and that, too, without deriving any advantage from them, other than the spreading of Christianity in these *provincias* of Nueva España.

Each of the *padres* has several horses for his own use, and when one starts out on an expedition for finding prospective *neófitos*, he is always escorted by one or more soldiers, who precede him on the way. At such times the soldiers commonly throw over their breast and shoulders a deerskin in mantle, which is intended as a protection against the arrows of the Indians, these being incapable of piercing leather. This mantle is worn on other occasions, also, as on dress parade, and when approaching a *presidio* or *misión*. By a royal command, it is not permissible for the *misioneros* to go any distance without military protection. As they carry only the Bible and the cross as their personal protection, a military escort accompanies them at such times.

This information was imparted while we were enjoying our breakfast, after which we were taken around to see whatever was worthy of notice.

Behind the residence of the *padres* there is a large courtyard, enclosed by houses. Here live the Indian women of the *misión*, who are employed under the immediate supervision of the *padres* in useful occupations, such as cleaning and combing wool, spinning, weaving, etc. Their principal business is the manufacture of a woolen cloth and blankets for the Indians' own use. The wool of the sheep here is very fine and of superior quality, but the tools and looms are of a crude make. As the *misioneros* are the sole instructors of these people, who themselves know very little about such matters—scarcely even understanding the fulling—the cloth is far from the perfection that might be achieved.

All the girls and women are closely guarded in separate houses—as though under lock and key—and kept at work. They are but seldom permitted to go out in the day, and never at night. As soon, however, as a girl marries, she is free, and, with her husband, lives in one of the Indian villages belonging to the *misión*. These villages are called *"las rancherías."* Through such arrangements or precautions, the *misioneros* hope to bind the *neófitos* to the *misión* and spread their faith with more ease and security. About a hundred paces from the buildings properly called the *misión* lies one of these Indian villages or barracks. It consists of eight long rows of houses, where each family lives separate and apart from the others. The Indian *neófitos* here are about twelve hundred in number.

The principal food of the Indians is a thick soup composed of meat, vegetables, and pulse. Because of the scarcity of fish here, or the want of proper means of catching them, the *misioneros* obtained a special dispensation from the pope allowing the eating of meat on fast days. The food is apportioned three times a day—morning, noon, and evening—in large ladlefuls. At mealtimes a big bell is rung, and each family sends a vessel to the kitchen and is served as many measures as there are members. I was present once at the time the soup was served, and it appeared incomprehensible to me how anyone could consume so much nourishing food three times a day. According to what we were told by our *cicerone*, from forty to fifty oxen are killed every week for the community. Besides this meal, bread, Indian corn, peas, beans, and other kinds of pulse are distributed in abundance, without any regular or stated allowance.

After satisfying our curiosity at the *ranchería*, we inspected several other serviceable institutions for the promotion of production and economy in the establishment. There was a building for melting tallow and another for making soap; there were workshops for locksmiths and blacksmiths, and for cabinet-makers and carpenters; there were houses for the storage of tallow, soap, butter, salt, wool, and ox-hides (these being articles of exportation), with storerooms for corn, peas, beans, and other kinds of pulse.

When one considers that in this way two or three *misionero padres* take upon themselves such a sort of voluntary exile from their country, only to spread Christianity, and to civilize a wild and uncultivated race of men, to teach them husbandry and various useful arts, cherishing and instructing them as if they were their own children, providing them with dwellings, food, and clothing, with everything else necessary for their subsistence, and maintaining the utmost order and regularity of conduct—when all these particulars, I say, are considered, one cannot sufficiently admire the zeal and activity that carry them through labors so arduous, nor forbear to wish the most complete success to their undertaking.

Meanwhile, we were called to dinner and were served with a very appetizing soup seasoned with herbs and vegetables of different kinds, roast fowl, leg of mutton, different kinds of vegetables dressed in different ways, salad, pastry, preserved fruits, and many fine sorts of food dishes prepared with milk. All these were things to which our palates had been so long strangers that we were not a little pleased with them. The wine offered us had been brought from the peninsula of Antigua [Baja] California and was of but an ordinary quality. Soon after dinner we were served with tea of poor quality and chocolate of superexcellence.

Thereafter we were shown the kitchen garden, but it did not equal our expectations. There was very little fruit, and that, of inferior quality. Most of the beds were overgrown with weeds. Of fine vegetables and herbs there were few. Northwest winds, which prevail on this coast, and a soil dry and sandy by nature, are insurmountable obstacles to horticulture. The only vegetables that grow well in the gardens are asparagus, cabbage, several kinds of lettuce, onions, and potatoes. In outlying fields, more sheltered from the winds, peas, beans, corn, and other pulse are cultivated and thrive fairly well. Corn is here less productive than it is in some other parts of Nueva California. Notwithstanding this, the Spanish government thought it necessary to establish a *misión* in the neighborhood of such an excellent port as that of San Francisco, with a *presidio* for its protection. Both establishments are in a flourishing condition, principally on account of the great number of cattle bred....

Although we acquired but a slight knowledge of the Indians of this *misión* on this day, I will combine here all that I learned concerning them with my observations during our entire stay.

The *neófitos* of the Misión San Francisco are the original inhabitants of these and the neighboring parts. A few come from the mouth of a large river that flows into the northernmost part of the harbor, and some from the neighborhood of Port Bodega, which lies to the north of San Francisco. All these people that inhabit the coasts of Nueva California are divided into tribes, under the names of Estero, Tuiban, and Tamien.[3] Some other tribes, who live more

---

[3] The Tuiban and Tamien Indians both spoke an Ohlone language and lived along the southern coast of San Francisco Bay; Estero (meaning "estuary") was not a tribal group but an arbitrary designation given by the *padres* to a variety of Indians, including the Alson and Tuiban.

inland to the eastward of these, and who were formerly in continual warfare with them, called themselves Cholvon and Tamcan.[4]

The former are nomadic, with no fixed abode. Their food consists partly of fish, sea dogs, shellfish, and other sea foods, partly of animals killed in the chase, and partly of seeds, herbs, and roots. The last mentioned are considered the greatest dainties.

Their habitations are small round huts of straw, cone-shaped, erected at any stopping place. These huts are burned upon their leaving, and the hut in which a person dies is also given to the flames. Both sexes go almost naked, wearing merely a girdle tied around the waist. Only in the coldest days of winter do they throw over their bodies a covering of deerskin or the skin of the sea otter. They also make for themselves garments of the feathers of several kinds of water fowl, particularly ducks and geese. These they bind closely together in a string-like fashion, which strings are afterwards joined tight, making a dress of a feather-fur appearance. Both sides are alike, and it is so warm that it would be an excellent protection against the cold of even a more northerly clime. Sea otter skins are also cut by them in small strips, and these they twist together and join in the same manner as with the feathers just described, and also as with the feathers, both sides alike. These coverings are worn principally by the women, and but very rarely by the males.

These Indians are of middling or rather short stature, and their color is of such a dark brown that it approaches black. This color is owing very much to their filthy mode of living, to the power of the sun's rays, to their custom of smearing their bodies with mud and ember dust, and their slovenly way of wearing their scanty covering.

Their lips are large, thick, and protruding; their noses broad, flat, and negro-like. Their features in many respects resemble those of the negro, and their color also, but their black hair, however, is

---

[4] The Cholvon and Tamcan Indians both spoke Northern Yokuts and lived along the Old River branch of the lower San Joaquín River.

111

in the highest degree different, being long and straight. Left to grow naturally, it would often hang down even below the hips, but they commonly cut it to the length of four or five inches, when it sticks out like bristles, and this to the eyes of a European is very repellent. The forehead appears extremely low, as the hair grows very far down towards the eyes. The eyebrows are not very hirsute. The beard is but moderately thick, and many pinch out the hairs with mussel shells.

None of the men that we saw were over five feet in height. They were badly proportioned, and their appearance was so dull, heavy, and neglectful that we were all agreed that we had never before seen the human race on such a low level.

Their weapons consist of the bow and arrow, and as these contribute essentially to the acquisition of many of the necessaries of life, their construction seems a principal object of their skill and industry. The shape of the bow is pleasing in appearance. It is made of wood, is from three to four-and-a-half feet long, neatly constructed, and drawn together very ingeniously with tendons of the deer. By this means the wood is kept in place securely, and the bow has such elasticity that very little strength and dexterity are required to draw the arrow. Both the bow and the arrow are very neatly made, and the arrows are pointed with vitrified lava, or obsidian, which is inserted in the shaft and bound with tendons. The Spaniards, on their first encounters in the country, had reason to remember with sorrow the skill of the Indians in the use of this weapon.

Among the articles in use in their habitations, I saw baskets made of the bark of trees.[5] These were so ingeniously woven, compact, and impervious to water that they are used as drinking-vessels, food dishes, and even as roasting-pans. Corn and pulse are put in them, and the Indians, by turning them quickly and dexterously over a slow charcoal fire, get every grain thoroughly browned

---

[5] Actually split roots and stalks.

without the basket being scorched in the least.[6] Many of these baskets, or vessels, are ornamented with the scarlet feathers of the *Oriolus phoeniceous,* or with the black crest-feathers of the California partridge *(Tetraonis cristati),* or with shells and corals.

However dull and heavy, however filthy, ugly, and disgusting these people appear, they show a great fondness for ornaments and sports. Their ornaments are of many kinds and are generally fashioned of shells and feathers. Among the shells chiefly used is a sort of sea-ear—probably the *Haliotis gigantea* [abalone]—which abounds on these coasts, chiefly in the vicinity of Monterey, and which, in brilliancy of color, is scarcely inferior to the *Haliotis iris* of New Zealand. Small rings are made of another sort of shell [clams], but I never saw a perfect one. These rings are all of the same size, and are of perfectly accurate make and bored through the middle without the aid of any kind of instrument. In appearance they are much like glass beads and are strung together to make necklaces.

Their most beautiful head ornament is made of the two middle tail feathers of the golden-winged woodpecker *(Picus auratus),* the shafts of which are naturally of a brilliant vermilion color. They are stripped to within an inch of the end, and then very cleverly strung and bound together so as to form a sort of bandeau for the head, the effect of which is very pleasing.

Among other curiosities that I procured from these people—in exchange for European glass beads, silk ribbons, knives, and other articles—was one of these bandeaus, which consisted of 450 feathers; hence 225 birds were required in the making of it. I could not imagine, nor did I learn, how so large a number of these birds was procured, as the golden-winged woodpecker is a bird that frequents only a heavily-timbered territory, and there is very little timber within the region of San Francisco. Another head ornament, which is usually worn by these Indians at their dances, is made of

---

[6] Rather, hot rocks were added to heat up grains and soups.

113

the feathers of a vulture very common in these parts, the *Vultus aura*. The tail and wing feathers are woven together in such a way that the ornament resembles a Turkish fez.

Tattooing is a common practice, but principally among the women. Some have a double or triple line from each corner of the mouth down to the chin, while others have, in the middle of the chin only, a few concentrical stripes, which converge. Most have simple long and cross stripes from the chin over the neck down to the breast and upon the shoulders.

Among all their amusements there is none in which they take so much delight as in their dances. But of these I shall speak more particularly later. Another of their games or pastimes they call *tussi*. A number sit together in a circle, one of whom has a little stick in his hand. This he passes, in a covert manner, from one hand to the other, singing the while. When he thinks he has twirled and twisted it about so effectually that the company does not know the hand that holds it, he turns suddenly to some one of them, and, with both hands shut and looking at him steadfastly, utters a loud "Ha!" It is the part of the one so addressed to guess in which hand the stick is. Should his guess prove accurate, he takes the stick and juggles with it in turn, but if he misses, a loud laugh is raised against him by the whole company.

When it is considered that two or three *padres* and four or five soldiers keep in order a community of from a thousand to fifteen hundred rough and uncivilized men, and make them pursue a course of life wholly different from that to which they had always been accustomed, it must be presumed that the cause is principally to be found in the mildness and forbearance with which they are treated, and in the paternal care and kindness extended toward them. I must, however, also attribute the cause, in no small measure, to the simplicity of these poor creatures, who, in stature no less than in mind, are certainly of a very inferior race of human beings. I believe them wholly incapable of forming among themselves any regular and combined plan for their own emancipation.

Although it must be allowed generally, as facts incontestable, that a moderate climate is the most favorable to the human species, and that the mild regions of the globe are those which nature points out to man as the most friendly for his habitation, here we find a most striking exception to the general rule.

Here, on this western coast of North America in the thirty-eighth degree of north latitude, where the aborigines live in a very moderate and equable climate, where there is no lack of food and no care about habitations or clothing, where by hunting they can obtain sustenance, where an abundance of roots, seeds, fruits, and the products of the sea, in many varieties, are at their hands—these people are, notwithstanding, small, ugly, and of bad proportion in their persons, and heavy and dull in their minds. Yet several tribes living on the same coast, on the contrary, as, for example, the Kolosh, in the fifty-eighth and fifty-ninth degrees of north latitude, are strong, well built, and handsome, and possessing so much acuteness of mind that by their shrewdness or cunning they have often foiled both the English and the Russians. I frankly acknowledge that the phenomenon of these Californian pigmies, in such a mild climate and with an abundance of food, is to me a puzzle.

But I will return to the *religiosos* of the *misiones*. Properly speaking, they are merely the stewards through whose instruction the *neófitos* obtain the comforts of life, a habitation, and food and clothing. The *neófitos* are principally employed in such work as husbandry, tending cattle, and shearing sheep, or in handiwork, such as building, preparing tallow, and making soap and household articles. They are also employed in the transportation of provisions, as well as other goods, from one *misión* or *presidio* to another. The most laborious work, the grinding of the corn, is left almost entirely to the women. It is rubbed between two quadrangular oblong stones until ground into meal. Although the flour made is very white, the bread is very heavy and hard. The excellent and friendly La Pérouse, with the object of overcoming this fault in the bread, left a hand mill here, but it was not in existence at the time of our visit, neither had it been used as a model for the manufacture of others.[7]

When we consider that in the whole world there is no other country in which windmills are more numerous than in Spain, it appears incredible that these very useful machines have never been put to use here. I learned, however, that in preferring the poorly ground flour produced by the methods just described, the good *misioneros* are really actuated by economic motives. As they have more Indians of both sexes under their care than they can keep constantly employed the whole year, they fear that the introduction of mills would only be productive of idleness, whereas under the present system the *neófitos* can be kept busy making flour during the periods of unemployment.

The cattle, horses, and sheep do not require any particular attention. The herds are left in the open the whole year through. Only a sufficient number are kept in the neighborhood of the establishment to serve immediate wants. When a supply of cattle is wanted, some of the *neófitos* and soldiers are sent out to the pastures on horseback, and with riatas, which they throw very dexterously, catch by the horns the number required.

The immense herds of cattle now seen here are supposed to have sprung from five head brought to this *misión* in the year 1776. The *gobernador* of Monterey,[8] and with whom we became acquainted during our stay, informed me that the cattle had increased

---

[7] In reality, French navigator Jean François de La Pérouse (who visited California for ten days in 1786) left the hand mill at Mission San Carlos in Monterey.

[8] José Joaquin de Arrillaga (ca.1750–1814), twice *gobernador* of California (1792–1794 and 1800–1806), arrived from Monterey ten days after the Russians anchored at San Francisco.

to such a degree in the years immediately preceding—in the three northerly and contiguous *misiones* of San Francisco, Santa Clara, and Santa Cruz—that some months ago he had been compelled to send out a party of soldiers to kill not less than 20,000, wherever they should meet them, as he began to be afraid that from the immense increase there might in a short time be a lack of sufficient pasturage.

Plowing, etc., is done by oxen. Horses are kept principally for military service and for the use of the *misioneros,* and for the transportation of goods and provisions from one establishment to another one. Mules are also employed for similar transportation. The carts and wagons are of rough construction. Here, as in Spain and Portugal, block-wheels are in use, and they are generally very far from being perfectly round.

The government has not, nor have the *padres*, anything in view other than the propagation of the Christian religion. Hence it may be supposed that the Indians, to whose maintenance and instruction all their efforts are devoted, must be much happier in their condition of comparative civilization than they were before, since they are permitted to retain their former habits and customs not interdicted by the *misioneros.*

In their dances, amusements, sports, ornaments, etc., they are liberally indulged. They have a little property of their own in fowls and pigeons. Upon obtaining permission, they may go hunting and fishing. Altogether, they can live much more free from care than in their previous wild, natural state.

Notwithstanding all that has been said in favor of the treatment of the Indians at the *misiones*, an irresistible desire for freedom sometimes breaks out in individuals. This may probably be referred to the natural genius of the race. Their attachment to a wandering life, their love of alternate diversion from hunting and fishing to entire idleness, seem, in their eyes, to overbalance all the benefits they enjoy at the *misiones*, and these to us appear very great. The result is every now and then attempts to escape are made. On such occasions, no sooner is the *neófito* missed than search for him is at once begun, and as it is always known to what tribe he belongs, and on account of the enmity that subsists among the different tribes, he can never take refuge with any other—a circumstance which perhaps he thought not of beforehand—it is hardly possible for him to escape those sent in his pursuit. He is almost always brought back to the *misión*, where he is bastinadoed, and an iron rod a foot or a foot-and-a-half long and an inch in diameter is fastened to one of his feet. This has a twofold use, in that it prevents the Indian from making another attempt to escape, and has the effect of terrifying the others and deterring them from indulging in escapades of a similar nature....

As soon as we were informed of the arrival of the *gobernador* [Arrillaga], Lieutenant Davidov was sent ashore to welcome the company and extend our warmest acknowledgments for the friendly manner in which we had been received. On the following morning, when we expected our visit to be returned, there came two *religiosos* tendering the apologies of the *gobernador* that, being advanced in years and of a feeble constitution, he hoped to be excused from returning the visit, and at the same time requesting Rezanov, with all of the officers, to visit him at the *presidio*. The invitation was accepted, and we all went to the *presidio*, where we became acquainted with the *gobernador*, a venerable-looking man of sixty years. He had come a distance of no less than twenty-five German miles,[9] solely for the purpose of showing respect to us and of making our stay as agreeable as possible.

The principal matter to be agreed upon between Rezanov and the *gobernador* was the furnishing of food supplies and other

---

[9] Monterey to San Francisco is about 100 miles; Rezanov commented that Arrillaga, "whose hair was white, was actually fagged out from the journey on horseback, as there is no other mode of traveling overland in California."

necessaries to the Russian settlements. Rezanov thought that a trade might be established between these and the *provincias* of Nueva España, which would be of mutual benefit, and that it might be carried on by vessels running from one to the other at stated periods.

The *gobernador*, however, did not think he had the authority to establish such an intercourse, but he agreed that the proposition was one worthy of consideration as being mutually advantageous. He said that the proposal should be submitted to the cabinet at Madrid, as not even the viceroy of Nueva España had the authority to entertain it.

There was, however, no difficulty about getting the supplies necessary for the continuance of our voyage. The *gobernador* even dispatched couriers to all the neighboring *misiones*, authorizing the sending of corn, meal, flour, meat, salt, and other supplies. We were permitted, as we could not pay in cash, to make payments in such merchandise as we carried and as was desired....

We often amused ourselves with shooting the crested partridges and rabbits, which abound upon the surrounding sand hills. One day we went out, accompanied by a party of twelve, and conducted by some thirty or forty Indians, to catch hares and rabbits. This was done by a peculiar kind of snare. Inside of three hours, without firing a shot, we had taken seventy-five, and most of them alive. In vain we sought for [mountain] lions *(Felis concolor)*, tigers *(Felis onca)*, and bears. The last are very numerous here, while the others are found but rarely. On the north shore of the bay the roe abounds, and the chase of it is very alluring, and yields an abundance. In a number of aquatic trips, I found most of the birds with which I had become familiar at Sitka, e.g., *Pelicanus, Colymbus, Anas perspicillata* and *A. nigra, Haematopus ostralegus*, and others. There were also seals of various kinds, and, pre-eminent, the precious sea otter, which, almost unheeded, was swimming about the bay in numbers.

Almost every afternoon some of us were at the *presidio*, and the evening parties were ordinarily enlivened by dancing and music. The sternness of Fray José Uría, who was almost a daily visitor at the *presidio*, was in striking contrast with the vivacity of Fray Pedro De la Cueva, who lived there with the Argüello family. When the former spoke, all was silence and profound attention, but hardly had the latter opened his lips than laughter followed from the whole company. He seemed to abound in wit and humor, and entertained us in a manner most agreeable.

The popular dance here is called *barrego*. It is performed by two couples, who stand opposite each other. They sing a tune in six-eighths time and stamp the measure with their feet, making the figure of a half-chain, then balance opposite each other to a slow tune, when they recommence the dance. We were at some pains to teach the *señoras* English country dances, which they liked so much that we afterwards commonly danced them. They seemed particularly well pleased that all could dance at one time. Some soldiers of the garrison, who could play the violin and guitar, were our musicians.

Don Luís Argüello had talked much to us ever since we arrived of the combats between animals. These form a part of the amusements of the place. On the 10th of April he sent out eight soldiers on horseback to catch a live bear to fight with a wild bull at the *presidio*. They returned on the evening of the same day with a large dark-brown bear, taken by means of ropes and slings. He lay upon an ox hide stretched over branches of trees bound together, and had been drawn on this for some miles by a pair of oxen. He had been muzzled, and his paws were tied fast together. This confinement, together with the way in which he had been dragged, and his rage, had heated him exceedingly. When he arrived at the *presidio* most of the bands securing him were loosened. Water was thrown over his body, and he seemed much refreshed by this. Afterwards he was tied, by his hind feet only, to a stake driven into the ground near a pool. He soon began to drink of the water and splashed about in it to cool himself. No one dared to venture near him, for he growled and glanced about furiously.

An order was now given to catch some wild bulls to fight with the bear, and the next day was set for the combat. We awaited the time impatiently, and at the appointed hour looked eagerly for the horses, but when they arrived we were greatly disappointed, as we were told that the bear had died in the night. According to what we were told by the Spaniards, the bear generally gets the worst of the fight.

To make some amends for our disappointment, the *comandante* promised that we should have a bullfight, and this fight was had in the afternoon. Several soldiers, on foot and on horseback, killed one bull after another with spears, but the animals did not fall until they had received many wounds.

As these bullfights are well known as one of the national sports of the Spaniards and Portuguese, and have been often described, it would be useless here to repeat such descriptions, especially as none of the combatants on this occasion displayed any dexterity or skill. I ought, however, to say that I could not help being impressed upon seeing that the *padres*, who in all their instructions to their *neófitos* insist so strongly upon the cultivation of tenderness of heart and feelings of compassion, never offer any opposition to these national sports, though there is no denying that they are very cruel and barbarous. Perhaps, accustomed as they are to the sport from their youth up, all sense of cruelty is lost, and they are no more affected by the sight of this worthless slaughter of animals, in a manner revolting to those unaccustomed to it, than the natives of Nukahiva[10] are by the eating of human flesh.

In the same light must be regarded cockfights, which are quite frequent in Nueva California, and are, it must be admitted, to the

[10] Possibly Nukualofa, capital of Tonga, a group of islands in the South Pacific visited by Captain James Cook in the 1770s and colonized by British missionaries after 1797.

humane, no less cruel and repugnant. We saw no more of this sport than the little knives that are fastened to the legs of the birds when they fight.

Our intimate association daily with the Argüello family—the music and dancing, the sports—aroused in the mind of Rezanov some new and important speculations. These led to the formation of a plan of a very different nature from the original scheme for the establishment of commercial relations.

The bright, sparkling eyes of Doña Concepción had made upon him a deep impression and pierced his inmost soul. He conceived the idea that through a marriage with the daughter of the *comandante* of the Presidio de San Francisco a close bond would be formed for future business intercourse between the Russian-American Company and the *provincia* of Nueva California. He had therefore decided to sacrifice himself, by wedding Doña Concepción, to the welfare of his country, and to bind in friendly alliance both Spain and Russia.

Rezanov: Seeing that our situation was not getting better, expecting every day that some serious unpleasantness would arise, and having but little confidence in my own men, I decided that I should assume a serious bearing where I had before been but formally polite and gracious.

Associating daily with and paying my addresses to the beautiful Spanish *señorita*, I could not fail to perceive her active, venturesome disposition and character, her unlimited and overweening desire for rank and honors, which, with her age of fifteen years, made her, alone among her family, dissatisfied with the land of her birth. She always referred to it jokingly, thus, as "a beautiful country, a warm climate, an abundance of grain and cattle—and nothing else."

I described Russia to her as a colder country, but still abounding in everything, and she was willing to live there, and at length I imperceptibly created in her an impatient desire to hear something more explicit from me, and when I proffered my hand, she accepted.

My proposal was a shock to her parents, whose religious upbringing was fanatical. The difference in religion, besides the prospective separation from their daughter, was, in contemplation, a dreadful blow to them.

They sought the counsel of the *misioneros,* who did not know what to do. The parents forced their daughter to church and had her confessed. They urged her to refuse me, but her brave front finally quieted them all. The holy *padres* decided to leave the final decision to the throne of Rome.

Not being able to bring about the marriage, I had a written conditional agreement made and forced a betrothal. Consent was given on condition that the agreement be kept secret pending the decision of the pope. Thereafter my deportment in the house of Comandante Argüello was that of a near relative, and I managed this *puerto* of his Catholic majesty as my interests called for.

LANGSDORFF: Misiones de San Francisco de Asís, Santa Clara de Asís, San José—the three most northerly of the Franciscan *misiones* of Nueva California—lie near the southeast part of the Puerto de San Francisco; and although water communication from one to the other would be of the utmost benefit, it seems almost incredible that in not one of them, no, not even in the Presidio or Puerto de San Francisco, is there a vessel or boat of any kind.

Perhaps the *misioneros* are afraid that if they had boats the escape of the Indians—who never wholly lose their love of freedom or attachment to their original habits—might be facilitated, and

therefore consider it better to confine their communication with one
another to the means afforded by land—to the horse.

The Spaniard, as well as his nursling the Indian, is but seldom
forced to trust himself to the waves, and this may be the reason that
communication by water here is hardly yet in its infancy. When such
an occasion does arise, they make a kind of boat of straw, reeds, and
rushes, bound so compactly that it is water-tight, and in this they
manage to go very well from one shore to the other.[11] It is called by
the Spaniards *balsa*. The oar used is a long, narrow pole, somewhat
wider at the ends, with which they row, sometimes on one side and
sometimes on the other.

This total lack of vessels—which are, so to speak, keys to all
their southern and eastern possessions—is a strong proof of the
recklessness of the Spanish government. It is because of this lack that
they had to wait so long on shore on the day of our arrival, and were
thus precluded from all communication with us until we sent out
our ship's boat

As Misión San José[12] lies on the opposite or southeastern shore
of the *puerto*, at a distance of sixteen leagues, communication by
water would prove of infinite benefit to the *misioneros*. Notwithstanding that this convenience is so easily within their reach, they
have no other means of intercourse than that by land. Thus they are
obliged to go round the bay—at least three times the distance.

The difficulty of conveyance by land, the small number of
neófitos at the Misión San José, and the breaking out, this year, of
an infectious disease (the measles, hitherto unknown in California)—which had spread from Antigua California to the northern
settlements and had for some weeks attacked great numbers of the

---

[11] A *balsa* is not watertight, but buoyant because of the lightness of its tule reeds.

[12] Mission San José de Guadalupe was founded by Father-President Fermín de Lasuén
in 1797. It is in present-day Fremont.

Indians in the contiguous *misiones*—caused much delay in the delivery of the supplies agreed upon. Count Rezanov therefore applied to Gobernador Arrillaga for permission to send our ship's boats to Misión San José, so that the delivery of the supplies might be expedited. The advantage accruing, in saving the labor of men and horses, was so obvious that the *gobernador* readily consented....

On the 20th, therefore, with a sailor and a huntsman, I set out in a three-seated *bidarka* that I had brought from Sitka. We left San Francisco early in the morning and about noon reached the plain lying in front of the *misión*. We then sought for the principal channel, which is supposed to be in the vicinity of several hills, and these are indeed the principal guides in finding it. They stretch from the northwest to the southeast and are surrounded by a muddy shallow extending a considerable distance along the shore, to avoid which one must steer to the west until the southern hills (which on our first attempt on the 14th we had mistaken for an island) lie to the east. The channel that must then be taken winds among the heights, and the lowest two of these left to the north and the others, which are much higher, to the south. This channel runs at first in a northwesterly direction, and then, after many windings, southeasterly into the interior. At flood-tide the depth of water is from six to nine feet, but even at ebb-tide it is navigable by small boats. At low water it is almost impossible to land, on account of the muddy shore, and at high water the landing is not unattended with difficulty. The many little channels intersecting this flat land make it an absolute labyrinth, and as we were not acquainted with the terrain, we were mistaken at many times and had to turn back, often missing the main by turning into a side channel.

Wearied at length by continually going astray, I ascended a hill nearby, where I could get a better view of the terrain, and saw a landing place from which we could proceed overland to the *misión*, which lay three-and-a-half leagues east-northeast. The country now to be traveled over rises gradually over the low-lying plain, and is bounded by a chain of moderately high hills, which stretch from the north-northwest to the south-southeast. Numerous herds of horses and cattle were running wild here without any attention being paid to them. The bulls even render the country unsafe for foot-passengers. We also saw many foxes and a large wolf that ran away frightened. The foxes seemed to live on the most peaceable terms with the young calves and followed the cows like the calves.

Shortly before sunset we arrived at the *misión*, very much fatigued. It was now under the charge of two *misioneros*, Padre Luís [Gil y Taboada] and Padre Pedro De la Cueva. The latter only was at the *misión*. He received us with open arms and sent at once horses to the shore to fetch our baggage and the sailor. We had left the sailor to take care of the *bidarka*, and he was now relieved by some Indians. Fray Luís was now at San Francisco on a short visit. On the morning of the 21st, all the Indian *neófitos* were assembled to receive from Fray Pedro their allotted work for the day. He had promised, when I saw him at San Francisco, to entertain me with an Indian dance at his *misión*, and he therefore now announced to them that they should have a holiday, and that they might dress themselves in their best and prepare for the dance. He distributed, for this purpose, a number of ornaments among the best dancers, who immediately withdrew with them to make the necessary preparations.

In the meantime, Fray Pedro showed me about the buildings and grounds belonging to his *misión*. They are of considerable extent, although it is only eight years since work was begun on them. Grain in the storehouses, as to quantity, greatly exceeded my expectations, there being over 2,000 fanegas of wheat, and a proportionate quantity of maize, barley, peas, beans, etc. The kitchen-garden is exceptionally well laid out and kept in very good order. The soil is everywhere productive, and the fruit trees, although still small, are doing very well. A rivulet runs through the garden, with sufficient water to irrigate. Some vineyards have been planted within the past few years, with vines now yielding exceedingly well. The wine is sweet and resembles Málaga.

The site of the establishment is exceedingly well chosen, and the common opinion is that the *misión* will in a few years be one of the richest and best in Nueva California. The one and only disadvantage is an entire lack of forests of tall timber. The native Indians have, now and then, thoughtlessly, simply to make a bonfire, set fire to the forests and burned down large tracts, leaving few trees standing;[13] hence timber for building purposes must be brought from a distance of several miles. But, in comparison with other *misiones*, this disadvantage is compensated by the presence, in the neighborhood, of chalk hills and an excellent clay, whereby brick kilns may be erected and the main structures built of brick.

The *misión* is richer in grain than in cattle, and the number of cattle slaughtered weekly is hence much smaller than at Misión San Francisco, but the distribution of corn and pulse is much greater. The interior arrangement and organization of this *misión* is entirely the same as that of Misión San Francisco. The habitations of the Indians—*las rancherías*—are not yet finished, so that the *neófitos* live for the most part in families, in straw huts of a conical form.

Fray Pedro, who showed me about everywhere, invited me—when we had seen all that was worth seeing—to go and see the Indians getting ready for the dance. We went to a rivulet, by the side of which the dancers were gathered, very busy in smearing their bodies over with charcoal, red clay, and chalk. While one Indian was ornamenting his own breast, abdomen, and thighs, another was painting his back with various regular figures. Some were covering their nude bodies all over with down, which gave them rather the appearance of monkeys than of human beings. Their heads, ears,

---

[13] Actually, Indian burning practices—mimicking lightning fires—carefully managed the landscape, maintaining open woodlands and meadows.

and necks were set off with a great variety of ornaments, but, except a covering tied around the waist, their entire bodies were nude. The women were at the same time, in their huts, performing the offices of the toilet, and were all, consistently with the customs of decorum, dressed. Their faces and necks, only, were painted, and they were adorned with a profusion of shells, feathers, corals, etc.

The Indians assembled in the courtyard toward noon. They are very different from the Indians of Misión San Francisco, as to size, appearance, and build. The men are well-built and almost all are above middling stature. Very few indeed are what may be called undersized. Their complexions are dark, but not negro-like, and if their physiognomy cannot absolutely be called pleasing, there is nothing about it that would provoke aversion. I thought that they strongly resembled the northern tribes. They have very coarse black hair, and some are possessed of extraordinary strength. In general, the women seem proportionately taller than the men, and many are over five feet high. If there were not any, either among the men or women, that I could call handsome, I did not note in one the dull, heavy, and repugnant look of the *neófitos* of San Francisco. The Indians of this *misión* are indeed generally considered the handsomest in Nueva California, and hence the Spanish soldiers, in the absence of Spanish women, often marry the Indian women of this *misión*.[14]

The dancers were divided into two companies. Each distinguished itself by specific ornaments and a special kind of song. One of these companies was composed of Indians inhabiting the coast, and the other of Indians belonging to inland tribes. The coast Indians were not so well made, nor so strong, nor so good-looking, as those of the interior. These neighboring tribes formerly lived at great mutual enmity. Although they are now united here by the bond of

---

[14] Perhaps the relative "handsomeness" of the neophytes of Mission San José was due to the fact that they had been living at the mission a far shorter time than those at Mission San Francisco.

religion, the old hostility is so rooted in them that it is still apparent. As an instance of this, the *misioneros* cannot induce them to intermarry. They will unite themselves with only those of their own tribe, and it is an exception that they mingle or associate with members of any tribe other than their own.

In their dances the Indians remain almost always in the same place, endeavoring—partly with their bows and arrows, partly with the feathers they hold in their hands and wear on their heads, and also by measured springs, by different movements of their bodies, and by facial contortions—to imitate scenes of battle or of domestic life. Their music consists of singing and clapping with a stick split at one end. The women have their own particular song and their own particular manner of dancing. They hop about near the men, but never in time with them. Their principal action or practice is in pressing the abdomen with the thumb and forefinger, first to one side and then to the other, in regular measure. As soon as the men begin to dance, the women also begin, and cease the moment the men cease.

At about two o'clock we sat down to a very fine dinner, and afterwards went again to see the Indians, who were still engaged in dancing and were now about to enact a mock battle. A large straw figure represented the enemy, and a number of the men, armed with bows and arrows, sprang and danced about with fierce gesticulations and contortions to defy their adversary, who, had he been able, would have done likewise. One of the Indians finally gave a signal, and at the same moment the straw figure was pierced with many arrows, whereupon it was presented in triumph to the man who personated the chief.

Upon this occasion I perceived that most of the Indians were skillful marksmen. Yet it appeared to me that if the enemy was courageous and would attend more to the use of his weapons and less to gesticulations, he could hardly fail to win. These people were

"A Dance of the Indians at the Mission of St. Joseph [San Jose] in New California," 1806, by Georg von Langsdorff. "The hair of these people is very coarse, thick, and stands erect; in some it is powdered with down feathers," noted Langsdorff. "Their bodies are fantastically painted with charcoal dust, red clay, and chalk. The foremost dancer is ornamented all over with down feathers, which gives him a monkey-like appearance; the hindermost has had the whimsical idea of painting his body to imitate the uniform of a Spanish soldier, with his boots, stockings, breeches, and upper garments." *Courtesy of The Bancroft Library.*

never in the habit of eating the enemy killed in battle, the greatest endeavor of each party being to steal the young girls and the wives of the enemy.

Another party of Indians danced before a large fire, from which each one, apparently for his own gratification, took, now and then, a glowing ember as large as a walnut, and without further ceremony put it into his mouth and swallowed it. It was not deception. I watched them very closely and saw it done repeatedly, although it is utterly beyond my comprehension how it could be done without the mouth being burned.

I was also entertained with a representation of a hunting party. The Indians fasten the horns of a deer on their heads and throw a portion of the skin over their shoulders. Thus disguised, they lurk in the high grass, where the stags and the roes come to feed, imitating their actions so well that, though naturally shy and timid, they are duped and allow the Indians, with their bows and arrows, to come within a few feet of them. Several are often killed without the others having any idea of their peril.

Directly east, about seven leagues from Misión San José, there is an arm of a great river [San Joaquín River] that first winds toward the north, and then, making a turn to the west, empties itself at last into the bay of San Francisco at its northeastern part. In the region of this river there are numerous Indian villages, but the natives do not yet consort with the Spaniards or the baptized Indians. When Misión San José was first founded they became troublesome from time to time. Only a year-and-a-half before I was there, they had murdered five soldiers and dangerously wounded one of the *padres* and another soldier. Upon this a strong military expedition was sent out against them, and a great slaughter of the Indians was the result, whereupon they were compelled to conclude a peace. There has been no trouble with them since. The Spaniards and the Indian *neófitos* occasionally go among these Indians, remaining with them for perhaps a fortnight or longer, with the intention of gaining *neófitos*, if possible. Some of them make visits to the *misión*, at which times they always return home enriched with presents of various kinds.

Three leagues from the Misión San José, to the southwest, lies the Pueblo de San José de Guadalupe. The word *pueblo* is used here to indicate a sort of village composed of *inválidos*, who are released from military service. They cultivate the soil and raise cattle, and live in the midst of plenty. There are several *pueblos* such as this, in different parts of Nueva and Antigua California, and here there is a yearly increase in population. Gobernador Arrillaga assured me that in twenty years the population of the Pueblo de San José de Guadalupe had increased from 100 to 700. It is peculiar that, conversely, and notwithstanding their good treatment, there is a continuous diminution in the number of the *misión* Indian *neófitos*.

On the 23rd I took leave of Fray Pedro, to whom I owe my public acknowledgments for his kindly reception and hospitality. He had horses saddled for us, and we went, accompanied by a soldier, in search of our *bidarka,* which we found at the very spot where we had left it. Some wild bulls followed us on our way and caused us much uneasiness. A number of foxes, on the contrary, ran off terrified.

We rowed in shallow water, through the channel that winds among the hills, down to the bay. The muddy banks that stretched on either side were overspread with sandpipers, snipes, wild ducks, and sea-mews [gulls]; but we did not attempt to shoot any of them, as it would have been impossible to get them out of the deep mire. We saw also a great number of sea otters, one of which we shot, but as it took refuge in one of the smaller channels, we had not the disposition to lose time in its pursuit.

Scarcely had we reached the open waters of the bay than a strong north wind arose. It was now an impossibility to proceed. Wet through and through by the dashing waves, held back by the rush of the current, and suffering from hunger and thirst, we were forced at sunset to relinquish all hope of going forward and resign ourselves to the probability of the open, in a low boggy place near the landing. Not having anticipated such a condition, we had brought with us provisions for only one day, and now nothing was left but a little bread and cheese and an insignificant quantity of brandy. We laid ourselves down to rest with empty stomachs, not being able even to quench our thirst, since we were surrounded by the saline tidewater. We endeavored to shelter ourselves somewhat from the force of the strong winds by means of our wet sailcloth, and in this situation and stiff with cold, waited for daybreak.

By the morning our clothes, which had been wet through by the storm yesterday, were tolerably dry, and at ten o'clock we were ready to leave. But we found that on account of the tide being still at low ebb there was still a larger extent of muddy shore than it was possible to cross. Nor would it admit of our re-embarking until about noon. Scarcely, then, had we seated ourselves in the boat than the same north and northwest wind returned, and left not a probability of our being able, even on that day, to reach San Francisco [*presidio*]. We consequently decided to row to the opposite shore, which looked to be much higher and well-wooded, and reached that side at about three o'clock in the afternoon. But here we found a low boggy plain, overgrown merely by a saltwort *(Salsola),* and, like the plain on the eastern shore, intersected by many little channels, so that there was no possibility of our reaching the woods on foot.

However, we followed, in our *bidarka,* the widest channel, and, rowing amidst the many windings for about three-quarters of an hour, were lucky enough to find a place to land and from which there was reason to hope that we might soon reach the wood, where we hoped to find fresh water. Armed with guns and pistols, and taking with us our last morsel of bread and cheese and an empty bottle, we went on our way. Infinitely annoyed, we traveled about in search of some brook or spring where we might quench our thirst. We reached the wood before nightfall, after walking more than a German mile, but nowhere found a drop of water. We at length saw a numerous herd of bulls and cows, feeding wild among luxuriant wild grass in a meadow. Keeping these off with our guns and pistols, we searched in a thorough manner for water, but all in vain— again not a drop could we find. Exhausted by fatigue and suffering from hunger and thirst, in listless despair we laid ourselves down, when suddenly we heard, at some distance, the croak of a frog.

Never did the tuneful notes of the nightingale sound to our ears half so delightful. We started up, and, following the call and seeming invitation of this creature, soon found ourselves, in the darkness of the night, by the side of a little stream of excellent water. As for two days we had been upon a short allowance of food and with nothing to quench our thirst, we drank the water with such avidity that in two hours we consumed fourteen bottlefuls. It should be stated that we were a party of only three.

The night was cool and damp. So we made a fire to warm ourselves and rested 'til midnight, when, the moon being very bright, we decided to return to our *bidarka*. On the way we encountered several bears and wild bulls, which we kept off with our guns, and at about three o'clock in the morning we reached our *bidarka*. It was then perfectly calm. In a very fine morning we set out upon our return to [the harbor of the Presidio de] San Francisco. The channel that we followed to reach the bay was full of sea otters and sea dogs [seals]. Many were lying on the muddy shores, and many swimming, their heads just above the water. The trials of the past few days were so fresh in our memories, and the craving of our stomachs for nourishment so insistent, that we renounced all the joys and advantages that might accrue from a chase of these animals. Despite this, three sea otters that lay sleeping almost beside our *bidarka* presented a temptation that could not be resisted. These we did kill and carry off with us.

Towards noon we were pretty near the Misión San Francisco, but a northwest wind that arose at the moment again retarded us so much that we did not reach the ship until about three, exhausted by hunger, thirst, and fatigue.

To my inexpressible regret, a number of objects of natural history collected by me on my journey, chiefly plants and birds, had become a prey to the stormy waters, and I brought nothing back with me but the three sea otters.

ADELBERT VON CHAMISSO
1816

—————⊳•⊲—————

Before leaving Sitka, Rezanov advised Governor Baranov that the Russians' only chance for survival lay in establishing a colony a few miles north of San Francisco Bay. A base there, he argued, could assure a steady supply of grain to Alaska; it would be far enough away to avoid conflict with Spain, and still be close enough to trade with the missions and hunt otter on the bay. Three years after Rezanov's visit to San Francisco, the Russian-American Company sent a preliminary expedition to Bodega Bay, about fifty miles north of San Francisco. For most of 1809 the surrounding lands were explored and the ship returned with 2,000 otter skins. By 1812 two colonies were established—Bodega Bay for otter hunting and, eighteen miles to the north, Fort Ross, an agricultural post. Initially Fort Ross housed ninety-five Russians and eighty Aleuts, making the little fort larger than any Spanish *presidio* in California.

For the next ten years an uneasy peace prevailed between Russian and Spanish California. The Russians were repeatedly asked to leave, and they in turn replied with equivocations, complaining they could not understand demands made in an unfamiliar language. Trade with Fort Ross, at first unthinkable, became a necessity after 1808 when Spain's always flimsy grip on Alta California was severed by the French invasion of Spain, ending the dispatching of supply ships from San Blas. Mexico had no military or economic support to lend, for it was embroiled in a revolution begun by Father Miguel Hidalgo in 1810. California's military leaders, reduced to wearing rags and eating what the mission *padres* doled out, acknowledged that trade with Fort Ross could provide at least some of life's essentials. "Necessity makes licit what is not licit by law," admitted Gobernador Argüello. From San Francisco to San Diego, the declining fortunes of Spain were seen as no more than a temporary wrinkle of fate—surely the order of the king would soon be re-established throughout his possessions and the Russians would be driven out.

Against this backdrop of colonial intrigue sailed the *Rurik* in 1816. A round-the-world expedition launched from St. Petersburg in July 1815, the *Rurik* was sponsored by Count Nikolai Rumjanzoff, the recently retired chancellor of the Russian Empire. It had two stated goals—to explore the islands of the South Pacific and to search for a passage to the Atlantic around the tip of Alaska. It also sailed with a third, ulterior objective—to intimidate Californian officials with a show of Russian strength.

The *Rurik* itself seemed unimpressive—a modest, 180-ton, two-masted brig commanded by a twenty-six-year-old German lieutenant named Otto von Kotzebue. In reality, the expedition of the *Rurik* set a new standard of efficiency, free from traditional naval practices. The small size of the ship was ideal for sailing through ice-covered arctic seas. With a tiny crew of only thirty-one (including a surgeon, an artist, and two naturalists), it could carry state-of-the-art navigational devices and plenty of anti-scorbutic rations with no worry of overcrowding. In fifteen months at sea it had sailed from its home port of Kronstadt through the Baltic Sea, across the Atlantic Ocean, around Cape Horn, through the South Seas, and up the Pacific Coast to the Bering Strait. It was there that depleted supplies required the *Rurik* to head back down the coast to San Francisco.

The chief naturalist of the expedition, Adelbert von Chamisso, a literate scientist and poet with a wry sense a humor, kept a personal diary of the expedition. He was born in Château de Boncourt in Champagne in 1781, the youngest son of a count from the highest strata of the French aristocracy. His family was forced into exile during the French Revolution, their cattle destroyed and lands confiscated. Chamisso's youth was spent traveling extensively through Europe, staying at Liége, Aachen, the Hague, Düsseldorf, Würzburg, and Bavaria before moving permanently to Berlin in 1796. Notwithstanding a French background and education, he came to identify strongly with his adopted country and entered the Prussian army as an ensign in 1798. More interested in science and literature than politics or war, he turned down a comfortable future as an officer in 1809 to study botany and zoology at the University of Berlin. He also tried his hand at writing—his fable *Peter Schlemihl's Wonderful History*, the story of a man who sells his shadow and wanders from place to place in a pair of seven-league boots, was published to wide acclaim a few months before Chamisso signed up for the *Rurik* expedition.

Onboard the *Rurik*, Chamisso collected and named hundreds of unusual plants and flowers from all over the world. His most famous find was the golden poppy (later designated the state flower of California), which he named *Eschscholtzia californica* in honor of the *Rurik*'s surgeon, Johann Friedrich Eschscholtz. Chamisso's assistant, a twenty-year-old Russian artist named Louis Choris, made evocative sketches of the landscapes and native peoples he encountered during the trip that are today perhaps the *Rurik*'s most important legacy.

The *Rurik* left San Francisco on November 1, 1816, and visited the Hawaiian Islands for three weeks. Hawaii, like California, was undergoing a gradual but relentless transformation in the early nineteenth century as European and American traders and explorers unwittingly introduced diseases that devastated its native population. After 1820, American missionaries and planters would establish extensive sugar plantations on the islands and come to increasingly dominate Hawaii's economy, religion, and government. Anglo-Americans were also expanding across North America in these years, using dubious treaties, violence, and sheer numbers to overrun and usurp vast tracts of Native American lands. In 1803, the Louisiana Purchase extended the U.S. border to the Rocky Mountains, encouraging westward migration and notions of "manifest destiny." In short, the Europeanization process that was reshaping California was by no means exceptional.

Chamisso pleaded with Kotzebue to allow him to spend a year at Hawaii so he could study in depth the native languages and literature of the islands before they disappeared. Kotzebue refused, but Chamisso obtained enough information to later compile a book on Hawaiian grammar. The *Rurik* returned to Europe in August 1818, almost three years after it left. Chamisso went on to become director of Berlin's Royal Herbarium and an accomplished lyrical poet. His poetic cycle *Frauenliebe und Leben* was later made famous when set to music by German composer Robert Schumann. Chamisso died in Berlin in 1838. His private diary of the voyage of the *Rurik* was published the following year. This excerpt from his diary begins on October 2, 1816.

ADELBERT VON CHAMISSO

from *A Voyage Around the World*

*O*n October 2, 1816, at four o'clock in the afternoon, we sail into San Francisco harbor. There is great activity in the fort on the southern entrance of the channel. They hoist their flag, we show ours, which does not seem to be known here, and salute the Spanish flag with seven guns, which, according to Spanish regulation, are returned with two fewer. We drop anchor in front of the *presidio*, and no boat pushes out from the shore to come to us, because Spain does not have a single boat on this bay.

I was immediately ordered to accompany Lieutenant Shishmarev to the *presidio*. Lieutenant Don Luís de Argüello[1]—after the death of the colonel, the interim commandant—received us in an exceptionally friendly manner, immediately saw to the most pressing needs of the *Rurik* by sending fruit and vegetables on board, and on the same evening, sent a messenger to the governor of New California in Monterey to report our arrival to him.

On the next morning (the 3rd) I met Artillery Officer Don Miguel de la Luz Gómez and a pater of the local mission, who came aboard ship just as I was about to go to the *presidio* on an errand of the captain's. I accompanied them on board; they were the bearers of the friendliest promises of assistance on the part of the commandant and the very powerful mission. The clerical gentleman also invited us to the mission of San Francisco on the following day,

---

[1] Luís Antonio Argüello, now age thirty-two, was officially appointed *comandante* of San Francisco *presidio* a few months after Chamisso's visit, a post he held until becoming *gobernador* in 1822.

Adelbert von Chamisso (1781–1838). *Courtesy of the California Historical Society, North Baker Research Library, FN-31309.*

which was a saint's festival day, for which purpose we would find riding horses ready. At the express wish of the captain, we were most abundantly supplied with beef cattle and vegetables. In the afternoon the tents were set up on the land, as were the observatory and the Russian bath. In the evening we paid the commandant a visit. Eight guns were fired from the *presidio* to receive the captain.

But it was not these superfluous courtesy guns that the captain desired, but rather the two that were still owed to the Russian flag, and he insisted tenaciously upon their delivery. There were long negotiations on this subject, and only against his will and under compulsion (I don't know, but it took a command from the governor) did Don Luís de Argüello finally agree to provide belatedly the two missing cannon shots. Also, one of our crew had to be sent to the fort to repair the line for hoisting the flag, for it had broken when last used, and there was no one among the inhabitants who could climb up the pole to fix it.

The feast of St. Francis [October 9] gave us the opportunity to observe the missionaries at their work and the peoples to whom they are sent when these peoples are in a subjugated condition[2]....

Here, as in Chile, the captain was able to accustom the commandant and his officers to our table. We dined on land under the tent, and our friends of the *presidio* were usually not slow in arriving. This relationship occurred almost automatically. The misery in which they had been wallowing for six to seven years, forgotten and forsaken by Mexico, the motherland, did not permit them to be

---

[2] In his "Notes and Opinions," Chamisso had this to say about the mission *padres*: "The contempt that the missionaries feel toward the peoples to whom they are sent seems to us to be an unhappy circumstance in view of their pious purpose. None of them seem to have concerned themselves with their history, customs, beliefs, or languages. 'They are unreasoning savages and there is no more to be said about them!'" *Rurik* artist Louis Choris noted that "severe fevers occur constantly among the [mission] Indians. These maladies commonly carry off a great number....I have never seen one laugh. I have never seen one look [you] in the face. They look as though they were interested in nothing."

Indian neophytes gambling at Mission San Francisco de Asís, 1816, by Louis Choris.
Courtesy of the California Historical Society, Templeton Crocker Collection, FN-30509.

hosts, and the need to pour out their hearts in speech impelled them to approach us, as life was easy and pleasant with us. They spoke only with bitterness of the missionaries, who in the face of a deficiency in imported goods nonetheless enjoyed a superfluity of the products of the earth and would let them have nothing now that their money had run out, except in return for a promissory note—and, even so, only what is absolutely necessary to maintain life, among which things bread and flour are not included. For years they had lived on maize, without seeing bread. Even the detachments of soldiers who are placed in every mission for their protection were only provided with absolute essentials against promissory notes. "Our leaders are too good!" cried Don Miguel, meaning the commandant. "They should requisition, demand that they provide what we need!" One soldier went even further and complained to us that the commandant would not permit them to secure natives in order to get them to work for them, as they did in the missions. It also caused dissatisfaction that the new governor of Monterey, Don Pablo Vicente de Solá,[3] since he assumed office had wished to oppose smuggling, which is the only way they have of obtaining their most essential necessities.

On October 8 the courier came back from Monterey. He brought the captain a letter from the governor, announcing his imminent arrival in San Francisco. In accordance with Mr. von Kotzebue's wish, Don Luís de Argüello had been empowered to send a messenger to Mr. Kuskov[4] in Port Bodega, and the captain wrote to the latter in order to draw from his flourishing trading center some of the things that were beginning to be lacking on the *Rurik*.

"Mr. Kuskov," says Mr. von Kotzebue, "Mr. Kuskov, agent of the Russian-American Company, settled at Bodega at the command of Mr. [Aleksandr] Baranov, who is the head of all the possessions in America, in order to provide the possessions of the company with supplies." But Bodega, situated about thirty miles, a half-day's journey, north of San Francisco, was counted by Spain, not without some appearance of justice, as part of its territory; and on Spanish territory, therefore, Mr. Kuskov, with twenty Russians and fifty Kadiakans [Kodiakans], had erected a fort in the midst of peace, a fort that was equipped with a dozen cannon, and there he practiced agriculture, possessed horses, cattle, sheep, a windmill, etc. He had a trading center there for smuggling with the Spanish harbors, and from there he sent out his Kadiakans each year to catch a few thousand sea otters along the California coast, the skins of which, according to [Louis] Choris, who may have been well informed, were sold in Canton [China] at an average price of sixty *piastres*, thirty-five *piastres* for the poorer skins and seventy-five for

---

[3] Pablo Vicente de Solá (1761–ca.1826), a fierce royalist, was California's last Spanish *gobernador* (1814–1822).

[4] Ivan Aleksandrovich Kuskov, an official with the Russian-American Fur Company, was Fort Ross's manager.

the better ones. It was only regrettable that the port of Bodega could only take ships that did not draw more than nine feet of water.

It does not seem incomprehensible to me that the governor, when he obtained late information about this settlement, was outraged about it. Different steps were taken to force Mr. Kuskov to vacate the premises. For everything they directed toward him, he had referred the Spanish authorities to Mr. Baranov, who had sent him there and at whose command, in case they could get him to make it, he would very gladly withdraw again. This is the way matters stood when we entered San Francisco. The governor now placed his hopes in us. I, too, will have conferences and negotiations to talk about and shall reveal to the world the memorable events of my diplomatic career. But we haven't gotten to this point yet.

On October 9 some Spaniards were shipped to the northern shore to use the *lasso* to catch some horses for the courier to be sent to Mr. Kuskov, and I seized the opportunity to look around over there....The year was already old, and the area—which in the spring months, the way Langsdorff saw it, should resemble a flower garden—now offered the botanist nothing but a dry, dead field. In a swamp in the vicinity of our tents, a water plant is said to have been green, and [*Rurik* surgeon Johann Friedrich] Eschscholtz asked me about its pedigree. I hadn't noticed it, but he had calculated that a water plant, my special fancy, would not have escaped me and so had not wanted to get his feet wet. That's the kind of thing you can expect from your closest friend.

On the naked plain that lies at the foot of the *presidio*, farther to the east, a solitary oak tree stands in the midst of a shorter growth of brush. Recently my young friend Adolph Erman saw it too; if he had observed it more closely he would have found my name carved in its bark.

On October 15 the courier dispatched to Kuskov returned; and on the evening of the 16th, artillery salvos from the *presidio* and the fort announced the arrival of the governor [Solá] from Monterey. Right after that a messenger came down from the *presidio* to request the help of our physician for two men who had been dangerously wounded firing off a cannon. Eschscholtz immediately acceded to the request.

On the morning of the 17th Mr. von Kotzebue waited on board ship for the first visit of the governor of the province, and the governor in turn, an old man and an officer of higher rank, waited in the *presidio* for the first visit of Lieutenant von Kotzebue. The captain was notified by chance that he was expected in the *presidio*, whereupon he sent me to the *presidio* with the unpleasant task of politely telling the governor that he, the captain, had been informed that he, the governor, wished to visit him on board this morning and that he expected him. I found the little man in dress uniform and all his decorations, except for a sleeping cap, which he still wore on his head, ready to take it off in time. I discharged my task to the best of my ability and saw the little man's face lengthen three times its normal size. He bit his lip and said he regretted that he could not bear the sea before eating and that he was sorry that for now he must forego the pleasure of meeting the captain. I saw it coming that the old man would mount his horse and start out again on his trip back through the wilderness to Monterey without having accomplished his mission, for it could not be assumed that Mr. von Kotzebue, once the rift had been expressed, could give in.

Pondering this, I slunk down to the beach again, when a good genius intervened and, before unpleasantness could occur, sealed the prevailing peace with the fairest bonds of friendship. The morning had gone by, and the hour came when Mr. von Kotzebue had to go ashore to sight the noonday sun and wind his chronometers. The lookouts in the *presidio* reported that the captain was coming, and when he stepped ashore, the governor strode down the incline toward him. He in turn ascended the incline toward the governor's reception, and Spain and Russia fell into each other's open arms halfway toward each other.

A meal was served under our tent, and in the matter of Port Bodega, which was discussed, the captain had the opportunity to regret that he was without instructions to counter the wrong that had been imposed against Spain. From that port a large baidare arrived on this day and brought everything from Mr. Kuskov that the captain had requested. With this same baidare, which returned on the next day, the 18th, Mr. von Kotzebue, in the governor's name, requested Mr. Kuskov to appear in San Francisco for a conference.

On the 18th we did not see the governor, who perhaps expected a state visit in the *presidio*. On the 19th we dined in the *presidio*, and artillery salvos accompanied the toast to the alliance of the sovereigns and the friendship of the nations. On the 20th we were again the hosts at noon and danced in the *presidio* in the evening. When the eight o'clock bell sounded, the music was silent for a while, and the evening prayer was read in the silence.

Mr. von Kotzebue was prepossessingly charming in social intercourse, and Don Pablo Vicente de Solá, who was very much a stickler for formalities and had eschewed any deficiency of them, had been consoled in this respect and now devoted himself completely to us. The popular spectacle here of a fight between a bear and a bull was promised to us. On the 21st ten to twelve soldiers went over to the mission on the northern shore—in the longboat—in order to *lasso* bears there. Some claimed that in the late evening they heard cries from the direction of the sea, which were interpreted as coming from the bear hunters on that coast; however, no campfire could be seen. The Indians are said to be able to raise a very piercing scream.

Not until the evening of the 22nd did the hunters bring in a very small she-bear. They had also caught a larger bear, but too far away from the sea for them to transport it to the shore. The animal,

"Dance of the California Indians at the Mission of San Francisco," 1816, by Louis Choris, twenty-year-old artist of the *Rurik* expedition. *Courtesy of the California Historical Society, North Baker Research Library, Templeton Crocker Collection, FN-00963.*

which was to fight the next day, stayed overnight in the longboat; and contrary to custom, its head and mouth were kept free so that it would stay fresher. The governor spent the whole day, noon and evening, in our tents. At night, on the land behind the harbor, great fires burned. The natives are in the habit of burning the grass in order to further its growth.

On the 23rd the bear-baiting took place on the beach. Unwilling and bound as the animals were, the spectacle had nothing great or uplifting about it. One must pity the poor creatures that are so shamefully treated. I was in the *presidio* with Gleb Simonovich for the evening. The governor had just received the news that the ship from Acapulco, which had stayed away for so many years, had finally again sailed into Monterey to provide California with supplies. Along with this news he also received at the same time the latest newspapers from Mexico. He shared these papers with me, to whom he showed himself inclined and obliging at every opportunity....

Don Pablo Vicente, when he descended the hill to our tents, once brought a present *a su amigo* Don Adelberto, a flower, which he had plucked by the wayside and which he solemnly handed to me, the botanist. By chance it was our cinquefoil or five-finger (*Pontentilla anserina*), as beautiful as it could grow near Berlin.

In Monterey at the time, there were prisoners of various nations, whom smuggling and sea otter hunting had enticed to seek adventure on these coasts, and these few individuals were paying for the derelictions of others. Among them were a few Aleuts or Kadiakans, with whom seven years ago an American sea captain had engaged in otter hunting in the Spanish harbors of this coast. The Russians not only misuse these northern peoples, they also deliver them over to others for misuse. I have even encountered dislodged Kadiakans in the Sandwich Islands. Among the prisoners in Monterey was a certain Mr. John Elliot de Castro, of whom I shall have more to say further on. After many adventures as supercargo of a ship of the Russian-American Company sent out to smuggle from Sitka by Mr. Baranov, he and others of the crew had fallen into the hands of the Spaniards. Besides the prisoners there were three other Russians there, former servants of the Russian-American Company who had deserted the settlement at Port Bodega and now, missing the language and customs of home, regretted having taken the step.

Don Pablo Vicente de Solá offered to deliver the Russians—among whom the Aleuts and Kadiakans also were numbered—to the captain, while he refused them to Mr. Kuskov. It does not seem that the Spaniards asked any service of or received any advantage from these people, whom foreign greed had deprived of their homeland to profit from their strength here. The king of Spain gave recompense, or was supposed to give recompense, of one-and-one-half *reales* a day for each prisoner of war. The captain, limited by circumstances, could take only the three Russian deserters on board and offer Mr. Elliot passage to the Sandwich Islands, from where he could easily get to Sitka or wherever else he chose. The governor sent for these Russians, and when they had arrived he handed them over to Mr. von Kotzebue after he had demanded and received from him his word of honor that they, who had sought and found protection in Spain, should not be punished in any way for this. I found his behavior on this occasion very noble.

Among these Russians there was one, Ivan Strogonov, an old man, who was sincerely happy to have come among his compatriots again. As he was hardly fit for duty as a seaman, the captain earmarked him for duty in the main cabin and made this known to us. On the last days we spent in port, he was sent out to hunt. The poor wretch! On the eve of departure his powder horn exploded, and he was brought back mortally wounded. He wanted only to die among Russians. The captain kept him on board out of pity, and he died on the third day of the passage. He was quietly lowered into the sea, and with him went the last hope our boots had of ever being polished again. Peace be with you, Ivan Strogonov!

But I am getting ahead of myself; let me turn back.

On October 25 Mr. Kuskov arrived from Port Bodega with seven small baidares. A clever man, capable in every way of taking care of his affairs.

On the 26th the diplomatic conference took place in the *presidio*. Don Pablo Vicente de Solá, governor of New California, elucidated fully Spain's indisputable right to the territory occupied by the Russian settlement under Mr. Kuskov and called upon Mr. Kuskov to vacate the area occupied counter to international law. Mr. Kuskov, agent of the Russian-American Trading Company and supervisor of the settlement at Port Bodega, without going into the question of law, which was not his concern, manifested the greatest willingness to depart from Port Bodega as soon as he was empowered to do so by his superior, Mr. Baranov, who had ordered

Indians at Mission San Francisco de Asís, 1816, by Louis Choris. *Courtesy of the California Historical Society, Templeton Crocker Collection, FN-30510.*

him here. Thereupon the governor called upon Mr. von Kotzebue to intervene in the name of the tsar and effect the evacuation of Bodega. Otto von Kotzebue, lieutenant in the Imperial Russian navy and captain of the *Rurik,* declared himself to be without jurisdiction to act in this case, even though the justice of the case seemed so clear that it merely had to be stated to be recognized. And so then we were as far as we had been before.

Hereupon it was decided to issue a statement about the day's negotiations and the state of affairs and to send it, *in duplo,* signed and sealed by all participants in said negotiations, to the two high sovereigns: His Majesty, the tsar of Russia, through the captain of the *Rurik;* and His Majesty, the king of Spain, through the governor of New California.

The editing of this document, I, as interpreter, had to supervise. I discarded the first draft, in which I felt that something was missing. "For," I said to Don Pablo Vicente, "by bringing this matter to the

Indians' feather headdresses, 1816, by Louis Choris. *Courtesy of the California Historical Society, North Baker Research Library, Templeton Crocker Collection, FN-31034.*

thrones of the high sovereigns and expecting to secure an alleviation of this wrong and the punishment of the servants responsible for it from the tsar of Russia himself, you are divesting yourself of the right that you indisputably have of taking action into your own hands against the invader, and then must not anticipate the high decision of the monarchs."

Pablo Vicente de Solá had no objection to this. He praised my insight, had the statement rewritten, and when it was signed in the *presidio* on the evening of the 28th, he gave his solemn word of honor not to undertake any act of force on his own initiative against the aforesaid Kuskov and the Russian settlement in Port Bodega and to leave affairs *in statu quo* until the decision of the high courts was made. I signed the document *en clase de intérprete*, as interpreter.

I do not mean to boast about this turn of things. For even if the good Don Pablo Vicente de Solá had not sworn this oath, he would hardly have opened hostilities and undertaken a campaign against the Russian fort at Port Bodega.

I have heard that the said statement did not fail to reach its real destination in St. Petersburg and, without ever being acted upon, was consigned to the files in the appropriate ministry. But a Russian order of merit is said to have been sent to Don Pablo Vicente de Solá, Gobernador de la Nueva California. I received a fine otter skin from Mr. Kuskov as a gift of recognition, and you can have it displayed to you in the Berlin Zoological Museum, to which I donated it.

An immediate consequence of the conference of October 26 was not a favorable one for the *Rurik*. The negotiations had stretched out beyond the noon hour, and someone else had wound up the chronometers for the captain. He confided to me that hereafter the large chronometer had changed its operation to such an extent that he must consider it ruined.

Spain's claims to the territory of this coast were not esteemed any more highly by the Americans and English than they were by the Russians. The mouth of the Columbia River was also counted by Spain as part of its territory. The history of the settlement there the Spaniards and Mr. Elliot both told in about the same way. The Americans from New York had gone there partly by land and partly by sea and founded a settlement. During the war between England and America [War of 1812], the frigate *Racoon*, Captain Black, was sent out to take possession of this post. The English merchants from Canada went there by land, and when the warship that threatened the colony was in sight of the harbor, for the sake of a prize of money—50,000 pounds sterling—they took possession of the colony and raised the English flag. A land trade route is supposed to connect the Columbia with Canada. I merely report what I have heard.

The time of our stay in California had run out. On October 26, a Sunday, after a ride to the mission, there was a festive farewell dinner in our tents. The *Rurik*'s artillery roared an accompaniment to the toast to the alliance of the monarchs and the peoples and to the health of the governor. A good missionary had dipped his cloak too deeply into the blood of the grapes and swayed visibly under the burden.

On the 28th camp was struck, and the tents brought aboard ship again. While we sealed our statement in the *presidio*, Mr. Kuskov, with the foreknowledge of Mr. von Kotzebue, had sent two baidares out to catch otters at the rear of the bay.

On the 29th Mr. Kuskov left early in the morning with his flotilla of baidares for Bodega on the one hand, and on the other, later in the day Don Pablo Vicente de Solá left for Monterey. The latter took our letters for transshipment to Europe, the last our friends received from us on our voyage. With them our trail vanished. For when in the fall of 1817 we did not return to Kamchatka, in Europe they gave us up for lost.

On the 30th all animals were aboard and vegetables in great abundance. At the same time a terrible number of flies came aboard, thickening the air. We had taken on fresh water, which in this port, especially in the summer, is a difficult business. We were obliged to the governor for a cask of wine from Monterey. Our friends from the *presidio* dined with us at noon on the *Rurik*. We were ready to sail.

On the 31st our friends were still with us for a last farewell, and some of us rode to the mission in the afternoon. Late in the evening Mr. John Elliot de Castro arrived, still undecided whether he would take advantage of the captain's offer or not. He finally decided to accept.

On November 1, 1816, All Saints' Day, at nine o'clock in the morning, we weighed anchor while our friends were in church. We saw them arrive at the fort just as we sailed past. They hoisted the Spanish flag to the accompaniment of a one-gun salute; we did the same with ours. They saluted us first with seven guns, which we returned shot for shot.

The water of the harbor of San Francisco was highly phospho-
rescent from very fine particles of light, and even the surf on the
beach of the coast outside of the bay unrolled with a perceptible
shimmer. I examined the water of the harbor under the microscope
and observed in it small amounts of exceptionally small infusoria,
to which I however cannot ascribe the luminescence.

Here we daily observed the play of the banks of fog, which
were blown across the sun-drenched land by the prevailing sea
breeze, where they broke apart and became dissipated. The spectacle that they prepared for us upon departure was especially fine,
as they first enshrouded and then unveiled various peaks and areas
of the coast.

PART III:

PICTURING A WORLD TRANSFORMED

The changing California Indians, from *The Annals of San Francisco*, 1855. The original caption read, "1. *Wahla*, chief of the Yuba tribe—civilized and employed by Mr. S. Brannan. 2. A Partly civilized Indian. 3. A Wild Indian." *Courtesy of the California Historical Society, North Baker Research Library, FN-31316.*

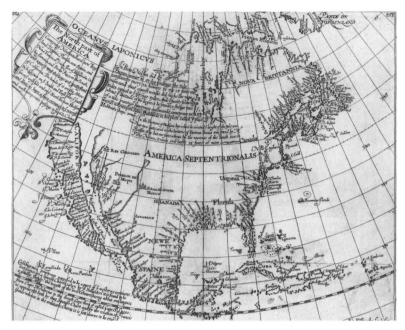

(above) "The North Part of America," 1625, by Henry Briggs, bearing the label "California, sometymes supposed to be a part of ye western continent, but scince by a Spanish Charte taken by ye Hollanders it is found to be a goodly ilande." Map-makers like Briggs continued to portray California as an island until the mid-eighteenth century. *Courtesy of The Bancroft Library.*

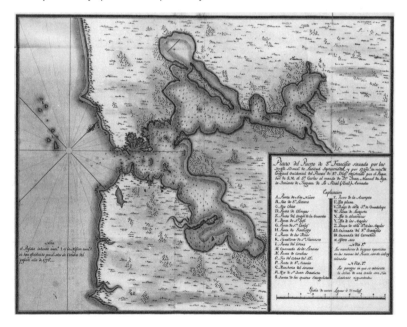

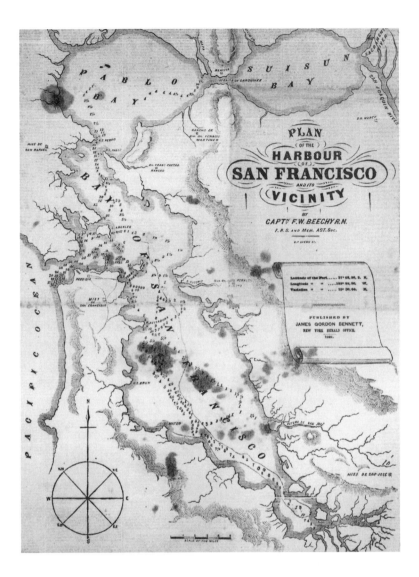

(above) This detailed map, drafted by Frederick William Beechey in 1826, provided ship captains with the first reliable map of San Francisco Bay. His map also permanently established many local place-names, although in the process he accidentally reversed the names for Yerba Buena and Alcatraz islands given by Captain Juan Manuel de Ayala fifty years earlier. *Courtesy of the California Historical Society, North Baker Research Library, Map Collection, gift of Miss F.L. Chace, FN-31308.*

(opposite) "Plano del Puerto de San Francisco," 1776, by José de Canizares, navigator and pilot of the *San Carlos* under Captain Ayala. *Courtesy of The Bancroft Library.*

158

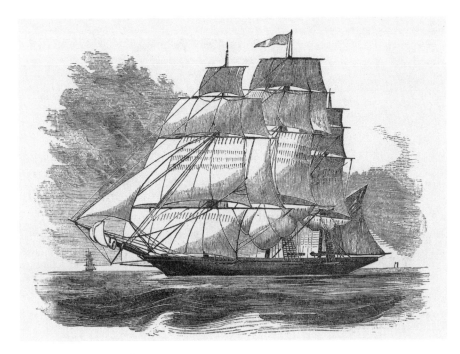

(above) Clipper ship, from *The Annals of San Francisco*, 1855. Speedy vessels named for their capacity to sail at a rapid "clip," clipper ships began appearing along the California coastline in the 1840s. Their swiftness encouraged trade with Asia and New England. *Courtesy of the California Historical Society, North Baker Research Library, FN-31315.*

(opposite, above) Indians paddling in San Francisco Bay, 1816, by Louis Choris. The native people of San Francisco Bay constructed canoes, binding together long, buoyant tule reeds. *Courtesy of the California Historical Society, Templeton Crocker Collection, FN-30512.*

(opposite, below) "The Golden Hinde," 1927, by Montague Dawson. Isolated and forbidding, California attracted few visitors in the sixteenth and seventeenth centuries. The *Golden Hind,* the first English ship to sail around the world, made an emergency landing in present-day Marin County in 1579. Only the ponderous Manila galleons—annual treasure ships laden with Asian silks, spices, and gems on their way from the Philippines to Acapulco—appeared off the California coast with any regularity. *Courtesy of The Bancroft Library.*

L'Ours gris de l'Amérique Septentrionale.
(Ursus griseus Cuv.)

European depictions of California's natural world: Grizzly bear, 1816, by Louis Choris. *Courtesy of the California Historical Society, North Baker Research Library, Templeton Crocker Collection, FN-31314.*

California quail, 1786, by Jean-Louis-Robert Prevost, botanist of the La Pérouse expedition. *Courtesy of The Bancroft Library.*

Sea lion, 1816, by Louis Choris. *Courtesy of the California Historical Society, North Baker Research Library, Templeton Crocker Collection, FN-31313.*

Raccoon, as reconstructed from an evidently damaged specimen obtained along the Sacramento River by British Captain Edward Belcher, 1837. From Zoology of the *Voyage of the Sulphur. Courtesy of The Bancroft Library.*

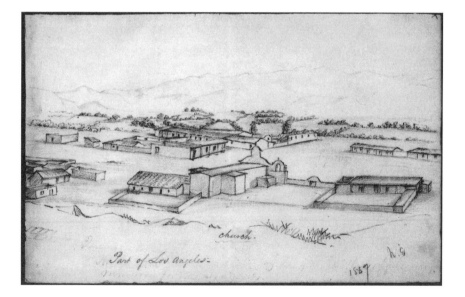

church.

Part of Los angeles.

1857

162

(above) Fort Ross, ca. 1827, by French captain Auguste Duhaut-Cilly. Founded in 1812 at the urging of Nikolai Petrovich Rezanov, Fort Ross featured extensive gardens and more than fifty buildings, including a boathouse, a barn large enough to house 200 cows, a posh governor's residence, and a chapel complete with a Russian-style dome and bells cast in St. Petersburg. After helping to hunt the California sea otter to the brink of extinction, the Russians sold Fort Ross to John Sutter in 1841. *Courtesy of the California Department of Parks and Recreation, State Museum Resource Center.*

(opposite, above) Monterey, 1792, by John Sykes, master's mate onboard the *Discovery*. Site of Alta California's second mission, Monterey served as Father-President Junípero Serra's headquarters and California's capital under Spanish and Mexican control. *Courtesy of the California Historical Society, FN-30520.*

(opposite, below) Los Angeles, 1847, by William Rich Hutton. Established by Felipe de Neve in 1781, Los Angeles began as home to a mere forty-four Spanish settlers but soon became the most populous *pueblo* in Alta California. In the early nineteenth century the town became a prosperous trade center, bolstered by the arrival of American merchants such as rancher William Wolfskill, trader John Temple, and cattleman Abel Stearns, many of whom married into local Californio families. *Courtesy of The Huntington Library, San Marino, California.*

PART IV:

MEXICAN CONTROL, YANKEE INFILTRATION AND CONQUEST

"Sickness in general prevails to an incredible extent in all the missions, and on comparing the census of the years 1786 and 1813, the proportion of deaths appears to be increasing. At the former period there had been only 7,701 Indians baptized, out of which 2,388 had died; but in 1813 there had been 37,437 deaths to only 57,328 baptisms."

—Frederick William Beechey, 1826

"Wherever the Anglo-Saxon race plant themselves, progess is certain to be displayed in some form or other. Such is their 'go-ahead' energy, that things cannot stand still where they are, whatever may be the circumstances surrounding them."

—Edwin Bryant, 1846

Frederick William Beechey
1826

After ten years of bloody revolution, Mexico finally declared its independence from Spain on September 28, 1821. Two years later, a new constitution established the Federal Republic of Mexico and, at least on paper, granted the right to vote and own property to all men, including Indians. The territories of California, Texas, and New Mexico were officially controlled by the Mexican Congress. However, widespread corruption and a series of civil wars would cripple Mexico's attempts at establishing consistent administrative or economic policies.

News of Mexico's independence did not reach California for seven months. When it did arrive, it changed little in day-to-day life, certainly not for the Indians living at the region's twenty missions, who were never informed of their new political freedom. Independence meant little more for them than the substitution of an eagle for a lion on a flag. The non-Indian residents of California (who haughtily called themselves *gente de razón*, meaning "people of reason") were more shaken by the news. Although few had been born in Spain, they viewed it, not Mexico, as their homeland. But most pledged allegiance to the new government in the hope of receiving much-needed economic aid.

Despite the change in government, California remained in the 1820s as poverty-stricken and lawless as ever. José María Echeandía, the first governor of California appointed by the Federal Republic of Mexico, arrived in 1825. A hypochondriac who left a wife and four daughters behind in Mexico City, Echeandía's administration was beset by nonstop crises and rebellions. When he rejected living in the foggy capitol of Monterey in favor of San Diego, he enraged northern officials, who elected their own governor in 1832. In 1826 American fur trapper Jedediah Strong Smith led the first overland party into California; Echeandía, frightened by the precedent, ousted him. In 1829 a group of destitute and demoralized presidial soldiers marched south from Monterey, demanding compensation for years of unpaid salaries. They backed down only when Echeandía met them near Santa Barbara with a battalion of troops. That same year, an escaped neophyte named Estanislao from Mission San José organized a large war band of Indians in the San Joaquín Valley; 100 Mexican soldiers could not quash the rebellion.

After 1822, the shadowy commerce between Californians and English, American, and Russian ships came out in the open as a permanent institution. Mexican independence ended many restrictions on foreign trade, and the new government's lack of authority and scattered coastal patrols made collecting import and export tariffs difficult. In 1821, the last year of Spanish control, nine ships visited California; the following year the number rose to twenty, and to forty-four in 1826.

One of those ships that anchored at California in 1826 was the *Blossom*, a sizable British sloop equipped with sixteen guns, a hull strengthened against icebergs, and a crew of 100 men, commanded by Frederick William Beechey. The *Blossom*'s expedition was not a single voyage, planned as a complete enterprise in itself, but rather a part of British polar exploration aimed at discovering the Northwest Passage before the Russians. Beechey was dispatched in May 1825 to meet up with an overland party led by Captain John Franklin that was charting the northern Alaskan shoreline. In order to secure sailors for what was sure to be a cold and dreary voyage, Beechey offered the men six months advance pay and stocked the *Blossom* with plenty of anti-scorbutics and unusual luxuries such as preserved meats, soup, pickles, spices, and chocolate.

The trip was actually Frederick Beechey's second foray into the icy waters of the North Pacific. He was born in 1796, the second of eighteen children of Sir William Beechey, a painter who had worked his way out of obscurity to high social position by painting portraits of the royal family and aristocracy. In keeping with his new-found status, Sir William was anxious that his sons should establish respectable careers and so entered Frederick into the navy at the age of ten. As a young midshipman, Frederick Beechey saw little action during the Napoleonic wars, although he took part in a campaign against New Orleans. His entry into polar exploration came in 1817, when he was appointed second-in-command on the *Trent* under Captain Franklin. While attempting to sail around the northern tip of Greenland, the ship encountered ice that Franklin had expected to be melted. The *Trent* nearly capsized near Spitzbergen. Although a disaster, the voyage prepared Beechey for command of the *Blossom* a few years later.

As instructed, the *Blossom* sailed around Cape Horn, stopped for supplies at Chile, and spent a few weeks in the South Pacific surveying and collecting "rare and curious specimens" for the ship's team of scientists. Onboard were two artists, William Smyth and Richard Brydges Beechey (Frederick's younger brother), who painted superb watercolors of scenes along the way. They reached the rendezvous point in Kotzebue Sound near the Bering Strait, but Franklin's land party never arrived. In September, Beechey decided to leave supplies there for Franklin and sail south for warmer waters. He anchored in the bay of San Francisco on November 6, 1826.

While resupplying, Beechey asked *presidio* commander Ignacio Martinez for permission to make a detailed survey of the bay. Martinez agreed, providing that Beechey left a copy of the map for the Mexican government. Taking soundings throughout the bay,

Beechey discovered a dangerous sunken rock he named after the *Blossom*, leaving what he thought would be a permanent memento of the voyage. His precise map of the bay, along with his charts of the coast south of San Francisco, became the standards used by later visitors. Beechey did make one mistake—he accidentally and permanently reversed the names for Yerba Buena and Alcatraz islands given by Captain Ayala fifty years earlier.

Today, the most important aspect of the *Blossom*'s fifty-two-day stay at San Francisco is Beechey's description of the missions in their heyday. The number of missions had swelled to twenty-one, each sitting upon an enormous tract of land and equipped with a grain-mill and sawmill. Nearly 30,000 neophytes tended the missions' ten million acres of fields and gardens and watched over nearly two million head of cattle, sheep, horses, goats, and mules. With Mexico unable to send much aid, California's soldiers and civilians were forced to barter with the missions for food, clothing, soap, leather goods, and furniture, all produced by Indian laborers. The missions supported approximately two-thirds of California's Spanish-speaking population.

Narrative of a Voyage to the Pacific and Beering's Strait, Beechey's journal of the voyage of the *Blossom*, was published in London in 1831 during an era when travel diaries were enjoying considerable popularity throughout Europe. Narratives of even minor voyages often ran through several printings almost as soon as they appeared. But by the 1830s almost all of the major discoveries that could be made by sea voyage had already been accomplished; if a naval explorer wished to gain public recognition, he had to write something more than a bare record of his travels. Beechey's account epitomized this new genre—the popularized travel narrative. Only after the *Blossom*'s return to England did Beechey compile the final version of *Narrative of a Voyage to the Pacific*, carefully arranging his selection of material from his own log and several crew members' diaries so that even the most mundane parts of the voyage would seem exciting. Beechey's generally fine writing is marred only by its heavy moralistic overtone, especially present when condemning Californian society.

After seeing San Francisco, the *Blossom* visited Monterey, the Sandwich Islands, China, and Kamchatka before returning to the Bering Strait. There was still no sign of Franklin (who was delayed and never actually reached the Strait), so Beechey stopped again for supplies at California in the autumn of 1827 before rounding Cape Horn and sailing for England. The command of the *Blossom* was the last voyage of exploration Beechey undertook. Health failing, he spent the last thirty years of his life living in semi-retirement, overseeing minor surveying work along the coast of Ireland while keeping appraised of new explorations through the Royal Geographic Society. At the time of his death in 1857, he was serving as its president. In 1870, in a great explosion that drew thousands of onlookers, Blossom Rock was destroyed as a hazard to navigation, and the last tangible reminder of the *Blossom*'s visit vanished from the bay. This excerpt from Beechey's *Narrative* begins November 6, 1826.

FREDERICK WILLIAM BEECHEY

from *Narrative of a Voyage to the Pacific and Beering's Strait*

*W*hen the day broke, we found ourselves about four miles from the land. It was a beautiful morning, with just sufficient freshness in the air to exhilarate without chilling. The tops of the mountains, the only part of the land visible, formed two ranges—between which our port [San Francisco Bay] was situated—though its entrance, as well as the valleys and the low lands, were still covered with the morning mist condensed around the bases of the mountains. We bore up for the opening between the ranges, anxious for the rising sun to withdraw the veil, that we might obtain a view of the harbor and form our judgment of the country in which we were about to pass the next few weeks. As we advanced, the beams of the rising sun gradually descended the hills, until the mist, dispelled from the land, rolled on before the refreshing sea wind, discovering cape after cape, and exhibiting a luxuriant country apparently abounding in wood and rivers. At length two low promontories—the southern one distinguished by a fort and a Mexican flag—marked the narrow entrance of the port.

We spread our sails with all the anxiety of persons who had long been secluded from civilized society and deprived of wholesome aliment; but after the first effort of the breeze, it died away and left us becalmed in a heavy NW swell....

The fort, which we passed upon our right, mounts nine guns and is built upon a promontory on the south side of the entrance, apparently so near to the precipice that one side will, before long,

172

San Francisco Bay and *presidio*, 1826, by Richard Brydges Beechey, the younger sibling of Captain Frederick William Beechey, who accompanied his brother to California onboard the *Blossom. Courtesy of Mr. and Mrs. Henry S. Dakin. Photograph courtesy of North Point Gallery.*

be precipitated over it by the gradual breaking away of the rock. Its situation, nevertheless, is good, as regards the defense of the entrance; but it is commanded by a rising ground behind it. As we passed, a soldier protruded a speaking-trumpet through one of the embrasures and hailed us with a stentorian voice, but we could not distinguish what was said. This custom of hailing vessels has arisen from there being no boat belonging to the garrison and the inconvenience felt by the governor in having to wait for a report of arrivals until the masters of the vessels could send their boats on shore.

The port of San Francisco does not show itself to advantage until after the fort is passed, when it breaks upon the view and forcibly impresses the spectator with the magnificence of the harbor. He then beholds a broad sheet of water—sufficiently extensive to contain all the British navy—with convenient coves, anchorage in every part, and, around, a country diversified with hill and dale, partly wooded and partly disposed in pasture lands of the richest kind, abounding in herds of cattle. In short, the only objects wanting to complete the interest of the scene are some useful establishments and comfortable residences on the grassy borders of the harbor, the absence of which creates an involuntary regret that so fine a country, abounding in all that is essential to man, should be allowed to remain in such a state of neglect. So poorly did the place appear to be peopled that a sickly column of smoke rising from within some dilapidated walls—misnamed the *presidio* or protection—was the only indication we had of the country being inhabited....

As we opened out the several islands and stopping places in the harbor, we noticed seven American whalers at anchor at Sausalito, not one of which showed their colors. We passed them and anchored off a small bay named Yerba Buena—from the luxuriance of its vegetation, about a league distant from both the *presidio* and the mission of San Francisco. I immediately went on shore to pay my respects to Don Ignacio Martinez,[1] a lieutenant in the Mexican army, acting governor in the absence of Don Luís [Antonio Argüello],[2] and to the priest, whose name was Tomaso, both of whom gave me a very hospitable and friendly reception, and offered their services in any way they might be required. Our first inquiries naturally related to supplies, which we were disappointed to find not at all equal to what had been reported. In short, it seemed that with the exception of flour, fresh beef, vegetables, and salt, which might be procured through the missions, we should have to depend upon the American vessels for whatever else we might want, or upon what might chance to be in store at Monterey, a port of more

---

[1] Ignacio Martínez was later named *comandante* of San Francisco *presidio* (1822–1827). His daughter, Maria Antonia, married William A. Richardson, an Englishman who founded the town of Yerba Buena in 1835.

[2] Beechey was misinformed; Luís Antonio Argüello, *gobernador* from 1822 to 1825, had been recently replaced by José María Echeandía, California's first *gobernador* appointed by the Federal Republic of Mexico.

importance than San Francisco, and from being the residence of a branch of a respectable firm in Lima, [Peru,] better supplied with the means of refitting vessels after a long sea voyage.

It was evident from this report that the supplies were likely to be very inadequate to our wants, but that no opportunity of obtaining them might be lost, I dispatched Mr. Collie the surgeon and Mr. Marsh the purser overland to Monterey—with Mr. Evans as interpreter—with orders to procure for the ship what medicines, provisions, and other stores were to be had, and to negotiate government bills, on which the exchange was far more favorable there than at the Sandwich Islands. The governor politely furnished a passport and a guard for this service; and our hospitable friend Tomaso, the *padre* of the mission, provided horses for them free of any charge. In the meantime we arranged with a relation of the governor for the daily supply of the ship's company, an arrangement which it afterwards appeared increased the jealousy that had long existed between the *presidio* and the missions by transferring to the pocket of the commandant the profits that would otherwise have been reaped by the *padre*.

We were happy to find the country around our anchorage abounding in game of all kinds, so plentiful, indeed, as soon to lessen the desire of pursuit. Still there were many inducements to both the officers and seamen to land and enjoy themselves, and as it was for the benefit of the service that they should recruit their health and strength as soon as possible, every facility was afforded them. Horses were fortunately very cheap, from nine shillings to seven pounds apiece, so that riding became a favorite amusement; and the Spaniards, finding they could make a good market by letting out their stud, appeared with them every Sunday opposite the ship, ready saddled for the occasion, as this was a day on which I allowed every man to go out of the ship. Some of the officers purchased horses and tethered them near the place, but the Spaniards, finding this to interfere with their market, contrived to let them loose on the Saturday night in order that the officers might be compelled to hire others on the following day. The only difficulty to the enjoyment of this amusement was the scarcity of saddles and bridles, some of which cost ten times as much as a decent horse. The ingenuity of the seamen generally obviated these difficulties, while some borrowed or hired saddles of the natives. For my own part, I purchased a decent-looking horse for about thirty-five shillings sterling, and on my departure presented it to a Spaniard who had lent me the necessary accoutrements for it during my stay, which answered the purpose of both parties, as he was pleased with his present, and I had my ride for about a shilling a day—a useful hint to persons who may be similarly circumstanced.

Such of the seamen as would not venture on horseback made parties to visit the *presidio* and mission, where they found themselves welcome guests with the Spanish soldiers. These two places were the only buildings within many miles of us, and they fortunately supplied just enough spirits to allow the people to enjoy themselves with their friends, without indulging in much excess—a very great advantage in a seaport.

The roads leading to these two great places of attraction in a short time became well-beaten, and that to the mission very much improved by having the boughs removed which before overhung it. It was at first in contemplation to hire a Spaniard to lop them, but our pioneers, who stopped at nothing, soon tore them all away, except one, a large stump, which resisted every attack and unhorsed several of its assailants.

Martinez was always glad to see the officers at the *presidio* and made them welcome to what he had. Indeed, nothing seemed to give him greater pleasure than our partaking of his family dinner; the greater part of which was dressed by his wife and daughters, who prided themselves on their proficiency in the art of cooking. It was not, however, entirely for the satisfaction of presenting us with a well-prepared repast that they were induced to indulge in this humble occupation; poor Martinez, besides his legitimate offspring, had eighteen others to provide for out of his salary, which was then eleven years in arrears. He had a sorry prospect before him, as, a short time previous to our visit, the government, by way of paying up these arrears, sent a brig with a cargo of paper cigars to be issued to the troops in lieu of dollars; but, as Martinez justly observed, cigars would not satisfy the families of the soldiers, and the compromise was refused. The cargo was, however, landed at Monterey and placed under the charge of the governor, where all other tobacco is contraband; and as the Spaniards are fond of smoking, it stands a fair chance, in the course of time, of answering the intention of the government, particularly as the troops apply for these oftener than they otherwise would, under the impression of clearing off a score of wages that will never be settled in any other manner. Fortunately for Martinez and other veterans in this country, both vegetable and animal food are uncommonly cheap, and there are no fashions to create any expense of dress.

The governor's abode was in a corner of the *presidio* and formed one end of a row, of which the other was occupied by a chapel. The opposite side was broken down and little better than a heap of rubbish and bones, on which jackals, dogs, and vultures were constantly preying. The other two sides of the quadrangle contained storehouses, artificers' shops, and the jail, all built in the humblest style with badly-burnt bricks and roofed with tiles. The chapel and the governor's house were distinguished by being whitewashed.

Whether viewed at a distance or near, the establishment impresses a spectator with any other sentiment than that of its being a place of authority; and but for a tottering flagstaff, upon which was occasionally displayed the tri-colored flag of Mexico, three rusty field pieces, and a half accoutred sentinel parading the gateway in charge of a few poor wretches heavily-shackled, a visitor would be ignorant of the importance of the place. The neglect of the government to its establishments could not be more thoroughly evinced than in the dilapidated condition of the building in question, and such was the dissatisfaction of the people that there was no inclination to improve their situation or even to remedy many of the evils which they appeared to us to have the power to remove.

The plain upon which the *presidio* stands is well adapted to cultivation, but it is scarcely ever touched by the plow, and the garrison is entirely beholden to the missions for its resources. Each soldier has nominally about three pounds a month, out of which he is obliged to purchase his provision. If the governor were active and the means were supplied, the country in the vicinity of the establishment might be made to yield enough wheat and vegetables for the troops, by which they would save that portion of their pay that now goes to the purchase of these necessary articles.

The garrison of San Francisco consists of seventy-six cavalry soldiers and a few artillerymen, distributed between the *presidios* and the missions, and consequently not more than half a dozen are at anytime in one place.

They appeared to us to be very dissatisfied, owing not only to their pay being so many years in arrear, but to the duties that had been imposed both on the importation of foreign articles and on those of the Mexican territory, amounting in the first instance to 42 1/2 percent, whereas, under the old government, two ships were annually sent from Acapulco with goods, which were sold duty free, and at their original cost in that country, and then, also, their pay being regularly discharged, they were able to purchase what they wanted. A further grievance has arisen by the refusal of the government to continue certain privileges that were enjoyed under the old system. At that time soldiers entered for a term of ten years, at the expiration of which they were allowed to retire to the *pueblos*—

villages erected for this purpose and attached to the missions, where the men have a portion of ground allotted to them for the support of their families. This afforded a competency to many; and while it benefited them, it was of service to the government, as the country by that means became settled and its security increased. But this privilege has latterly been withheld, and the applicants have been allowed only to possess the land and feed their cattle upon it, until it shall please the government to turn them off. The reason of this, I believe, was that Mexico was beginning to turn her attention to California and was desirous of having settlers there from the southern districts, to whom it would be necessary to give lands; and until they could see what would be required for this purpose and for the government establishments—and had the limits of the property already allotted, defined—they did not wish to make any new grants. The real cause, however, was not explained to the soldiers; they merely heard that they could not have the land ceded to them for life as usual, and they were consequently much dissatisfied

The same feeling of discontent that was experienced by the garrison pervaded the missions, in consequence of some new regulations of the republican government, the first and most grievous of which was the discontinuance of a salary of 400 dollars per annum heretofore allowed to each of the *padres*; the support the former government had given to the missions amounted, according to Langsdorff, to a million *piastres* a year. Another grievance was the requisition of an oath of allegiance to the reigning authorities, which these holy men considered so egregious a violation of their former pledge to the king of Spain that, until he renounced his sovereignty over the country, they could not conscientiously take it; and, much as they were attached to the place in which they had passed a large portion of their lives, and though by quitting it they would be reduced to the utmost penury—yet, so much did they regard this pledge that they were prepared to leave the country and to seek an asylum in any other that would afford it them. Indeed, the prefect preferring his expulsion to renouncing his allegiance had already received his dismissal and was ready at the seaport of Monterey to embark in any vessel the government might appoint to receive him. A third grievance—and one which, when duly considered, was of some importance, not only to the missions but to the country in general—was an order to liberate all those converted Indians from the missions who bore good characters and had been taught the art of agriculture or were masters of a trade, and were capable of supporting themselves, giving them portions of land to cultivate, so arranged that they should be divided into parishes, with curates to superintend them, subservient to the clergy of the missions who were to proceed in the conversion of the Indians as usual, and to train them for the domesticated state of society in contemplation.

This philanthropic system at first sight appeared to be a very excellent one, and every friend of the rights of man would naturally join in a wish for its prosperity; but the Mexican government could not have sufficiently considered the state of California and the disposition of the Indians, or they would have known it could not possibly succeed without long previous training, and then it would require to be introduced by slow degrees.

The Indians whom this law emancipated were essential to the support of the missions, not only for conducting their agricultural concerns but for keeping in subordination by force and example those whom disobedience and ignorance would exempt from the privilege; and as a necessary consequence of this indulgence, the missions would be ruined before the system could be brought into effect, even supposing the Indians capable of conducting their own affairs. So far from this being the case, however, they were known to possess neither the will, the steadiness, nor the patience to provide for themselves. Accustomed, many of them from their infancy, to as much restraint as children and to execute, mechanically, what they were desired and no more, without even entertaining a thought for their future welfare, it was natural that such persons, when released from this discipline, should abandon themselves entirely to their favorite amusements, pastimes, and vices. Those also who had been converted in later life would return to their former habits, and having once again tasted the blessings of freedom, which confinement and discipline must have rendered doubly desirable, would forget all restraint; and then being joined by the wild discontented Indians, they would be more formidable enemies to the missions than before, inasmuch as they would be more enlightened. But I will not anticipate the result, which we had an opportunity of seeing on our return the following year, and from which the reader will be able to judge how the system worked.

The *padres*, however, dreading the worst, were very discontented, and many would willingly have quitted the country for Manila. The government appeared to be aware of this feeling, as they sent some young priests from Mexico to supplant those who were disaffected, and desired that they should be trained up in the mission and should make themselves acquainted with the language and usages of the Indians, in order that they might not promote discontent by any sudden innovation....

The object of the missions is to convert as many of the wild Indians as possible and to train them up within the walls of the establishment in the exercise of a good life, and of some trade, so that they may in time be able to provide for themselves and become useful members of civilized society. As to the various methods employed for the purpose of bringing proselytes to the mission, there are several reports, of which some were not very creditable to the institution. Nevertheless, on the whole I am of opinion that the priests are innocent, from a conviction that they are ignorant of the means employed by those who are under them. Whatever may be the system, and whether the Indians be really dragged from their homes and families by armed parties, as some assert, or not, and forced to exchange their life of freedom and wandering for one of confinement and restraint in the missions, the change according to our ideas of happiness would seem advantageous to them, as they lead a far better life in the missions than in their forests, where they are in a state of nudity and are frequently obliged to depend solely upon wild acorns for their subsistence.

Immediately the Indians are brought to the mission. They are placed under the tuition of some of the most enlightened of their countrymen, who teach them to repeat in Spanish the Lord's Prayer and certain passages in the Romish litany, and also, to cross themselves properly on entering the church. In a few days, a willing Indian becomes a proficient in these mysteries and suffers himself to be baptized and duly initiated into the church. If, however, as it not infrequently happens, any of the captured Indians show a repugnance to conversion, it is the practice to imprison them for a few days and then to allow them to breathe a little fresh air in a walk 'round the mission, to observe the happy mode of life of their converted countrymen; after which they are again shut up, and thus continue to be incarcerated until they declare their readiness to renounce the religion of their forefathers.

I do not suppose that this apparently unjustifiable conduct would be pursued for any length of time; and I had never an opportunity of ascertaining the fact, as the Indians are so averse to confinement that they very soon become impressed with the manifestly superior and more comfortable mode of life of those who are at liberty, and in a very few days declare their readiness to have the new religion explained to them. A person acquainted with the language of the parties, of which there are sometimes several dialects in the same mission, is then selected to train them, and having duly prepared them takes them to the *padre* to be baptized and to receive the sacrament. Having become Christians, they are put to trades, or if they have good voices, they are taught music and form part of the choir of the church.[3] Thus there are in almost every mission weavers, tanners, shoemakers, bricklayers, carpenters, blacksmiths, and other artificers. Others again are taught husbandry, to rear cattle and horses, and some to cook for the mission; while the females card, clean, and spin wool, weave, and sew, and those who are married attend to their domestic concerns.

In requital of these benefits, the services of the Indian, for life, belong to the mission, and if any neophyte should repent of his apostasy from the religion of his ancestors and desert, an armed force is sent in pursuit of him and drags him back to punishment apportioned to the degree of aggravation attached to his crime. It does not often happen that a voluntary convert succeeds in his attempt to escape, as the wild Indians have a great contempt and dislike for those who have entered the missions, and they will frequently not only refuse to readmit them to their tribe, but will sometimes even discover their retreat to their pursuers. This animosity between the wild and converted Indians is of great importance to the missions, as it checks desertion and is at the same time a powerful defense against the wild tribes, who consider their territory invaded and have other just causes of complaint. The Indians, besides, from political motives, are, I fear, frequently encouraged in a contemptuous feeling toward their unconverted countrymen by hearing them constantly held up to them in the degrading light of *bestias!* and in hearing the Spaniards distinguished by the appellation of *gente de razón*.

The produce of the land and of the labor of the Indians is appropriated to the support of the mission, and the overplus to amass a fund that is entirely at the disposal of the *padres*. In some of the establishments this must be very large, although the *padres* will not admit it and always plead poverty. The government has lately

---

[3] In fact, at Mission San José, Father Narcisco Durán taught neophytes to read music and organized a thirty-piece orchestra.

demanded a part of this profit, but the priests who, it is said, think the Indians are more entitled to it than the government, make small donations to them, and thus evade the tax by taking care there shall be no overplus. These donations in some of the missions are greater than in others, according as one establishment is more prosperous than another; and on this also, in a great measure, depends the comforts of the dwellings and the neatness, the cleanliness, and the clothing of the people. In some of the missions much misery prevails, while in others there is a degree of cheerfulness and cleanliness which shows that many of the Indians require only care and proper management to make them as happy as their dull senses will admit of under a life of constraint.

The two missions of San Francisco and San José are examples of the contrast alluded to. The former in 1817 contained a thousand converts, who were housed in small huts around the mission; but at present only 260 remain—some have been sent, it is true, to the new mission of San Francisco Solano,[4] but sickness and death have dealt with an unsparing hand among the others. The huts of the absentees, at the time of our visit, had all fallen to decay and presented heaps of filth and rubbish; while the remaining inmates of the mission were in as miserable a condition as it was possible to conceive and were entirely regardless of their own comfort. Their hovels afforded scarcely any protection against the weather and were black with smoke. Some of the Indians were sleeping on the greasy floor; others were grinding baked acorns to make into cakes, which constitute a large portion of their food. So little attention indeed had been paid even to health that in one hut there was a quarter of beef suspended opposite a window in a very offensive and unwholesome state, but its owners were too indolent to throw it out. San José, on

---

[4] Mission San Francisco Solano, located in the present-day city of Sonoma, was the last mission to be founded in California (1823)—and the only one established under Mexican control.

Mission San Carlos Borromeo [Mission Carmel-Monterey], 1827, by William Smyth, an admiralty mate aboard the *Blossom*. *Courtesy of the California Historical Society.*

the other hand, was all neatness, cleanliness, and comfort. The Indians were amusing themselves between the hours of labor at their games; and the children, uniformly dressed in white bodices and scarlet petticoats, were playing at bat and ball. Part of this difference may arise from the habits of the people, who are of different tribes. Langsdorff observes that the Indians of the mission of San José are the handsomest tribe in California and in every way a finer race of men, and terms the neophytes of San Francisco pygmies compared with them. I cannot say that this remark occurred to me, and I think it probable that he may have been deceived by the apparently miserable condition of the people of San Francisco.

The children and adults of both sexes, in all the missions, are carefully locked up every night in separate apartments, and the keys are delivered into the possession of the *padre*; and as, in the daytime, their occupations lead to distinct places, unless they form a matrimonial alliance they enjoy very little of each other's society.

It, however, sometimes happens that they endeavor to evade the vigilance of their keepers and are locked up with the opposite sex; but severe corporeal punishment—inflicted in the same manner as is practiced in our schools, but with a whip instead of a rod—is sure to ensue if they are discovered. Though there may be occasional acts of tyranny, the general character of the *padres* is kind and benevolent, and in some of the missions the converts are so much attached to them that I have heard them declare they would go with them if they were obliged to quit the country. It is greatly to be regretted that with the influence these men have over their pupils, and with the regard those pupils seem to have for their masters, that the priests do not interest themselves a little more in the education of their converts, the first step to which would be in making themselves acquainted with the Indian language. Many of the Indians surpass their pastors in this respect and can speak the Spanish language, while scarcely one of the *padres* can make themselves understood by the Indians. They have besides, in general, a lamentable contempt for the intellect of these simple people and think them incapable of improvement beyond a certain point. Notwithstanding this, the Indians are, in general, well clothed and fed; they have houses of their own, and if they are not comfortable, it is, in a great measure, their own fault; their meals are given to them three times a day, and consist of thick gruel made of wheat, Indian corn, and sometimes acorns, to which at noon is generally added meat. Clothing of a better kind than that worn by the Indians is given to the officers of the missions, both as a reward for their services and to create an emulation in others.

If it should happen that there is a scarcity of provisions, either through failure in the crop or damage of that which is in store, as they have always two or three years in reserve, the Indians are sent off to the woods to provide for themselves, where, accustomed to hunt and fish, and game being very abundant, they find enough to subsist upon and return to the mission when they are required to reap the next year's harvest.

Having served ten years in the mission, an Indian may claim his liberty, provided any respectable settler will become surety for his future good conduct. A piece of ground is then allotted for his support, but he is never wholly free from the establishment, as part of his earnings must still be given to them. We heard of very few to whom this reward for servitude and good conduct had been granted; and it is not improbable that the *padres* are averse to it, as it deprives them of their best scholars. When these establishments were first founded, the Indians flocked to them in great numbers for the clothing with which the neophytes were supplied; but after they became acquainted with the nature of the institution and felt themselves under restraint, many absconded. Even now, notwithstanding the difficulty of escaping, desertions are of frequent occurrence, owing probably, in some cases, to the fear of punishment; in others to the deserters having been originally inveigled into the mission by the converted Indians or neophytes, as they are called by way of distinction to *los gentiles,* or the wild Indians; in other cases again to the fickleness of their own disposition.

Some of the converted Indians are occasionally stationed in places that are resorted to by the wild tribes for the purpose of offering them flattering accounts of the advantages of the mission and of persuading them to abandon their barbarous life; while others obtain leave to go into the territory of the gentiles to visit their friends and are expected to bring back converts with them when they return. At a particular period of the year, also, when the Indians can be spared from the agricultural concerns of the establishment, many of them are permitted to take the launch of the mission and make excursions to the Indian territory. All are anxious to go on such occasions, some to visit their friends, some to procure the manufactures of their barbarous countrymen (which, by the by, are often better than their own), and some with the secret determination never to return. On these occasions the *padres* desire them to induce as many of their unconverted brethren as possible to accompany them back to the mission, of course—implying that this is to be done only by persuasion—but the boat being furnished with a cannon and musketry, and in every respect equipped for war, it too often happens that the neophytes and the *gente de razón,* who superintend the direction of the boat, avail themselves of their superiority, with the desire of ingratiating themselves with their masters and of receiving a reward. There are, besides, repeated acts of aggression that it is necessary to punish, all of which furnish proselytes. Women and children are generally the first objects of capture, as their husbands and parents sometimes voluntarily follow them into captivity. These misunderstandings and captivities keep up a perpetual enmity amongst the tribes, whose thirst for revenge is almost insatiable.

We had an opportunity of witnessing the tragical issue of one of these holy day excursions of the neophytes of the mission of San José. The launch was armed as usual and placed under the superintendence of an *alcalde* [a town's leading civil officer] of the mission, who, it appears from one statement (for there were several), converted the party of pleasure either into one of attack for the purpose of procuring proselytes or of revenge upon a particular tribe for some aggression in which they were concerned. They proceeded up the Río San Joaquín until they came to the territory of a particular tribe named Cosemenes [sic],[5] when they disembarked with the gun and encamped for the night near the village of *los gentiles,* intending to make an attack upon them the next morning. But before they were prepared, the gentiles, who had been apprised of their intention and had collected a large body of friends, became the assail-

---

[5] The Cosumnes Indians, a Miwok-speaking people, lived in present-day El Dorado County on the banks of the Cosumnes River.

ants and pressed so hard upon the party that—notwithstanding they dealt death in every direction with their cannon and musketry, and were inspired with confidence by the contempt in which they held the valor and tactics of their unconverted countrymen—they were overpowered by numbers and obliged to seek their safety in flight, and to leave the guns in the woods. Some regained the launch and were saved, and others found their way over land to the mission, but thirty-four of the party never returned to tell their tale.

There were other accounts of this unfortunate affair, one of which accused the *padre* of authorizing the attack, and another stated that it was made in self defense; but that which I have given appeared to be the most probable. That the reverend father should have sanctioned such a proceeding is a supposition so totally at variance with his character that it will not obtain credit; and the other was in all probability the report of the *alcalde* to excuse his own conduct. They all agreed, however, in the fatal termination of their excursion, and the neophytes became so enraged at the news of the slaughter of their companions that it was almost impossible to prevent them from proceeding forthwith to revenge their deaths. The *padre* was also greatly displeased at the result of the excursion, as the loss of so many Indians to the mission was of the greatest consequence, and the confidence with which the victory would inspire the Indians was equally alarming. He therefore joined with the converted Indians in a determination to chastise and strike terror into the victorious tribe, and in concert with the governor planned an expedition against them. The mission furnished money, arms, Indians, and horses, and the *presidio* provided troops headed by the *alférez,* Sanchez, a veteran who had been frequently engaged with the Indians and was acquainted with every part of the country. The troops carried with them their armor and shields, as a defense against the arrows of the Indians. The armor consisted of a helmet and jerkin made of stout skins, quite impenetrable to an arrow, and the shields might almost vie with that of [Greek warrior] Ajax in the number of its folds.

The expedition set out on the 19th of November, and we heard nothing of it until the 27th. But two days after the troops had taken the field, some immense columns of smoke, rising above the mountains in the direction of the Cosemenes, bespoke the conflagration of the village of the persecuted gentiles. And on the day above mentioned, the veteran Sanchez made a triumphant entry into the mission of San José, escorting forty miserable women and children, the gun that had been taken in the first battle, and other trophies of the field. This victory, so glorious, according to the ideas of the conqueror, was achieved with the loss of only one man on the part of the Christians, who was mortally wounded by the bursting of his own gun; but on the part of the enemy it was considerable, as Sanchez the morning after the battle counted forty-one men, women, and children, dead. It is remarkable that none of the prisoners were wounded, and it is greatly to be feared that the Christians, who could scarcely be prevented from revenging the death of their relations upon those who were brought to the mission, glutted their brutal passion on all the wounded who fell into their hands....

The prisoners they had captured were immediately enrolled in the list of the mission, except a nice little boy whose mother was shot while running away with him in her arms, and he was sent to the *presidio*, and was, I heard, given to the alferez as a reward for his services. The poor little orphan had received a slight wound in his forehead. He wept bitterly at first and refused to eat, but in time became reconciled to his fate.

Those who were taken to the mission were immediately converted and were daily taught by the neophytes to repeat the Lord's Prayer and certain hymns in the Spanish language. I happened to visit the mission about this time and saw these unfortunate beings under tuition. They were clothed in blankets and arranged in a row before a blind Indian, who understood their dialect and was assisted by an *alcalde* to keep order. Their tutor began by desiring them to kneel, informing them that he was going to teach them the names of the persons composing the Trinity, and that they were to repeat in Spanish what he dictated.

The neophytes being thus arranged, the speaker began, *"Santisima Trinidada, Dios, Jesu Christo, Espiritu Santo"*—pausing between each name to listen if the simple Indians, who had never spoken a Spanish word before, pronounced it correctly or anything near the mark. After they had repeated these names satisfactorily, their blind tutor, after a pause, added *"Santos"* and recapitulated the names of a great many saints, which finished the morning's tuition. I did not attend the next schooling to hear what was the ensuing task, but saw them arranged on their knees repeating Spanish words as before.

They did not appear to me to pay much attention to what was going forward, and I observed to the *padre* that I thought their teachers had an arduous task. But he said they had never found any difficulty, that the Indians were accustomed to change their own gods, and that their conversion was in a measure habitual to them. I could not help smiling at this reason of the *padre*, but have no doubt it was very true, and that the party I saw would feel as little compunction at apostatizing again whenever they should have an opportunity of returning to their own tribe.

The expenses of the late expedition fell heavy upon the mission, and I was glad to find that the *padre* thought it was paying very dear for so few converts—as in all probability it will lessen his desire to undertake another expedition, and the poor Indians will be spared the horrors of being butchered by their own countrymen or dragged from their homes into perpetual captivity. He was also much concerned to think the Cosemenes had stood their ground so firmly, and he was under some little apprehension of an attack upon the mission. Impressed with this idea, and in order to defend himself the more effectually, he begged me to furnish him with a few fireworks, which he thought would strike terror into his enemies in case of necessity.

Morning and evening Mass are daily performed in the missions, and high Mass as it is appointed by the Romish church, at which all the converted Indians are obliged to attend. The commemoration of the anniversary of the patroness saint took place during my visit at San José, and high Mass was celebrated in the church. Before the prayers began, there was a procession of the young female Indians, with which I was highly pleased. They were neatly dressed in scarlet petticoats and white bodices, and walked in a very orderly manner to the church, where they had places assigned to them apart from the males. After the bell had done tolling, several *alguaziles* went 'round to the huts to see if all the Indians were at church, and if they found any loitering within them, they exercised with tolerable freedom a long lash with a broad thong at the end of it—a discipline which appeared the more tyrannical, as the church was not sufficiently capacious for all the attendants, and several sat upon the steps without. But the Indian women who had been captured in the affair with the Cosemenes were placed in a situation where they could see the costly images, vessels of burning incense, and everything that was going forward.

The congregation was arranged on both sides of the building, separated by a wide aisle passing along the center, in which were stationed several *alguaziles* with whips, canes, and goads to preserve silence and maintain order, and, what seemed more difficult than either, to keep the congregation in their kneeling posture. The goads were better adapted to this purpose than the whips, as they would reach a long way and inflict a sharp puncture without making any noise. The end of the church was occupied by a guard of soldiers under arms with fixed bayonets—a precaution which I suppose experience had taught the necessity of observing. Above them there was a choir consisting of several Indian musicians, who performed very well indeed on various instruments and sang the "Te Deum" in a very passable manner. The congregation was very attentive, but the gratification they appeared to derive from the music furnished another proof of the strong hold this portion of the ceremonies of the Romish church takes upon uninformed minds.

The worthy and benevolent priests of the mission devote almost the whole of their time to the duties of the establishment and have a fatherly regard for those placed under them who are obedient and diligent; and too much praise cannot be bestowed upon them, considering that they have relinquished many of the enjoyments of life and have embraced a voluntary exile in a distant and barbarous country. The only amusement which my hospitable host of the mission of San José indulged in during my visit to that place was during mealtimes, when he amused himself by throwing pancakes to the *muchachos,* a number of little Indian domestics who stood gaping 'round the table. For this purpose, he had every day two piles of pancakes made of Indian corn; and as soon as the *olla* was removed, he would fix his eyes upon one of the boys, who immediately opened his mouth and the *padre*, rolling up a cake, would say something ludicrous in allusion to the boy's appetite or to the size of his mouth and pitch the cake at him, which the imp would catch between his teeth and devour with incredible rapidity, in order that he might be ready the sooner for another, as well as to please the *padre*, whose amusement consisted in a great measure in witnessing the sudden disappearance of the cake. In this manner the piles of cakes were gradually distributed among the boys, amidst much laughter and occasional squabbling.

Nothing could exceed the kindness and consideration of these excellent men to their guests and to travelers, and they were seldom more pleased than when anyone paid their mission a visit. We always fared well there and even on fast days were provided with fish dressed in various ways and preserves made with the fruit of the country. We had, however, occasionally some difficulty in maintaining our good temper, in consequence of the unpleasant remarks that the difference of our religion brought from the *padres*, who were very bigoted men and invariably introduced this subject. At other times they were very conversable, and some of them were ingenious and clever men; but they had been so long excluded from the civilized world that their ideas and their politics, like the maps pinned against the walls, bore date of 1772, as near as I could read it for fly spots. Their geographical knowledge was equally backward, as my host at San José had never heard of the discoveries of Captain Cook, and because Otaheite [Tahiti] was not placed upon his chart, he would scarcely credit its existence....

At some of the missions they pursue a custom said to be of great antiquity among the aborigines and which appears to afford them much enjoyment. A mud house or rather a large oven, called *temescál* by the Spaniards, is built in a circular form, with a small entrance and an aperture in the top for the smoke to escape through. Several persons enter this place quite naked and make a fire near the door, which they continue to feed with wood as long as they can bear the heat. In a short time they are thrown into a most profuse perspiration; they wring their hair and scrape their skin with a sharp piece of wood or an iron hoop, in the same manner as coach horses are sometimes treated when they come in heated; and then plunge into a river or pond of cold water, which they always take care shall be near the *temescál*....

Formerly the missions had small villages attached to them, in which the Indians lived in a very filthy state. These have almost all disappeared since Vancouver's visit, and the converts are disposed of in huts as before described; and it is only when sickness prevails to a great extent that it is necessary to erect these habitations, in order to separate the sick from those who are in health. Sickness in general prevails to an incredible extent in all the missions, and on comparing the census of the years 1786 and 1813, the proportion of deaths appears to be increasing. At the former period there had been only 7,701 Indians baptized, out of which 2,388 had died; but in 1813 there had been 37,437 deaths to only 57,328 baptisms.

The establishments are badly supplied with medicines, and the reverend fathers, their only medical advisers, are inconceivably ignorant of the use of them. In one mission, there was a seaman who pretended to some skill in pharmacy, but he knew little or nothing of it and perhaps often did more harm than good. The Indians are also extremely careless and obstinate and prefer their own simples to any other remedies, which is not infrequently the occasion of their disease having a fatal termination.

The Indians in general submit quietly to the discipline of the missions, yet insurrections have occasionally broken out, particularly in the early stage of the settlement, when Father Tamoral and other priests suffered martyrdom. In 1823, also, a priest was murdered in a general insurrection in the vicinity of San Luis Rey; in 1827, the soldiers of the garrison were summoned to quell another riot in the same quarter.

The situations of the missions, particularly that of San José, are in general advantageously chosen. Each establishment has fifteen square miles of ground, of which part is cultivated, and the rest appropriated to the grazing and rearing of cattle; for in portioning out the ground, care has been taken to avoid that which is barren. The most productive farms are held by the missions of San José, Santa Clara, San Juan [Bautísta], and Santa Cruz. That of San Francisco appears to be badly situated, in consequence of the cold fogs from the sea, which approach the mission through several deep valleys and turn all the vegetation brown that is exposed to them, as is the case in Shetland with the tops of every tree that rises above the

Vaqueros lassoing cattle near Mission San José, 1826, by William Smyth. *Courtesy of the California History Room, California State Library, Sacramento, California.*

walls. Still, with care, more might be grown in this mission than it is at present made to produce. Santa Cruz is rich in supplies, probably on account of the greater demand by merchant vessels—whalers in particular—who not infrequently touch there the last thing on leaving the coast and take on board what vegetables they require; the quantity of which is so considerable, that it not infrequently happens that the missions are for a time completely drained. On this account it is advisable, on arriving at any of the ports, to take an early opportunity of ordering everything that may be required.

A quantity of grain, such as wheat and Indian corn, is annually raised in all the missions, except San Francisco, which, notwithstanding it has a farm at Burri Burri, is sometimes obliged to have recourse to the other establishments. Barley and oats are said to be scarcely worth the cultivation, but beans, peas, and other leguminous vegetables are in abundance, and fruit is plentiful. The land requires no manure at present and yields on an average twenty for one....

Hides and tallow constitute the principal riches of the missions and the staple commodity of the commerce of the country. A profitable revenue might also be derived from grain, were the demand for it on the coast such as to encourage them to cultivate a larger quantity than is required by the Indians attached to the missions. San José, which possesses 15,000 head of cattle, cures about 2,000 hides annually, and as many botas of tallow, which are either disposed of by contract to a mercantile establishment at Monterey or to vessels in the harbor. The price of these hides may be judged by their finding a ready market on the Lima coast. Though there are a great many sheep in the country—as may be seen by the Mission San José alone possessing 3,000—yet there is no export of wool, in consequence of the consumption of that article in the manufacture of cloth for the missions.

Husbandry is still in a very backward state, and it is fortunate that the soil is so fertile and that there are abundance of laborers to perform the work, or I verily believe the people would be contented to live upon acorns. Their plows appear to have descended from the patriarchal ages, and it is only a pity that a little of the skill and industry then employed upon them should not have devolved upon the present generation. It will scarcely be credited by agriculturists in other countries that there were seventy plows and 200 oxen at work upon a piece of light ground of ten acres; nor did the overseers appear to consider that number unnecessary, as the *padre* called our attention to this extraordinary advancement of the Indians in civilization and pointed out the most able workmen as the plows passed us in succession. The greater part of these plows followed in the same furrow without making much impression until they approached the *padre*, when the plowman gave the necessary inclination of the hand, and the share got hold of the ground. It would have been good policy for the *padre* to have moved gradually along the field, by which he would have had it properly plowed; but he seemed to be quite satisfied with the performance. Several of the missions, but particularly that of Santa Barbara, make a wine resembling claret, though not near so palatable, and they also distill an ardent spirit resembling arrack [Middle Eastern liquor].

In this part of California, besides the missions, there are several *pueblos*, or villages, occupied by Spaniards and their families, who have availed themselves of the privileges granted by the old government, and have relinquished the sword for the plowshare. There are also a few settlers who are farmers, but, with these exceptions, the country is almost uninhabited....

By Christmas day we had all remained sufficiently long in the harbor to contemplate our departure without regret: the eye had become familiar to the picturesque scenery of the bay, the pleasure of the chase had lost its fascination, and the roads to the mission and *presidio* were grown tedious and insipid. There was no society to enliven the hours, no incidents to vary one day from the other, and to use the expression of Donna Gonzales, California appeared to be as much out of the world as Kamschatka.

On the 26th, being ready for sea, I was obliged to relinquish the survey of this magnificent port, which possesses almost all the requisites for a great naval establishment and is so advantageously situated with regard to North America and China, and the Pacific in general, that it will, no doubt, at some future time, be of great importance.

Richard Henry Dana, Jr.
1835–36

By the 1820s, aggressive fur hunting had nearly exterminated the sea otters and seals once plentiful along the California coast. Foreign interest then turned to the region's 400,000 head of cattle—between 1822 and 1848, California exported more than a million hides and 7,000 pounds of tallow (rendered from cow carcasses). Most of this trade was conducted by New England merchants who sold the hides to Bostonian tanneries and leather-goods factories and the tallow to South American candle and soap factories. The Yankee ships returned from New England filled with manufactured goods to sell in California, turning into "floating department stores" hawking everything from shoes, furniture, liquor, and jewelry to fireworks, pianos, and fine silk handkerchiefs. Mexican officials, whose main source of revenue came from fat tariffs, encouraged the trade. In 1822 Bostonian William A. Gale set up shop in Monterey and spread the word that his firm, Bryant and Sturgis, was willing to pay two dollars a hide. By outbidding all British and Russian competitors, Bryant and Sturgis enjoyed a near-monopoly on the California hide-and-tallow trade for the next twenty years.

Possessing forced labor and abundant land, California's twenty-one missions dominated the production of hides and tallow through 1834. On August 9 of that year, governor José Figueroa, of partial Indian descent himself, issued a proclamation that began the secularization of the missions and turned half of all mission property over to the neophytes. The Franciscans had feared this day ever since Mexico had won its independence in 1821 and adopted a constitution based on republican ideals. There was widespread resentment among *gente de razón* toward the missions for their wealth and mistreatment of the Indians, a resentment laced with a healthy dose of self-interest, to be sure.

The disassembling of the mission system opened the door for approximately 700 private land grants, most for about 15,000 acres but some exceeding 200,000. This led to the rise of California's next dominant institution—the family *rancho*. Located along the coast (along with a few in the Central Valley), the *ranchos* mainly raised cattle for the booming hide-and-tallow trade but also grazed sheep and horses and cultivated grain and wine grapes. Any Californian could petition the governor for a land grant by submitting a hand-drawn *diseño* roughly outlining the dimensions of the desired land. Well-connected families (such as the Vallejos, Alvarados, and Peraltas in the north and the Carillos, de la Guerras, and Picos in the south) could secure grants for each family member, creating an elite class of *rancheros* who controlled hundreds of thousands of prime acreage. Surprisingly, about sixty grants went to women.

Secularization proved to be a mixed blessing for the 18,000 Indians still in the missions. They were freed from the institution that had virtually enslaved them for sixty years, but resuming their old way of life was unthinkable given all the changes wrought by diseases and subjugation. Furthermore, much of their former land was by now inhabited by *rancheros* and their huge cattle herds. Many Indians were never informed that they legally owned mission property, and those who tried to work their land were forcibly bought out by rapacious *gente de razón*. Strangers in their own homeland, most Indians abandoned the missions and found work as *vaqueros* and servants in nearby *ranchos* and towns. A few disappeared into

California's interior, reappearing from time to time to lead raids on *rancho* herds. The mission buildings themselves, looted by Indian and Californio alike, fell into disrepair.

The first Anglo-American residents of California came as traders in the 1820s and settled there permanently, often marrying into local Californio families. The Californians welcomed foreigners into their midst, granting them citizenship and land, provided they naturalized and adopted Catholicism. In return, most Americans derided Californio culture as lazy, wasteful, and immoral. This stemmed from what historian Leonard Pitt has described as "a deep-seated clash of values between the Anglo-American and the Latin-American culture," involving such elements as "the Protestant's condescension toward Catholicism; the Puritan's dedication to work, now familiarly known as the 'Protestant Ethic'; the republican's loathing of aristocracy; the Yankee's belief in Manifest Destiny; and the Anglo-Saxon's generalized fear of racial mixture." Racist scorn of Californio culture trickled back to the East Coast, reinforcing the notion that bountiful California was languishing under Mexican control.

The most widely read description of California was Richard Henry Dana, Jr.'s *Two Years Before the Mast*, a riveting account of the author's experiences onboard a Bryant and Sturgis hide-and-tallow brig in 1835 and 1836. Born in Cambridge, Massachusetts, in 1815, Dana was a sensitive, melancholy child whose mother died when he was seven years old. He enrolled in Harvard at age sixteen but had to withdraw during his junior year when measles left him with raw nerves and weakened eyesight. Instead of embarking on a tour of Europe to regain his health, as was customary for many affluent young men, Dana elected to enlist as a sailor onboard the California-bound *Pilgrim*.

He sailed from Boston in August 1834, rounded Cape Horn, and spent about sixteen months collecting hides up and down the California coast. It was exhausting work—because California had so few harbors, the heavy hides (which would spoil if wet) often had to be loaded by hand into small boats and ferried two or three miles out to the *Pilgrim*. In contrast to sea captains like Vancouver and Beechey, Dana's concerns were those of the common sailor—namely, seeing the country, avoiding work, and meeting women.

Dana, like most American visitors, disparaged Californios as "an idle, thriftless people" while simultaneously praising the exceptional California landscape, climate, and soil. In a typical passage, he wrote, "Such are the people who inhabit a country embracing four or five hundred miles of sea-coast, with several good harbors; with fine forests to the north; the waters filled with fish, and the plains covered with thousands of herds of cattle; blessed with a climate, that which there can be no better in the world; free from all manner of diseases, whether epidemic or endemic, and with a soil in which corn yields from seventy to eighty fold. In the hands of an enterprising people, what a country this might be!" More than any other work, *Two Years Before the Mast* shaped American attitudes toward distant California.

Dana returned to Boston in September 1836. Now healthy and tanned, he spent the next three years rewriting his sailor's journal at night while attending law school during the day. *Two Years Before the Mast* was published in 1840 and proved to be an immediate and enduring bestseller. Dana's years in California turned out to be the best ones of his life. He married and opened a law office in Boston but continued to wear his hair long and frequent sailors' saloons and brothels, obsessed with memories of freedom and camaraderie onboard the *Pilgrim*. He wrote only one more book, *To Cuba and Back*, his account of an 1859 round-the-world trip. It featured a stop in California where he nostalgically wrote that he was "made for the sea" and that "life on shore is a mistake." In an 1873 letter to his son, he conceded, "My life has been a failure compared to what I might and ought to have done. My great success—my book—was a boy's work, done before I came to the bar." In his final years he moved with his wife to Europe and struggled in vain to finish a third book on international law. He died in Rome in 1882. More than a hundred years later, his "boy's work" continues to be hailed as California's first literary classic. This excerpt from Dana's narrative begins

December 4, 1835. Also included is his description of a wedding and *fandango* he attended in Santa Barbara a few weeks later, one of the liveliest—and most positive—portrayals of Californio culture penned by an American during this period.

Richard Henry Dana, Jr. (1815–1882). *Courtesy of The Bancroft Library.*

RICHARD HENRY DANA, JR.

from *Two Years Before the Mast*

*D*ecember 4, 1835. Our place of destination
had been Monterey, but as we were to the northward of it when the
wind hauled ahead, we made a fair wind for San Francisco. This
large bay, which lies in latitude 37°58′, was discovered by Sir
Francis Drake,[1] and by him represented to be (as indeed it is) a magnificent bay, containing several good harbors, great depth of water,
and surrounded by a fertile and finely-wooded country. About
thirty miles from the mouth of the bay, and on the southeast side,
is a high point upon which the *presidio* is built. Behind this point
is the little harbor, or bight, called Yerba Buena, in which trading
vessels anchor, and, near it, the Mission of Dolores. There was no
other habitation on this side of the bay except a shanty of rough
boards put up by a man named Richardson,[2] who was doing a little
trading between the vessels and the Indians. Here, at anchor, and
the only vessel, was a brig under Russian colors from Sitka, in Russian America, which had come down to winter and to take in a supply of tallow and grain, great quantities of which latter article are
raised in the missions at the head of the bay. The second day after our arrival, we went on board the brig, it being Sunday, as a

---

[1] San Francisco Bay was almost certainly "discovered" not by Drake but by Portolá and
his men in 1769; historians continue to debate where Drake actually landed in 1579.

[2] William A. Richardson (1795–1858), born in England, came to California in 1822
onboard a whaling ship. He stayed on, adopted Catholicism, and married the daughter
of Ignacio Martínez, *comandante* of San Francisco *presidio*. In 1835 Richardson
founded the town of Yerba Buena at the site of present-day San Francisco's Grant
Avenue between Clay and Washington streets.

matter of curiosity; and there was enough there to gratify it. Though no larger than the *Pilgrim,* she had five or six officers and a crew of between twenty and thirty; and such a stupid and greasy-looking set, I never saw before. Although it was quite comfortable weather, and we had nothing on but straw hats, shirts, and duck trousers and were barefooted, they had, every man of them, doubled-soled boots (coming up to the knees and well-greased), thick woolen trousers, frocks, waistcoats, pea-jackets, woollen caps, and everything in true Novaya Zembla rig; and in the warmest days they made no change. The clothing of one of these men would weigh nearly as much as that of half our crew. They had brutish faces, looked like the antipodes of sailors, and apparently dealt in nothing but grease. They lived upon grease, ate it, drank it, slept in the midst of it, and their clothes were covered with it. To a Russian, grease is the greatest luxury. They looked with greedy eyes upon the tallow-bags as they were taken into the vessel, and, no doubt, would have eaten one up whole, had not the officer kept watch over it. The grease appeared to fill their pores and to come out in their hair and on their faces. It seems as if it were this saturation which makes them stand cold and rain so well. If they were to go into a warm climate, they would melt and die of the scurvy.

The vessel was no better than the crew. Everything was in the oldest and most inconvenient fashion possible: running trusses and lifts on the yards, and large hawser cables, coiled all over the decks, and served and parceled in all directions. The topmasts, top-gallant-masts, and studding-sail booms were nearly black for want of scraping, and the decks would have turned the stomach of a man-of-war's-man. The galley was down in the forecastle; and there the crew lived, in the midst of the steam and grease of the cooking, in a place as hot as an oven, and apparently never cleaned out. Five minutes in the forecastle was enough for us, and we were glad to get into the open air. We made some trade with them, buying Indian curiosities, of which they had a great number, such as beadwork, feathers of birds, fur moccasins, etc. I purchased a large robe, made of the skins of some animal, dried and sewed nicely together, and covered all over on the outside with thick downy feathers, taken from the breasts of various birds, and arranged with their different colors so as to make a brilliant show.

A few days after our arrival the rainy season set in, and for three weeks, it rained almost every hour without cessation. This was bad for our trade, for the collecting of hides is managed differently in this port from what it is in any other on the coast. The Mission of Dolores, near the anchorage, has no trade at all; but those of San José, Santa Clara, and others situated on the large creeks or rivers that run into the bay, and distant between fifteen and forty miles from the anchorage, do a greater business in hides than any in California. Large boats, or launches, manned by Indians and capable of carrying from five to six hundred hides apiece, are attached to the missions and sent down to the vessels with hides to bring away goods in return. Some of the crews of the vessels are obliged to go and come in the boats to look out for the hides and goods. These are favorite expeditions with the sailors in fine weather; but now, to be gone three or four days—in open boats, in constant rain, without any shelter, and with cold food—was hard service. Two of our men went up to Santa Clara in one of these boats and were gone three days, during all which time they had a constant rain and did not sleep a wink, but passed three long nights walking fore and aft the boat in the open air. When they got on board they were completely exhausted and took a watch below of twelve hours. All the hides, too, that came down in the boats were soaked with water and unfit to put below, so that we were obliged to trice them up to dry, in the intervals of sunshine or wind, upon all parts of the vessel. We got up tricing-lines from the jibboom end to each arm of the foreyard, and thence to the main and cross-jack yard arms. Between the tops, too, and the mastheads, from the fore to the main swifters, and thence to the mizzen rigging, and in all directions athwartships, tricing-lines were run and strung with hides. The head stays and guys and the spritsail yard were lined, and, having still more, we got out the swinging-booms and strung them and the forward and after guys with hides. The rail, fore and aft, the windlass, capstan, the sides of the ship, and every vacant place on deck were covered with wet hides on the least sign of an interval for drying. Our ship was nothing but a mass of hides, from the cat-harpins to the water's edge, and from the jibboom end to the taffrail.

One cold, rainy evening, about eight o'clock, I received orders to get ready to start for San José at four the next morning, in one of these Indian boats, with four days' provisions. I got my oil-cloth clothes, southwester, and thick boots ready, and turned into my hammock early, determined to get some sleep in advance, as the boat was to be alongside before daybreak. I slept on 'til all hands were called in the morning; for, fortunately for me, the Indians, intentionally or from mistaking their orders, had gone off alone in the night and were far out of sight. Thus I escaped three or four days of very uncomfortable service.

Four of our men, a few days afterwards, went up in one of the quarter-boats to Santa Clara, to carry the agent, and remained out all night in a drenching rain in the small boat, in which there was not room for them to turn 'round; the agent having gone up to the mission and left the men to their fate, making no provision for their accommodation and not even sending them anything to eat. After this they had to pull thirty miles, and when they got on board, were so stiff that they could not come up the gangway ladder. This filled up the measure of the agent's unpopularity, and never after this could he get anything done for him by the crew; and many a delay and vexation, and many a good ducking in the surf, did he get to pay up old scores or "square the yards with the bloody quill-driver."

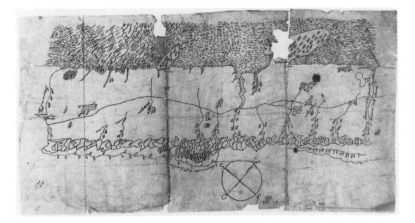

To request a land grant from the Spanish government, a Californio submitted a *diseño* roughly defining the boundaries of the proposed *rancho*. This *diseño* for Rancho San Antonio in the East Bay was submitted in 1820 by Luís María Peralta (1759–1851). His 46,800 acres of land (more than seventy square miles) extended from San Leandro Creek in the south to El Cerrito Creek in the north. *Courtesy of The Bancroft Library.*

Having collected nearly all the hides that were to be procured, we began our preparations for taking in a supply of wood and water, for both of which San Francisco is the best place on the coast. A small island [Angel Island], about two leagues from the anchorage, called by us "Wood Island," and by the Mexicans "Isla de los Angeles," was covered with trees to the water's edge; and to this two of our crew, who were Kennebec [Maine] men and could handle an axe like a plaything, were sent every morning to cut wood, with two boys to pile it up for them. In about a week they had cut enough to last us a year, and the third mate, with myself and three others, were sent over in a large, schooner-rigged, open launch, which we had hired of the mission, to take in the wood and bring it to the ship....

The next morning a water party was ordered off with all the casks. From this we escaped, having had a pretty good siege with the wooding. The water party was gone three days, during which time they narrowly escaped being carried out to sea and passed one day on an island, where one of them shot a deer, great numbers of which overrun the islands and hills of San Francisco Bay.

While not off on these wood and water parties or up the rivers to the missions, we had easy times on board the ship. We were moored, stem and stern, within a cable's length of the shore, safe from southeasters, and with little boating to do; and, as it rained nearly all the time, awnings were put over the hatchways and all hands sent down between decks, where we were at work, day after day, picking oakum, until we got enough to calk the ship all over and to last the whole voyage. Then we made a whole suit of gaskets for the voyage home, a pair of wheel-ropes from strips of green hide, great quantities of spun-yarn, and everything else that could be made between decks. It being now midwinter and in high latitude, the nights were very long, so that we were not turned-to until seven in the morning and were obliged to knock off at five in the evening, when we got supper, which gave us nearly three hours before eight bells, at which time the watch was set.

As we had now been about a year on the coast, it was time to think of the voyage home; and, knowing that the last two or three months of our stay would be very busy ones, and that we should never have so good an opportunity to work for ourselves as the present, we all employed our evenings in making clothes for the passage home, and more especially for Cape Horn. As soon as supper was over, the kids cleared away, and each man had taken his smoke, we seated ourselves on our chests 'round the lamp, which swung from a beam, and went to work each in his own way—some making hats, others trousers, others jackets, etc.—and no one was idle. The boys who could not sew well enough to make their own clothes laid up grass into sinnet for the men, who sewed for them in return. Several of us clubbed together and bought a large piece of twilled cotton, which we made into trousers and jackets, and, giving them several coats of linseed oil, laid them by for Cape Horn.

I also sewed and covered a tarpaulin hat, thick and strong enough to sit upon, and made myself a complete suit of flannel underclothing for bad weather. Those who had no southwester caps made them, and several of the crew got up for themselves tarpaulin jackets and trousers, lined on the inside with flannel. Industry was the order of the day, and everyone did something for himself; for we knew that as the season advanced and we went further south, we should have no evenings to work in.

Friday, December 25th. This day was Christmas, and, as it rained all day long, and there were no hides to take in, and nothing special to do, the captain gave us a holiday (the first we had had, except Sundays, since leaving Boston) and plum-duff for dinner. The Russian brig, following the Old Style, had celebrated their Christmas eleven days before, when they had a grand blowout and (as our men said) drank, in the forecastle, a barrel of gin, ate up a bag of tallow, and made a soup of the skin.

Sunday, December 27th. We had now finished all our business at this port, and, it being Sunday, we unmoored ship and got under way, firing a salute to the Russian brig and another to the *presidio*, which were both answered. The *commandante* of the *presidio*, Don Guadalupe Vallejo,[3] a young man, and the most popular among the Americans and English of any man in California, was on board when we got under way. He spoke English very well and was suspected of being favorably inclined to foreigners.

---

[3] Mariano Guadalupe Vallejo (1808–1890), one of the most important figures in Mexican California, was age twenty-seven at the time of Dana's visit. A lifelong soldier, in the early 1830s Vallejo was put in command of California's northern frontier by Gobernador José Figueroa. To forestall possible Russian encroachment, in 1835 Vallejo founded the town of Sonoma (near Mission San Francisco Solano), where he built a huge mansion called Casa Grande.

We sailed down this magnificent bay with a light wind—the tide, which was running out, carrying us at the rate of four or five knots. It was a fine day; the first of entire sunshine we had had for more than a month. We passed directly under the high cliff on which the *presidio* is built and stood into the middle of the bay, from whence we could see small bays making up into the interior, large and beautifully wooded islands, and the mouths of several small rivers. If California ever becomes a prosperous country, this bay will be the center of its prosperity. The abundance of wood and water; the extreme fertility of its shores; the excellence of its climate, which is as near to being perfect as any in the world; and its facilities for navigation, affording the best anchoring-grounds in the whole western coast of America—all fit it for a place of great importance.

The tide leaving us, we came to anchor near the mouth of the bay, under a high and beautifully sloping hill, upon which herds of hundreds and hundreds of red deer, and the stag, with his high branching antlers, were bounding about, looking at us for a moment, and then starting off, affrighted at the noises that we made for the purpose of seeing the variety of their beautiful attitudes and motions.

Sunday, January 10th. Arrived at Santa Barbara.... Great preparations were making on shore for the marriage of our agent, who was to marry Doña Anita de le Guerra de Noriega y Corillo, youngest daughter of Don Antonio Noriega, the grandee of the place, and the head of the first family in California. Our steward was ashore three days, making pastry and cake, and some of the best of our stores were sent off with him. On the day appointed for the wedding, we took the captain ashore in the gig, and had orders to come for him at night, with leave to go up to the house and see the *fandango*. Returning on board, we found preparations making for a salute. Our guns were loaded and run out, men appointed to each, cartridges served out, matches lighted, and all the flags ready to be

"Trying Out Tallow, Monterey," 1847, by William Rich Hutton. To produce tallow, Indian laborers boiled fat from cattle carcasses in enormous iron pots. After it cooled, they poured the liquid into fifty-pound hide bags called *botas* for transport to the market. *Courtesy of The Huntington Library, San Marino, California.*

run up. I took my place at the starboard after-gun, and we all waited for the signal from on shore. At ten o'clock the bride went up with her sister to the confessional, dressed in deep black. Nearly an hour intervened, when the great doors of the mission church opened, the bells rang out a loud discordant peal, the private signal for us was run up by the captain ashore, the bride, dressed in complete white, came out of the church with the bridegroom, followed by a long procession. Just as she stepped from the church door, a small white cloud issued from the bows of our ship, which was full in sight, the loud report echoed among the surrounding hills and over the bay, and instantly the ship was dressed in flags and pennants from stem to stern. Twenty-three guns followed in regular succession, with an interval of fifteen seconds between each, when the cloud blew off, and our ship lay dressed in her colors all day. At sundown another salute of the same number of guns was fired, and all the flags run down. This we thought was pretty well—a gun every fifteen seconds—for a merchantman with only four guns and a dozen or twenty men.

After supper the gig's crew were called, and we rowed ashore, dressed in our uniform, beached the boat, and went up to the *fandango*. The bride's father's house was the principal one in the place, with a large court in front, upon which a tent was built, capable of containing several hundred people. As we drew near, we heard the accustomed sound of violins and guitars, and saw a great motion of the people within. Going in, we found nearly all the people of the town—men, women, and children—collected and crowded together, leaving barely room for the dancers; for on these occasions no invitations are given, but everyone is expected to come, though there is always a private entertainment within the house for particular friends. The old women sat down in rows, clapping their hands to the music and applauding the young ones.

The music was lively, and among the tunes we recognized several of our popular airs, which we, without doubt, have taken from the Spanish. In the dancing I was much disappointed. The women stood upright with their hands down by their sides, their eyes fixed upon the ground before them, and slid about without any perceptible means of motion; for their feet were invisible, the hem of their dresses circle about them, reaching to the ground. They looked as grave as though they were going through some religious ceremony, their faces as little excited as their limbs; and on the whole, instead of the spirited, fascinating Spanish dances which I had expected, I found the Californian *fandango*, on the part of the women at least, a lifeless affair. The men did better. They danced with grace and spirit, moving in circles 'round their nearly stationary partners and showing their figures to advantage.

A great deal was said about our friend Don Juan Bandini,[4] and when he did appear, which was towards the close of the evening, he certainly gave us the most graceful dancing that I had ever seen. He was dressed in white pantaloons, neatly made, a short jacket of dark silk, gaily-figured, white stockings, and thin Morocco slippers upon his very small feet. His slight and graceful figure was well adapted to dancing, and he moved about with the grace and daintiness of a young fawn. An occasional touch of the toe to the ground seemed all that was necessary to give him a long interval of motion in the air. At the same time he was not fantastic or flourishing, but appeared to be rather repressing a strong tendency to motion. He was loudly applauded and danced frequently towards the close of the evening. After the supper the waltzing began, which was confined to a very few of the *gente de razón,* and was considered a high accomplishment and a mark of aristocracy. Here, too, Don Juan figured greatly, waltzing with the sister of the bride (Doña Angustia, a handsome woman and a general favorite) in a variety of beautiful figures, which lasted as much as half an hour, no one else taking the floor. They were repeatedly and loudly applauded, the old men and women jumping out of their seats in admiration, and the young people waving their hats and handkerchiefs.

The great amusement of the evening—owing to its being the Carnival—was the breaking of eggs, filled with cologne or other essences, upon the heads of the company. The women bring a great number of these secretly about them, and the amusement is to break one upon the head of a gentleman when his back is turned. He is bound in gallantry to find out the lady and return the compliment,

---

[4] Born in Peru, Juan Bandini (1800–1859) emigrated to southern California in the early 1820s and became a prominent *ranchero* and politician. "He had a slight and elegant figure, moved gracefully, danced and waltzed beautifully, spoke good Castilian...and had, throughout, the bearing of a man of birth and figure," wrote Dana. However, Bandini's fortunes turned downward after the U.S. conquest of California, when he was stripped of all his properties despite having three American sons-in-law.

though it must not be done if the person sees you. A tall, stately *don*, with immense gray whiskers and a look of great importance, was standing before me, when I felt a light hand on my shoulder, and, turning round, saw Doña Angustia (whom we all knew, as she had been up to Monterey, and down again, in the *Alert)*, with her finger upon her lip motioning me gently aside. I stepped back a little, when she went up behind the *don* and with one hand knocked off his huge *sombrero*, and at the same instant, with the other, broke the egg upon his head, and, springing behind me, was out of sight in a moment. The *don* turned slowly round, the cologne running down his face and over his clothes, and a loud laugh breaking out from every quarter. He looked round in vain for some time, until the direction of so many laughing eyes showed him the fair offender. She was his niece and a great favorite with him, so old Don Domingo had to join in the laugh. A great many such tricks were played, and many a war of sharp maneuvering was carried on between couples of the younger people, and at every successful exploit a general laugh was raised.

Another of their games I was for some time at a loss about. A pretty young girl was dancing, named—after what would appear to us an almost sacrilegious custom of the country—Espiritu Santo, when a young man went behind her and placed his hat directly upon her head, letting it fall down over her eyes, and sprang back among the crowd. She danced for some time with the hat on; when she threw it off, which called forth a general shout, the young man was obliged to go out upon the floor and pick it up. Some of the ladies, upon whose heads hats had been placed, threw them off at once, and a few kept them on throughout the dance, and took them off at the end, and held them out in their hands, when the owner stepped out, bowed, and took it from them. I soon began to suspect the meaning of the thing, and was afterwards told that it was a compliment, and an offer to become a lady's gallant for the rest of the evening and to wait upon her home. If the hat was thrown off the offer was refused, and the gentleman was obliged to pick up his hat amid a general laugh. Much amusement was caused sometimes by gentlemen putting hats on the ladies' heads without permitting them to see whom it was done by. This obliged them to throw them off or keep them on at a venture, and when they came to discover the owner the laugh was turned upon one or the other.

The captain sent for us about ten o'clock, and we went aboard in high spirits, having enjoyed the new scene much, and were of great importance among the crew, from having so much to tell, and from the prospect of going every night until it was over—for these *fandangos* generally last three days. The next day two of us were sent up to the town and took care to come back by way of Señor Noriega's and take a look into the booth. The musicians were again there, upon their platform, scraping and twanging away, and a few people, apparently of the lower classes, were dancing. The dancing is kept up at intervals throughout the day, but the crowd, the spirit, and the elite come in at night. The next night, which was the last, we went ashore in the same manner, until we got almost tired of the monotonous twang of the instruments, the drawling sounds which the women kept up, as an accompaniment, and the slapping of the hands in time with the music, in place of castanets. We found ourselves as great objects of attention as any persons or anything at the place. Our sailor dresses—and we took great pains to have them neat and ship-shape—were much admired, and we were invited, from every quarter, to give them an American dance; but after the ridiculous figure some of our countrymen cut in dancing after the Mexicans, we thought it best to leave it to their imaginations. Our agent, with a tight, black swallow-tailed coat just imported from Boston, a high stiff cravat, looking as if he had been pinned and skewered, with only his feet and hands left free, took the floor just after Bandini, and we thought they had had enough of Yankee grace.

SIR GEORGE SIMPSON
1841–42

———⟫●⟪———

Yerba Buena, the tiny anchorage in San Francisco Bay where Dana's ship docked in 1836, was founded a year earlier by William A. Richardson. An English whaler who deserted his ship in 1822, Richardson adopted Catholicism and married into a prominent Californio family. After the secularization order, he opened a modest trading post a few miles east of San Francisco's *presidio* opposite Yerba Buena island. The settlement began as a single tent, later a shanty of rough boards. By 1841 Yerba Buena consisted of several *adobe* buildings and a scattering of sheds and cattle pens.

California society managed to integrate most foreigners (like Richardson) who arrived in California via ship but had a harder time with the growing number of American mountain men who crossed the Sierra Nevada in the 1830s seeking beaver furs. Such trailblazers as James Ohio Pattie, Ewing Young, William Wolfskill, and Joseph Reddeford Walker improved upon Jedediah Strong Smith's 1826 route. They forged the Oregon and California trails and revived the Old Spanish Trail, routes used by subsequent wagon trains. Those mountain men who stayed in California (such as Job Dye, Isaac Graham, Isaac Sparks, Jonathan T. Warner, and Isaac Williams) usually kept their American citizenship and felt little desire to learn Spanish.

Americans were not the only trappers to penetrate California's borders in the 1830s. Britain's Hudson's Bay Company, enjoying a monopoly of the Canadian fur trade after merging with rival North West Company in 1821, began sending annual expeditions to hunt beaver in the streams of the Central Valley in the mid-1830s. In early 1841 it established a store and warehouse alongside William A. Richardson's trading post in Yerba Buena. There was talk in England of a possible British annexation of California.

It is telling that this British attention on California worried the United States more than Mexico. Every visitor to California remarked on the obvious weakness of Mexican control, and the U.S. was determined to be the nation to test it. In 1835 President Andrew Jackson unsuccessfully offered Mexico $3.5 million for San Francisco Bay and the land north of it. Soon after, American military expeditions—ostensibly exploring in the Pacific Northwest—increasingly began to wander into Mexican territory. The near-extinction of the sea otter meant Russia was no longer a threat, but France and England showed just enough interest in the region to make U.S. officials nervous.

Sir George Simpson's visit to California in 1841 grew directly out of this unsettled state of affairs. Born in Ross-shire, Scotland, in 1787, he worked during his teenage years as an apprentice for his uncle at the sugar trading company Graham & Simpson. As unscrupulous as he was ambitious, Simpson rose quickly through the ranks of the Hudson's Bay Company. Before his fortieth birthday, he was named governor of the company's extensive holdings in all of Canada, a title he held for thirty years.

Simpson was wise enough to realize that for the Company to remain in control of such a vast, trackless land with only a few hundred men, it would have to secure the trust of the region's Indians. Therefore he encouraged intermarriage between Company officers and the daughters of native potentates, acted as an impartial arbiter of local disputes, and did not attempt to force change into the Indians' lives. While Simpson dealt fairly with the Indians in business, he had little respect for them as individuals. In his early years with the Company, he kept a succession of Indian mistresses whom he referred to in letters as his "bits of brown" and "little articles." As he became jaded or they pregnant, they were replaced without hesitation. Simpson sired at least three mixed-blood sons with these mistresses; of illegitimate birth himself, he provided his sons with an elementary school education and jobs in the fur-trade business, but made it clear he would grant no further favors. In 1830, he married a respectable Englishwoman (who happened to be his first cousin) and adopted puritanical views that in his younger days he would have found most inconvenient to practice.

A great admirer of Napoleon, Simpson no doubt felt he deserved his nickname as the "Little Emperor" of the North. Like Junípero Serra, another diminutive and industrious leader, Simpson drove himself tirelessly. A contemporary described him as "the toughest-looking old fellow I ever saw, built…like one of those massy pillars one sees in an old country church….He is a man whom nothing will kill." To underlings he was a terrifying dictator; at one point in the 1830s he compiled a "character book" in which he expounded in considerable detail on the failings of each of the Company's servants.

For his achievements, Simpson was knighted by Queen Victoria in 1841. Sir George then embarked on a voyage around the world, crossing the Atlantic on steamer and trekking across Canada inspecting the many posts of the Hudson's Bay Company. Before turning north for Siberia, he decided on a lengthy detour to California to determine whether to invest the Company's considerable resources in a foreign land with an uncertain future. He was interested in purchasing Fort Ross from the Russians and suspected they were desperate to sell; they were asking for $30,000, but Simpson wrote the Hudson's Bay Company directors that he had "no doubt the whole might be purchased at from $15,000 to $20,000." When he reached Yerba Buena in December 1841 he learned the Russians had sold out two weeks earlier to a Swiss émigré named John Sutter. Simpson went on to visit Sonoma, Monterey, and Los Angeles. In Santa Barbara he met

Doña Concepción Argüello—by now a middle-aged nun—whom he boorishly informed that Count Rezanov, her betrothed, was long dead.

Rather than any special sensitivity or literary excellence, it is Simpson's consummate expertise in the economics of the frontier that gives his account of California lasting value. It is almost certain that the published version of *An Overland Journey Round the World,* while based on a journal Simpson dictated to his secretary, was polished and edited by a team of later writers. It was not published until 1847, two years after Simpson closed the Hudson's Bay Company outpost in Yerba Buena and conceded California to the United States. *An Overland Journey Round the World* offers Simpson's tantalizing vision of a British North Pacific that never came to pass.

The Hudson's Bay Company retreated out of California in 1845 but held its monopoly over Canadian lands until forcibly broken up by British Parliament in 1859. A lifelong Company man, Simpson himself testified before Parliament on behalf of his employer, but to no avail. He died the following year. This account of his visit to California begins on December 30, 1841.

from *An Overland Journey Around the World*

*O*n the morning of [December] 30th, a light breeze enabled us again to get under way and to work into the port. After crossing the bar, on which, however, there is a sufficient depth of water, we entered a strait of about two miles in width, just narrow enough for the purposes of military defense, observing, on the southern side of the mouth, a fort well-situated for commanding the passage, but itself commanded by a hill behind. This fort is now dismantled and dilapidated; nor are its remains likely to last long, for the soft rock, on the very verge of which they already hang, is fast crumbling into the undermining tide beneath. A short distance beyond the fort, and on the same side of the strait, is situated a square of huts, distinguished by the lofty title of "Presidio of San Francisco" and tenanted, for garrisoned it is not, by a commandant and as many soldiers as might, if all told, muster the rank and file of a corporal's party; and though here the softness of the rock does nothing to aid the national alacrity in decaying, yet the *adobes*, or unbaked bricks, of which Captain Prado's stronghold is composed, have already succeeded in rendering this establishment as much of a ruin as the other.

In addition to this *presidio* there are three others in the upper province, situated respectively at Monterey, Santa Barbara, and San Diego. But their principal occupation is gone. From the very commencement of the system, the pious fathers deemed it rash and inexpedient to encounter the heathen with spiritual arms only, and as neither the Jesuits nor the Franciscans could themselves lawfully carry carnal weapons, both the orders remedied this defect in their constitutions by enlisting soldiers in their service—a kind of fellow-laborers unknown to St. Paul's missionary experience. Now it was as the headquarters of these booted and spurred apostles of the faith that the *presidios* were primarily introduced, though each of them incidentally became the seat of government for its own subdivision of the province....

On proceeding along the strait, one of the most attractive scenes imaginable gradually opens on the mariner's view: a sheet of water, of about thirty miles in length by about twelve in breadth, sheltered from every wind by an amphitheater of green hills, while an intermediate belt of open plain, varying from two to six miles in depth, is dotted by the habitations of civilized men.

On emerging from the strait, which is about three miles long, we saw on our left, in a deep bay known as Whalers' Harbor [Sausalito Harbor], two vessels—the government schooner *California* and the Russian brig *Constantine,* now bound to Sitka with the last of the tenants of Bodega and Ross on board. As we observed the Russians getting under way, I dispatched Mr. Hopkins in one of our boats, in order to express my regret at being thus deprived of the anticipated pleasure of paying my respects in person. Mr. Hopkins found about a hundred souls—men, women, and children—all patriotically delighted to exchange the lovely climate of California for the ungenial skies of Sitka, and that, too, at the expense of making a long voyage in an old, crazy, clumsy tub, at the stormiest season of the year; but to this general rule there had been one exception, inasmuch as they had lost two days in waiting—but, alas, in vain—for a young woman who had abjured alike her country and her husband for the sake of one of the dons of San Francisco.

Mr. Hopkins further learned that though it was Thursday with us, it was Friday with our northern friends—a circumstance that,

Sir George Simpson (1792–1860). *Courtesy of the California Historical Society, North Baker Research Library, Templeton Crocker Collection, FN-31310.*

besides showing that the Russians had not the superstition of our tars as to days of sailing, forcibly reminded us that between them the two parties had passed round the globe in opposite directions to prosecute one and the same trade in furs, which the indolent inhabitants of the province were too lazy to appropriate at their very doors.

On our right, just opposite to the ground occupied by the *Constantine* and the *California,* stretched the pretty little bay of Yerba Buena, whose shores are doubtless destined, under better auspices, to be the site of a flourishing town, though at present they contain only eight or nine houses, in addition to the Hudson's Bay Company's establishment. Here we dropped anchor, in the neighborhood of four other vessels—the American ship *Alert* and brig *Bolivar,* the British bark *Index,* and the Mexican brig *Catalina*—and, after firing a salute, went ashore to visit Mr. Rae,[1] the Hudson's Bay Company's representative in this quarter....

In the face of all these advantages and temptations, the good folk of San Francisco, priests as well as laymen, and laymen as well as priests, have been contented to borrow, for their aquatic excursions, the native *balsa,* a kind of raft or basket, which, when wanted, can be constructed in a few minutes with the bulrushes that spring so luxuriantly on the margins of the lakes and rivers. In this miserable makeshift they contrive to cross the inland waters, and perhaps, in very choice weather, to venture a little way out to sea, there being, I believe, no other floating thing besides, neither boat nor canoe, neither barge nor scow, in any part of the harbor, or, in fact, in any part of Upper California, from San Diego on the south to San Francisco on the north. In consequence of this state of things, the people of the bay have been so far from availing themselves of their internal channels of communication that their numerous expeditions into the interior have all been conducted by land, seldom leading, of course, to any result commensurate with the delay and expense. But, inconvenient as the entire want of small craft must be to the dwellers on such an inlet as has been described, there are circumstances which do, to a certain extent, account for the protracted endurance of the evil. Horses are almost as plentiful as bulrushes; time is a perfect glut with a community of loungers; and, under the plea of having no means of catching fish, the faithful enjoy, by a standing dispensation, the comfortable privilege of fasting, at meager times, on their hecatombs of beef.

---

[1] William Glenn Rae, the unstable son-in-law of a high-ranking Hudson's Bay Company official, ran the Company's post in Yerba Buena until committing suicide in 1845.

The world at large has hitherto made nearly as little use of the peculiar facilities of San Francisco as the Californians themselves. Though at one time many whaling ships, as the name of Whalers' Harbor would imply, frequented the port, yet, through the operation of various causes, they have all gradually betaken themselves to the Sandwich Islands. In point of natural capabilities for such a purpose, the Sandwich Islands are, on the whole, inferior to San Francisco. If they excel it in position, as lying more directly in the track between the summer fishing of the north and the winter fishing of the south, and also as being more easy of access and departure by reason of the steadiness of the trade winds, they are, in turn, surpassed in all the elements for the refreshing and refitting of vessels by a place where beef may be had for little or nothing, where hemp grows spontaneously, where the pine offers an inexhaustible supply of resin, and where suitable timber for ship building invites the ax within an easy distance. But though nature may have done more for San Francisco than for the Sandwich Islands, yet man has certainly done less to promote her liberal intentions. The Sandwich Islands afford to the refitting whaler an ample supply of competent labor, both native and foreign, at reasonable wages, while San Francisco, turning the very bounty of Providence into a curse, corrupts a naturally indolent population by the superabundance of cattle and horses, by the readiness, in short, with which idleness can find both subsistence and recreation. Moreover, even on the score of fiscal regulations, the savage community has as decidedly the advantage of the civilized as in point of industrious habits. In the Sandwich Islands the whaler can enter at once into the port which is best adapted for his purposes, while in San Francisco he is by law forbidden to remain more than forty-eight hours, unless he has previously presented himself at Monterey and paid duty on the whole of his cargo. What wonder, then, is it that, with such a government and such a people, Whalers' Harbor is merely an empty name?

Few vessels, therefore, visit the port, excepting such as are engaged in collecting hides or tallow, the tallow going chiefly to Peru, and the hides exclusively either to Great Britain or to the United States. It was in the latter branch of the business that most of the vessels which we had found at anchor were employed, the mode of conducting it being worthy of a more detailed description.

To each ship there is attached a supercargo, or clerk, who, in a decked launch, carries an assortment of goods from farm to farm, collecting such hides as he can at the time, and securing, by his advances, as many as possible against the next *matanza,* or slaughtering season, which generally coincides with the months of July and August. The current rate of a hide is two dollars in goods, generally delivered beforehand, or a dollar and a half in specie, paid, as it were, across the counter; and the great difference arises from the circumstance that the goods are held at a price sufficient to cover the bad debts that the system of credit inevitably produces, the punctual debtor being thus obliged, in California as well as elsewhere, to pay for the defaulter. But even without this adventitious increase of their nominal value, the goods could not be sold for less than thrice their prime cost, so as to enable the vessels to meet a tariff of duties averaging about 100 percent in addition to very high tonnage dues, and the accumulating expenses of two tedious voyages, with a far more tedious detention on the coast. Thus, under the existing state of things, the farmer receives for his hide either about as many goods as may have been bought in London for half a crown or two shillings, or about as much hard cash as may here buy the same at ready-money rates.

The detention on the coast, to which I have alluded as an element in the price of goods, is occasioned by various circumstances. In the first place, there are too many competitors in the trade. The provincial exports of hides do not exceed, at the utmost, the number of 60,000, and though such a vessel as our neighbor the *Index* has room for two-thirds of the whole, yet there are at present on the coast fully sixteen ships of various sizes and denominations, all struggling and scrambling either for hides or for tallow. Supposing half of them to be engaged in the latter branch of business, there still remain eight vessels for such a number of hides as must take at least three years to fill them; and in illustration of this I may mention that our neighbor the *Alert,* belonging to one of the oldest and most experienced houses in the trade, has already spent eighteen months on the coast but is still about a third short of her full tale of 40,000. In the second place, the very nature of things necessarily involves considerable delay. As a vessel, whether large or small, cannot possibly load herself at any single point, she must keep paddling from post to pillar and from pillar to post, taking the chances of foul winds and bad anchorages through all the five ports of San Francisco, Monterey, Santa Barbara, San Pedro, and San Diego. But even if hides were more plentiful, the climate would, in a great measure, impose a similar necessity. As the hides are all green, or nearly so, for the skinning of the animal is pretty much the extent of Californian industry, each vessel must undertake the process of curing them for herself; and as the upper half of the coast to a depth of about fifteen miles is peculiarly exposed during the summer—which is of course the best time for the purpose—to the rains and fogs of the prevailing northwesters, the hides of each season, in order to be cured, must be carried to the drier climate of the southern ports, more particularly of San Diego. Moreover, the mere task of curing a cargo causes a great loss of time—a task too laborious to be undertaken by the sellers and too nice to be entrusted to them....

But to return to San Francisco. The trade of the bay, and in fact of the whole province, is entirely in the hands of foreigners, who are almost exclusively of the English race. Of that race, however, the Americans are considerably more numerous than the British, the former naturally flocking in greater force to neutral ground, such as this country and the Sandwich Islands, while the latter find a variety of advantageous outlets in their own national colonies. At present the foreigners are to the Californians in number as one to ten, being about 600 out of about 7,000, while, by their monopoly of trade and their command of resources, to say nothing of their superior energy and intelligence, they already possess vastly more than their numerical proportion of political influence. Their position in this respect excites the less jealousy, inasmuch as most of them have been induced, either by a desire of shaking off legal incapacities or by less interested motives, to profess the Catholic religion and to marry into provincial families.

The Californians of San Francisco number between 2,000 and 2,500, about 700 belonging to the village or *pueblo* of San José de Guadalupe and the remainder occupying about thirty farms of various sizes, generally subdivided among the families of the respective holders.

On the score of industry, these good folks, as also their brethren of the other ports, are perhaps the least promising colonists of a new country in the world, being in this respect decidedly inferior to what the savages themselves had become under the training of the priests, so that the spoliation of the missions, excepting that it has opened the province to general enterprise, has directly tended to nip civilization in the bud.

In the missions, there were large flocks of sheep, but now there are scarcely any left—the Hudson's Bay Company, last spring, having experienced great difficulty in collecting about 4,000 for its northern settlements.

In the missions the wool used to be manufactured into coarse cloth, and it is, in fact, because the Californians are too lazy to weave or spin—too lazy, I suspect, even to clip and wash the raw material—that the sheep have been literally destroyed to make more room for the horned cattle.

California man and woman of Monterey, 1837, by an unidentified artist who accompanied French explorer Abel Du Petit-Thouars to California. *Courtesy of The Bancroft Library.*

In the missions, soap and leather used to be made, but in such vulgar processes the Californians advance no further than nature herself has advanced before them, excepting to put each animal's tallow in one place and its hide in another.

In the missions, the dairy formed a principal object of attention, but now neither butter nor cheese, nor any other preparation of milk whatever, is to be found in the province.

In the missions, there were annually produced about 80,000 bushels of wheat and maize, the former, and perhaps part of the latter also, being converted into flour; but the present possessors of the soil do so little in the way of tilling the ground, that, when lying at Monterey, we sold to the government some barrels of flour at the famine rate of twenty-eight dollars, or nearly six pounds sterling, a sack—a price which could not be considered as merely local, for the stuff was intended to victual the same schooner which, on our first arrival, we had seen at anchor in Whalers' Harbor.

In the missions, beef was occasionally cured for exportation, but so miserably is the case now reversed, that, though meat enough to supply the fleets of England is annually either consumed by fire or left to the carrion birds, yet the authorities purchased from us, along with the flour just mentioned, some salted salmon as indispensable sea stores for the one paltry vessel that constituted the entire line of battle of the Californian navy.

In the missions, a great deal of wine was grown, good enough to be sent for sale to Mexico; but, with the exception of what we got at the Misión Santa Barbara, the native wine that we tasted was such trash as nothing but politeness could have induced us to swallow.

Various circumstances have conspired to render these dons so very peculiarly indolent. Independently of innate differences of national tastes, the objects of colonization exert an influence over the character of the colonists. Thus the energy of our republican brethren and the prosperity of the contiguous dependencies of the empire are to be traced, in a great degree, to the original and permanent necessity of relying on the steady and laborious use of the ax and the plow; and thus also the rival colonists of New France—a name which comprehended the valleys of the St. Lawrence and the Mississippi—dwindled and pined on much of the same ground, partly because the golden dreams of the fur trade carried them away from stationary pursuits to overrun half the breadth of the continent, and partly because the gigantic ambition of their government regarded them rather as soldiers than as settlers, rather as the instruments of political aggrandizement than as the germ of a kindred people. In like manner, Spanish America, with its sierras of silver, became the asylum and paradise of idlers, holding out to every adventurer, when leaving the shores of the old country, the prospect of earning his bread without the sweat of his brow.

But the population of California in particular has been drawn from the most indolent variety of an indolent species, being composed of superannuated troopers and retired office-holders and their descendants. In connection with the establishment of the missions, at least of those of the upper province, there had been projected three villages or *pueblos* as places of refuge for such of the old soldiers as might obtain leave to settle in the country; but as the priests were by no means friendly to the rise of a separate interest, they did all in their power to prevent the requisite licenses from being granted by the crown, so as to send to the villages as few denizens as possible and to send them only when they were past labor, as well in ability as in inclination. These villages were occasionally strengthened by congenial reinforcements of runaway sailors, and, in order to avoid such sinks of profligacy and riot, the better sort of functionaries, both civil and military, gradually established themselves elsewhere, but more particularly at Santa Barbara, while both classes were frequently coming into collision with the fathers, whose vexatious spirit of exclusiveness, even after the emancipation of the veterans, often prompted them nominally to preoccupy lands that they did not require.

Such settlers of either class were not likely to toil for much more than what the cheap bounty of nature afforded them—horses to ride and beef to eat, with hides and tallow to exchange for such other supplies as they wanted. In a word, they displayed more than the proverbial indolence of a pastoral people, for they did not even devote their idle hours to the tending of their herds. As one might have expected, the children improved on the example of the parents through the influence of a systematic education—an education which gave them the *lasso* as a toy in infancy and the horse as a companion in boyhood, which, in short, trained them from the cradle to be mounted bullock-hunters, and nothing else; and if anything could aggravate their laziness, it was the circumstance that many of them dropped, as it were, into ready-made competency by sharing in the lands and cattle of the plundered missions.

The only trouble which the Californians really take with their cattle is to brand them, when young, with their respective marks, and even this single task savors more of festivity than of labor. Once a year the cows and calves of a neighborhood, which, because of the absence of fences, all feed in common, are driven into a pen or *corral*, that every farmer may select his own stock for his own brand, at the same time keeping, if he is wise, a sharp eye on the proceedings of his associates, and after the cattle are all branded and again turned out to their pastures, the owners and their friends wind up the exciting business of the day with singing and dancing and feasting. In addition, however, to this, each farmer does occasionally collect his own cattle into his pen, partly to prevent them from becoming too wild and partly to ascertain how far his neighbors have kept the eighth commandment before their eyes.

Upon this latter point a man must be pretty vigilant in California, for a centaur of a fellow with a running noose in his hand is somewhat apt to disregard the distinctions between meum and tuum, and so common, in fact, is this free-and-easy system, that even passably honest men, merely as a precautionary measure of self-defense, occasionally catch and slay a fat bullock that they have never branded. In order to break the scent in such cases, the fortunate finder, knowing that the hide alone of a dead animal can tell any tales, obliterates the owner's mark by means of a little gunpowder and overlays it with his own in its stead. In the absence of evidence to the contrary, these brands are held to be a conclusive proof of property, and on this account a transfer, in order to be valid and safe, requires a sale brand to be placed over the seller's mark, so as to give the buyer's mark all the force of an original brand. In ignorance of this custom, Mr. Douglas, one of the Hudson's Bay Company's officers, lately committed a capital mistake. After collecting the sheep that I have already mentioned, he bought some horses for his drivers, which were subsequently sold on the *Columbia* to Commodore Wilkes[2] for the use of his party that went by land from the Willamette to San Francisco; and no sooner did the animals make their appearance in their old haunts than they were claimed by the sellers, whose marks still remained, as stolen property, to the no small astonishment of their real owners.

The income of every farmer may be pretty accurately ascertained from the number of his cattle, excepting that the owners of small stocks, as is the case at present with many of the plunderers of the missions, do not venture to kill so large a proportion of the whole as their more wealthy neighbors. The value of a single animal, without regard to the merely nominal worth of its beef, may average about five dollars, the hide fetching, as already mentioned, two dollars, and two or three *arrobas* of tallow, of twenty-five pounds each, yielding a dollar and a half by the *arroba*, and as the fourth part of a herd may generally be killed off every year without any improvidence, the farmer's revenue must be, as nearly as possible, a dollar and a quarter a head. Thus General Vallejo,[3] who is said to possess 8,000 cattle, must derive about 10,000 dollars a year from this source alone, and the next largest holders, an old man of the name of Sánchez and his sons, must draw rather more than half of that amount from their stock of 4,500 animals.

---

[2] American naval officer Charles Wilkes (1798–1877) led an exploratory and scientific expedition to the South Pacific, North Pacific, and Antarctica from 1838 to 1842. In 1841 he sailed into San Francisco Bay while an exploring party marched south to it from Astoria. In his widely read *Narrative of the United States Exploring Expedition,* published in 1845, he predictably praised California but disparaged the Californios. "Although I was prepared for anarchy and confusion, I was surprised when I found a total absence of all government in California, and even its forms and ceremonies thrown aside," he commented.

[3] By the time of Simpson's visit, Mariano Guadalupe Vallejo owned vast *ranchos* in present-day Solano and Sonoma counties.

On the same principles of calculation, the incomes of the missions must have been enormous, San José having possessed 30,000 head, and Santa Clara nearly half the number, and San Gabriel to the south being said to have owned more cattle than Santa Clara and San José put together. Even now, after all the pillage that has taken place for the benefit of individuals, the secularized wrecks of the establishments, if honestly administered, as they are not, would yield large returns to the government, Santa Clara alone, as an average instance, still mustering about 4,000 cattle. In addition to the value of hides and tallow, such of the farmers as understand the breaking of horses may turn their skill in this way to profitable account. A well-trained steed sometimes brings 150 dollars, the worth of thirty head of cattle, while the wild animal may be had at no great distance for the trouble of noosing him. In fact, horses had at one time become so numerous as to encroach on the pasturage of the cattle, and accordingly they were partly thinned out by slaughter and partly driven eastward into the valley of the San Joaquín....

Having celebrated New Year's Day to the best of our ability, we made preparations for starting on Monday, the 3rd of the month, to pay our respects to General Vallejo, who was residing at the Misión San Francisco Solano, situated, as already mentioned, on the northern side of the bay of San Pablo. Accordingly, at nine in the morning of the day appointed, we left the *Cowlitz* in the long and jolly boats, accompanied by Mr. Rae, and also by Mr. Forbes, living near the Misión San José, and acting in that neighborhood as an agent of the Hudson's Bay Company, and to whom we were much indebted during our stay, not only for his general politeness, but also for his special assistance as interpreter.

After a heavy pull of some hours against a stiff breeze, we reached the strait which communicates between Whalers' Harbor and the inner waters, having the point of San Pedro on our left and that of San Pablo on our right. As we here found the tide as well as the wind opposed to us, we were obliged to encamp on the former point a good while before it was dark. The place of our encampment, once a part of the lands of Misión San Rafael Arcángel, was now the property of an Irishman of the name of Murphy,[4] and as we had started without any stock of provisions, we were glad to find ourselves the guests of a gentleman who, besides our claims on him as his fellow-subjects, had got his cattle on such easy terms. Having made up our minds, therefore, to share with Mr. Murphy in the spoils of the church, we sent out several hunters to bring home a bullock for our supper, but, to our great mortification, we were less successful in plundering our host than he had been in plundering the priests, for our emissaries had not been able to approach within shot of a single animal, a man on foot being such a prodigy in this land of laziness as to make the very cattle scamper off in dismay. In addition to the want of beef, one of those heavy fogs, which here a northwester so frequently brings in its train, enveloped us in complete darkness, at the same time soaking through our clothes. In fact, our old fortune, whenever we slept ashore, seemed to pursue us from the Columbia to San Francisco.

Timothy Murphy, who unconsciously played the part of so inhospitable a landlord on this occasion, resides at the Misión San Rafael as *administrador* on behalf of General Vallejo, to whom, as one of the prime movers in the revolution of 1836, there fell the lion's share of prize money in the shape of the two nice snuggeries of San Rafael and San Francisco Solano. The general, who shows his sagacity by systematically allying himself with foreigners, selected Mr. Murphy as a fitting mate for one of his sisters, the prettiest girl of the family, giving him, in advance, as an earnest of the bargain, the management of San Rafael, with a good slice of the booty for his own private use. The lady, however, could not, or

---

[4] Timothy Murphy (1800–1853), an Irish-born rancher with holdings in present-day Marin County, came to California in 1829 on a hide-and-tallow brig.

Elk crossing the Carquinez Strait, 1889, by Emanuel Wyttenbach, based on a description by William Heath Davis. Davis, a Hawaiian-born merchant and ship owner who married into a prominent Californio family, described in his autobiography seeing elk herds of 3,000 or more near San Pablo Bay in the early 1840s. *Courtesy of the California Historical Society, gift of John Howell, FN-30528.*

would not, fancy Timothy, and the matter ended by the general's acquisition of two foreigners instead of one: Mr. Leese[5] having obtained the doña's hand, and Mr. Murphy having kept her dowry.

But the jilted *administrador* is not without his share of pleasant society, in the person of one of the few priests who remained in the country after the confiscation of their establishments. Father Quijas is one of those jovial souls who show that, in the New World as in the Old, power and wealth are more than a match for monastic austerities; nor has the removal of the corrupting influences

---

[5] In 1836, American merchant Jacob P. Leese (1809–1892) built Yerba Buena's first substantial structure, a house at the corner of present-day Clay Street and Grant Avenue. Earlier in 1841, he had sold the house to the Hudson's Bay Company, married Vallejo's sister, and moved to Sonoma.

rendered his reverence a more rigid observer of his vows, excepting always (thanks to Murphy and Vallejo) the single article of poverty. The two friends lately led each other into trouble in a way which forcibly illustrates the state of government in general and the character of Vallejo in particular.

As the bay of San Pablo is separated only by a ridge of green hills from the valley of Santa Rosa, in which are situated the settlements of Bodega and Ross, Murphy and Quijas, whether it was that the former was in search of stray bullocks, or that the latter wished to ease the schismatics of a little of their brandy, fell into the snare of visiting the Russians, against all rule and precedent. The treason soon came to the general's ears, and on the very evening after their return the delinquents were politely invited to attend at headquarters by a sergeant and five troopers. As the night was wet and stormy, they tried to bribe the soldiers with their best fare into a respite of a few hours, pleading at the same time the want of horses. But while the sergeant disclaimed all official knowledge of wind and weather, the troopers caught the requisite number of nags, and the next morning the luckless wights were thrown, all drenched and splashed, into the general's *calabozo* or dungeon, to chew the cud, in hunger and thirst, on the contraband hospitalities of Bodega and Ross. So much for the freedom and equity of Californian republicanism.

Early the next morning we got under way with a breeze from the southeast, and though the ebb tide was sweeping and tumbling through the straits like a rapid, we succeeded in crossing the bay to the entrance of the creek of Sonoma, which here flows, as do also several other creeks in the neighborhood, through one of the flats or marshes so common on the shores of the inlet of San Francisco. We tolled up the windings of this stream against a powerful current, looking in vain for a dry spot to put ashore, the banks being so low that they are regularly overflowed at high tide, and it was six in the evening before we reached the landing place, distant about ten miles from the bay and about three from the mission. Our standing luck here stuck to us, for we had no sooner pitched our tents and secured our baggage than the southeaster, after the day's reprieve, brought down its usual accompaniment of heavy rain. Finding an Indian at the landing place, we dispatched him with a note to the general explaining the object of our visit and requesting the favor of his sending us horses to enable us to pay our respects to him in the morning. During the night a northwest wind had taken the place of our southeaster, bringing, at this distance from the ocean, not the chilly fogs of the coast, but beautifully clear weather, rendered perhaps more pleasant by the bracing air of a sharp frost.

The sun, however, had hardly risen when the air became agreeably warm, and while we were making the most of a light breakfast the Indian returned with a polite message from the general, to the effect that horses would be with us immediately. In fact, before he had well delivered his errand, a band of thirty chargers came in sight, and soon after a still larger herd, the whole escorted by a sergeant and two troopers, with a rabble of native auxiliaries. Out of this supply nine or ten of the best-looking animals were quickly caught for us with the *lasso*, and the whole of the motley cavalcade now proceeded over a rich plain studded with scrub-oaks and embosomed within well-wooded hills of considerable height. In consequence of heavy rains, and more particularly of the bursting of a waterspout, the roads were flooded; for the plain, being low and level, not only receives far more than its share of whatever falls, but also retains nearly all it receives—a circumstance which, however inconvenient to the traveler, is, in general, peculiarly beneficial to agriculture. In fact, so dry is the climate during all the best seasons of the year that the valley is intersected in every direction by artificial ditches, which are fed from the creek for the purposes of irrigation. These artificial ditches, by the by, were the first symptom of human energy that we had seen in California, but, on inquiry, we found that they had been dug, under the direction of the priests, by the reluctant labor of the converts.

At Sonoma—for the very name of the mission has been secularized—we were received by the firing of a salute and the hoisting of the colors, the former mark of respect being complimentary in proportion to the scarcity of gunpowder in this land of *lassos*. Through a gateway and a courtyard we ascended a half-finished flight of steps to the principal room of the general's house, being of fifty feet in length and of other dimensions in proportion. Besides being disfigured by the doors of chambers, to which it appeared to be a passage, this apartment was very indifferently furnished, the only tolerable articles upon the bare floor being some gaudy chairs from Oahu, [Hawaii,] such as the native islanders themselves often make. This was California all over, the richest and most influential individual in a professedly civilized settlement obliged to borrow the means of sitting from savages who had never seen a white man 'til two years after San Francisco was colonized by the Spaniards. Here we were received by Don Salvador Vallejo and Mr. Leese, our host's brother and brother-in-law, and immediately afterwards the general, being somewhat indisposed, received us very courteously in his own chamber.

General Vallejo is a good-looking man of about forty-five years of age, who has risen in the world by his own talent and energy. His father, who was one of the most respectable men in California, died about ten years ago at Monterey, leaving to a large family of sons and daughters little other inheritance than a degree of intelligence and steadiness almost unknown in the country. The patrimonial estate, such as it was, descended to the eldest son, while the second, now the prop of the name, was an ensign in the army, with the command of the *presidio* of San Francisco. Having acquired considerable influence in the party, which styled itself democratic and aimed at something like independence, he was promoted by a conciliatory governor to be commandant of the frontier of Sonoma. Soon afterwards, taking advantage of this same governor's death, he became the leader in the revolution of 1836, securing for a nephew of the name of Alvarado the office of civil governor, and reserving to himself the important post of commander of the forces. As to the rest of the family, Don Salvador became a captain of cavalry, and another brother was made *administrador* of the Misión San José, while the girls were married off, most of them to foreigners with shrewd views to the strengthening of the general's influence.

In addition to what I have already said as to the power and value of foreigners, a recent rebellion [against the Mexican government], which has made Vallejo a great man, was brought to a crisis by the spirited conduct of an individual of that class. The insurgents, having entered the Presidio of Monterey, were brought to a stand by the Mexican commandant's refusal to surrender; but one of their foreign associates, after apostrophizing their "eyes" and ejaculating something about "humbug," loaded a gun to the muzzle and shot off part of the roof of the commandant's place of retreat— a hint to capitulate, which could no longer be misunderstood or neglected. The foreigners were pretty nearly unanimous in favor of the insurgents, some of them from the love of a row, many through matrimonial connections, and the Americans in the hope of seeing the new republic hoist the Stars and Stripes of the Union.

After spending about half an hour with our host, we left him to partake of a second breakfast, at which we were joined by the ladies of the family. First in honor and in place was Señora Vallejo, whose sister is married to Captain Wilson of the bark *Index*, an honest Scot from "Bonny Dundee"; next came one of her sisters-in-law, who is the wife of Captain Cooper[6] of the schooner *California*,

---

[6] John Rogers Cooper (1792–1872), born in England, emigrated to California in 1826. Known widely as Captain Cooper, he was a well-known shipmaster, merchant, and rancher during the Mexican era.

Mariano Guadalupe Vallejo (1808–1890) with his daughters and granddaughters. *Courtesy of The Bancroft Library.*

and who resides at Sonoma as a pledge for the fidelity of the provincial navy; and lastly followed Mrs. Leese with an unmarried sister and Mrs. Cooper's daughter. It won't be the general's fault if the

English race does not multiply in California. So far as names went, we might have supposed ourselves to be in London or in Boston.

In front of Mr. Leese, who sat at the head of the table as master of ceremonies, was placed an array of five dishes—two kinds of stewed beef, rice, fowl, and beans. As all the cooking is done in out-houses—for the dwellings, by reason of the mildness of the climate, have no chimneys or fireplaces—the dishes were by no means too hot when put on the table; while by being served out in succession to a party of about twenty people, they became each colder than the other before they reached their destinations. It was some consolation to know that the heat must once have been there, for everything had literally been seethed into chips, the beans or *frijoles* in particular having been first boiled and lastly fried, with an intermediate stewing to break the suddenness of the transition. Then every mouthful was poisoned with the everlasting compound of pepper and garlic, and this repast, be it observed, was quite an aristocratic specimen of the kind, for elsewhere we more than once saw, in one and the same dish, beef and tongue, and pumpkin and garlic, and potatoes in their jackets, and cabbage and onions, and tomatoes and peppers, and heaven knows what besides—this last indefinite ingredient being something more than a mere figure of speech, considering that all the cookery, as one may infer from the expenditure of so much labor, is the work of native drudges, unwashed and uncombed. When to the foregoing sketch are added bad tea and worse wine, the reader has picked up a perfect idea of a Californian breakfast, a Californian dinner, and a Californian supper, and is quite able to estimate the sacrifice which a naturalized John Bull makes for the pleasures of matrimony and the comforts of Roman Catholicism. Such varieties as cheese and butter and milk and mutton and fish are, as I have already mentioned, here unknown. Even game, whether of the land or of the water, is at a discount, not only as a matter of business, but also as an object of amusement; and the very beef has been parboiled in the feverish blood of the unfortunate bullock, first heated and infuriated by the chase, and then tortured and strangled with the *lasso*.

Immediately after breakfast our horses were brought to the door, and we started to see the country, accompanied by Don Salvador and an escort of three or four soldiers. We first ascended a steep hill at the back of the mission, whence we obtained an extensive view of the surrounding region. In the distance lay the waters of the magnificent harbor, while at our feet stretched a plain, for it exhibited nothing of the valley but its wall of mountains, about fifteen miles long and three broad. This plain is composed of alluvial soil, which is so fertile as to yield about fifty returns of wheat, and the hills present abundance of willow, poplar, pine, chestnut, and cedar. If one may judge from appearances, this valley once formed an arm of the bay of San Pablo, and in fact the whole harbor, in remote ages, was most probably an inland lake which has forced its way to the ocean through the same barrier of soft rock that, as already mentioned, still continues to melt into the tide.

In the course of our ride we saw several deer on the road, these animals being so tame as often to approach the houses in large herds. For beasts of chase, if here the phrase is not a misnomer, California is a perfect paradise. The Californian is too lazy to hunt for amusement, and as to any necessity of the kind, his bullocks supply all his wants, excepting that the red deer is occasionally pursued on account of the peculiar hardness and whiteness of its tallow. Hence the number of wild animals is very considerable. Beaver and otter have recently been caught within half a mile of the mission, and there are also the red deer, the wild goat [antelope], the bear, the panther, the wolf, the fox, the rabbit, etc.

Having descended from the hill, we traversed a great portion of the plain. The waterspout, which has been already mentioned, had done a great deal of damage, sweeping away the newly sown seed from several large fields of wheat. These fields had been highly prized by the general, as the grain had been procured from the Columbia River and was superior in quality to his own. As one might expect from the abundance of land, the fertility of the soil, and the indolence of the people, agriculture is conducted in the rudest possible way. As the surface of the plain presents so few obstacles to cultivation, the same land is never cropped for more than two successive years, and as General Vallejo's farm contains from 500 to 600 acres, he thus annually breaks up about 300 acres of what may be called wild land, either fresh from the hands of nature or refreshed by rest. In the fields that had been stripped by the waterspout, we saw several plows at work, or rather at what expects to be called work in this country. The machine consists of little more than a log of wood pointed with iron, from the top of which rises in a sloping direction a long pole for the oxen, while an upright handle for the plowman is fixed to the unpointed end of the share, or, if possible, is formed out of the same piece of timber as the share itself. The oxen, as if to prevent even them from putting forth their strength, are yoked by the horns, and considering that there are only two such animals to so clumsy a piece of workmanship, the topsoil alone is scratched to a depth of not more than two or three inches.

Having learned from us during our excursion that we wished to see an exhibition of the *lasso*, Don Salvador had kindly sent back orders to make the requisite preparations, and accordingly, on our return to the mission, we found everything ready for action. A band of wild horses had been driven into a pen or *corral* of very strong build. The door being thrown open, Don Salvador and one or two others entered on horseback, and the former, having his *lasso* coiled up in his hand, swung it 'round his head to give it an impetus, and then with a dexterous aim secured in the noose the neck of a fiery young steed. After plunging and rearing in vain, the animal was at length thrown down with great violence. Soon, however, it was again on its legs, and its captor, having attached the *lasso* to his saddle-bow, dragged it tottering out of the *corral*, 'til, with eyes staring from its head and nostrils fearfully distended, it fell panting and groaning to the ground. The *lasso* being now slackened, the animal regained its breath, and, infuriated with rage, started away at its utmost speed, Don Salvador, of course, following at an equal pace. One of the assistants now spurred forward his steed, and overtaking the victim, seized it by the tail with his hand, and at length, watching a favorable moment, he threw the animal by a jerk to the earth with such force as threatened to break every bone in its body. This cruel operation was repeated several times, 'til we begged hard that the wretched beast should be released from further torture. A second horse was then caught and thrown down in a manner still more painful. The captor suddenly stopped his horse when at full gallop, which, being well trained, threw its weight toward one side in expectation of the impending jerk, while the captive steed was instantaneously pitched head over heels to a distance of several yards.

Cruel as the sport was, we could not but admire the skill of the Californians in the management of their horses. One of the people, whether by accident or design dropped his *lasso*, of which the other end was attached to a wild horse in full career, and following 'til he came up with it as it trailed on the ground, he stooped to it from his saddle and picked it up without slackening his pace for a moment. But, with all their dexterity and experience, the riders often meet with serious, and even fatal, accidents by being thrown from their horses. Don Salvador himself had had his full share of this kind of thing. He had broken two ribs and fractured both his thighs, the one in two places and the other in three, so that he had now very little left in reserve but his neck. There is, moreover, one peculiar danger to which the thrower of the *lasso* is exposed. The saddle of the country has an elevated pommel, round which the *lasso*, after noosing its victim, is rapidly twisted, and in this operation the captor not unfrequently sees the first finger of his right hand torn off in an instant. These evils are, of course, often aggravated by the want of proper assistance, our host's present indisposition being a curious instance of this. While engaged with the *lasso* the general had dislocated his hip. The joint, however, was replaced, and he was doing well till he bruised it slightly. He sent a messenger to the only practitioner at San Francisco, one Bail from Manchester, for a strengthening plaster, but the doctor, who sometimes takes doses very different from those which he prescribes, sent by mistake a blister of cantharides, which, being supposed to be salutary in proportion to the pain of its application, was allowed to work double tides on the poor general's bruise so as to turn it into a very pretty sore, which had confined him to his bed.

During the day we visited a village of General Vallejo's Indians, about 300 in number, who were the most miserable of the race I ever saw, excepting always the slaves of the savages of the northwest coast. Though many of them are well-formed and well-grown, every face bears the impress of poverty and wretchedness, and they are, moreover, a prey to several malignant diseases, among which a hereditary syphilis ranks as the predominant scourge alike of old and young. They are badly clothed, badly lodged, and badly fed. As to clothing, they are pretty nearly in a state of nature. As to lodging, their hovels are made of boughs wattled with bulrushes in the form of beehives, with a hole in the top for a chimney, and with two holes at the bottom, towards the northwest and the southeast, so as to enable the poor creatures, by closing them in turns, to exclude both the prevailing winds. As to food, they eat the worst bullock's worst joints, with bread of acorns and chestnuts [buckeyes], which are most laboriously and carefully prepared by pounding and rinsing and grinding. Though not so recognized by law, they are thralls in all but the name, while, borne to the earth by the toils of civilization superadded to the privations of savage life, they vegetate rather than live, without the wish to enjoy their former pastimes or the skill to resume their former avocations.

This picture, which is a correct likeness not only of General Vallejo's Indians, but of all the civilized aborigines of California, is the only remaining monument of the zeal of the church and the munificence of the state. Nor is the result very different from what ought to have been expected. In a religious point of view, the priests were contented with merely external observances, and even this semblance of Christianity they systematically purchased and rewarded with the good things of this life, their very first step in the formation of a mission having been to barter maize-pottage, by a kind of regular tariff, for an unconscious attendance at church and the repetition of unintelligible catechisms.

With regard, again, to temporal improvement, the priests, instead of establishing each proselyte on a farm of his own, and thus gradually imbuing him with knowledge and industry, penned the whole like cattle and watched them like children, at the very most making them eye-servants through their dread of punishment and their reverence for a master. In truth, the Indians were then the same as now, excepting that they shared more liberally in the fruits of their own labor and possessed spirit enough to enjoy a holiday in the songs and dances of their race. The true tendency of the monkish discipline was displayed by the partial emancipation which took place, as already mentioned, in 1825; and when the missions were confiscated in 1836, the proselytes, almost as naturally as the cattle, were divided among the spoilers, either as menial drudges or as predial serfs, excepting that some of the more independent among them retired to the wilderness, in order, as the sequel will show, to avenge their wrongs by a life of rapine.

These sons and daughters of bondage—many of them too sadly broken in spirit even to marry—are so rapidly diminishing in numbers that they must soon pass away from the land of their fathers, a result which, as it seems uniformly to spring from all the conflicting varieties of civilized agency, is to be ultimately ascribed to the inscrutable wisdom of a mysterious Providence. If anything could render such a state of things more melancholy, it would be the reflection that many of these victims of a hollow civilization must have been born in the missions, inasmuch as, even at San Francisco, those establishments had taken root sixty years before the revolution, and it was truly pitiable to hear Vallejo's beasts of burden speaking the Spanish language, as an evidence that the system, wherever the fault lay, had not failed through want of time.

Previously to dressing for dinner we took a closer survey of the buildings and premises. The general's plan seems to be to throw his principal edifices into the form of a square, or rather of three sides of a square. The center is already filled up with the general's own house, flanked on one side by a barrack and on the other by Don Salvador's residence, but as yet the wings contain respectively only a billiard room and Mr. Leese's dwelling, opposite to each other. On the outside of this square are many detached buildings, such as the *calabozo*, the church, etc. The *calabozo* is most probably a part of the original establishment, for every mission had its cage for refractory converts; but the church, which even now is large, has been built by Vallejo to replace a still larger one, though no priest lives at Sonoma, and Father Quijas of San Rafael, after his experience of the dungeon, has but little stomach for officiating at headquarters.

All the buildings are of *adobes*, or unbaked bricks, which are cemented with mud instead of mortar, and in order to protect such perishable materials from the rain, besides keeping off the rays of the sun, the houses are very neatly finished with verandas and overhanging eaves. If tolerably protected for a time, the walls, which are generally four or five feet thick, become, in a measure, vitrified, and are nearly as durable as stone. To increase the expenditure of labor and materials, the partitions are nearly as thick as the outer walls, each room of any size having its own separate roof, a circumstance which explained what at first surprised us—the great length and breadth of the apartments.

At this season of the year [January] we found the houses very comfortless in consequence of the want of fireplaces, for the warmth of the day only rendered us more sensible of the chilliness of the night. The Californians remedy or mitigate the evil by the ludicrous makeshift of wearing their cloaks, and even among the foreigners not more than two or three dwellings with chimneys will be found from one end of the province to the other.

The garrison of Sonoma is certainly well officered, for the general and the captain have only thirteen troopers under their command, this force and Prado's corps, if they could only get *balsas* enough to effect a junction, forming a standing army of about twenty men for San Francisco alone. The absurdity of the thing consists not in the number of soldiers, for they are sixteen times more numerous in proportion than the Army of the United States. The essential folly is this: that a scattered population of 7,000 men, women, and children should ever think of an independence that must either ruin them for the maintenance of an adequate force or expose them at one and the same time to the horrors of popular anarchy and of military insubordination.

If one may judge from the variety of uniforms, each of the thirteen warriors constitutes his own regiment, one being the "Blues," another the "Buffs," and so on; and as they are all mere boys, this nucleus of a formidable cavalry has at least the merit of being a growing one. The only articles common to the whole of this baker's dozen are an enormous sword, a pair of nascent *mostachos,* deerskin boots, and that everlasting *serape* or blanket with a hole in the middle of it for the head. This troop the general turns to useful account, being clearly of opinion that idleness is the very rust of discipline. He makes them catch his cattle, and, in short, discharge the duty of servants-of-all-work—an example highly worthy of the imitation of all military autocrats. The system, however, has led to two or three revolts. On one occasion a regiment of native infantry, being an awkward squad of fifteen Indians, having conspired against the general, were shot for their pains; and more recently the Californian soldiers, disdaining to drive bullocks, were cashiered on the spot and replaced by new levies. Besides the garrison, the general possesses several field-pieces and carronades, which, however, are, by reason of the low state of the ammunition, rather ornamental than useful.

There is a small vineyard behind the house, of about 300 feet square, which, in the days of the priests, used to yield about 1,000 gallons of wine. The general, on coming into possession, replanted the vines, which bore abundantly in the third season, and now, at the end of only five years, they have just yielded twenty barrels of wine and four of spirits, equal to sixteen more of wine, of fifteen gallons each, or about 540 gallons of wine in all. The peaches and pears also, though only three years old, were from fifteen to twenty feet high and had borne fruit this season. In short, almost any plant might here be cultivated with success.

During the short winter, snow is never seen, excepting occasionally on the summits of the highest hills, while at noon the heat generally ranges from sixty-five degrees to seventy degrees in the shade, and in summer the average temperature of the day is seldom lower than ninety degrees. As the northwest fogs do not penetrate into the interior more than fifteen miles, there are, in fact, two climates at San Francisco, and General Vallejo has chosen the better one for himself, as also for his brother [Don José de Jesús], the *administrador* of Misión San José.

At dinner the general made his appearance, wrapped in a cloak, and we had now also the pleasure of being introduced to the dowager *señora*, an agreeable dame of about sixty, and we could

not help envying the old lady the very rare luxury of being immediately surrounded, at her time of life, by so many as five grown sons
and daughters. This meal was merely a counterpart of the breakfast—the same Mr. Leese, the same stews, the same *frijoles*, and the
same pepper and garlic, with the same dead-and-alive temperature
in every morsel—and the only difference was, that, as we were a
little better appetized, we took more notice of the want of attendance, the only servant, besides my own, being a miserable Indian
dressed in a shirt, with bare legs and cropped hair.

Immediately after dinner the ladies retired, the gentlemen at
the same time going out for a stroll, but soon afterwards the ladies
again met us at tea, reinforced by one or two of the more juvenile
doñas of the establishment. Dancing was now the order of the day.
Don Salvador and one of his troopers played the guitar while we
were "toeing it and heeling it" at the *fandango*, the cotillion, and
the waltz. The scene was rather peculiar for a ballroom, both gentlemen and ladies, when not on active service, smoking furiously, with
fully more, in some cases, than the usual accompaniments.

Among the persons present was a very fierce, punchy little man
enveloped in an immense cloak. He proved to be no less a person-
age than Commandant Prado of the *presidio* of San Francisco, suc-
cessor, in fact, of Vallejo in the same office that formed the stepping-
stone to his present elevation. Besides having been engaged in many
skirmishes against both Californians and Indians, he has had several narrow escapes with his life in private brawls. About two years
ago a religious festival was celebrated at the Misión San Francisco
de Asís in honor of the patron saint, passing through all the usual
gradations of Mass, bullfight, supper, and ball. In the course of the
evening, Don Francisco Guerrero, the steward of the mission,
stabbed Prado with the ever-ready knife for presuming to interpose
in an altercation between himself and his mistress; but the corpu-
lent commandant was not to be so easily run through, for though

breadth of beam is not generally an advantage to a soldier, on this occasion Prado's fat did succeed in saving his bacon. Such a termination of a religious festival is so much a matter of course that at one that took place a few months back, one of Prado's numerous enemies came up to him, and, drawing his knife, said, "What! here's daylight, and no one yet stabbed!" and it required all the influence of Vallejo, who happened to be present, to nip so very promising a quarrel in the bud. On such occasions the cloak is often invaluable as a shield, and in fact, when both parties are on their guard, there is commonly far more of noise than of mischief.

Our evening, however, passed over most amicably and agreeably, winding up, after several other songs, with "Auld Lang Syne," in which the Californians joined the foreigners very heartily, so that, as next day was Old Christmas, I could almost have fancied that I was welcoming Auld Yule in the north of Scotland.

On the morning of the 6th we left the mission about seven o'clock, under a pretty heavy rain, to the great surprise of its amiable and hospitable inmates. We breakfasted at the landing place, on the site of our old camp, after which we made our way to the mouth of the creek with the ebb tide, but as the wind was blowing hard from the southeast, we could not face the bay and were obliged to retrace our steps, encamping for the third time at the landing place, after nearly a whole day's exposure and toil. In all the course of my traveling I never had occasion to go so far in search of an encampment as I did this day, but between our encampment and the bay there really was not a single spot where, even in the direst necessity, we could have obtained a footing. The banks of the creek were a mere marsh, and we saw and heard thousands upon thousands of cranes, geese, ducks, curlew snipe, plover, heron, etc. These birds enjoy a perpetual holiday. They, of course, are quite safe from the *lasso*, and so long as the Californians can get beef without gunpowder, they are not likely to expend it on any less profitable quarry.

By next morning the wind had returned to the northwest. We accordingly got under way at six o'clock, and, after a pleasant run down the creek, we stood across the bay of San Pablo, passed our old encampment on Murphy's estate, and at four in the afternoon arrived in safety on board of the *Cowlitz.*

It had been our intention on this trip to visit Captain Sutter,[7] the purchaser, as already mentioned, of the Russian-American Company's stock in Ross and Bodega, who had settled, under the sanction of the government, on the banks of the Sacramento, but as this prolongation of our excursion would have occupied us at least eight or ten days, we were reluctantly obliged to return without beating up the captain's quarters. Besides having thus lost the opportunity of seeing a little of the interior, we had reasons of a less romantic character for regretting our disappointment, as Sutter, a man of speculative turn and good address, had given to the Hudson's Bay Company, in common with many others less able to pay for the compliment, particular grounds for taking an interest in his welfare and prosperity. He was understood to have served in the bodyguard of Charles X and to have emigrated, after the three glorious days of 1830, to the United States, a country that, by its acquisition of Louisiana, offers far more powerful inducements to French enterprise than any one of the rickety colonies of the grand nation. He had successively tried his fortune in St. Louis, among the Shawnee Indians, in the Snake country, on the Columbia River, at the Sandwich Islands, at Sitka, and at San Francisco, uniformly illustrating the proverb of the rolling stone, but yet generally contriving to leave anxious and inquisitive friends behind him.

Sutter was now living on a grant of land about sixty miles long and twelve broad, trapping, farming, trading, bullying the

---

[7] Swiss émigré Johann Augustus Sutter (1803–1880) oversaw a huge *rancho* at the confluence of the Sacramento and American rivers. In early 1841, he bought Fort Ross from the Russians—to Simpson's chagrin.

government, and letting out Indians on hire—being, in short, in a fairer way of figuring in the world as a territorial potentate than his royal patron's heir, the Duke of Bordeaux. If he really has the talent and the courage to make the most of his position, he is not unlikely to render California a second Texas. Even now the Americans only want a rallying point for carrying into effect their theory that the English race is destined by "right divine" to expel the Spaniards from their ancient seats, a theory which has already begun to develop itself in more ways than one.

American adventurers have repeatedly stolen cattle and horses by wholesale, with as little compunction as if they had merely helped themselves to an installment of their own property. American trappers have frequently stalked into the Californian towns with their long rifles, ready for all sorts of mischief, practically setting the government at defiance and putting the inhabitants in bodily fear; and in 1836 the American residents, as also some of the American skippers on the coast, supported the revolution, in the hope of its merely transferring California from Mexico to the United States.

Now, for fostering and maturing Brother Jonathan's ambitious views, Captain Sutter's establishment is admirably situated. Besides lying on the direct route between San Francisco on the one hand and the Missouri and the Willamette on the other, it virtually excludes the Californians from all the best parts of their own country—the valleys of the San Joaquín, the Sacramento, and the Colorado. Hitherto the Spaniards have confined themselves to the comparatively barren slip of land, varying from ten to forty miles in width, which lies between the ocean and the first range of mountains; and beyond this slip they will never penetrate with their present character and their present force, if Captain Sutter, or any other adventurer, can gather 'round him a score of such marksmen as won Texas on the field of San Jacinto. But this is not all, for the Americans, if masters of the interior, will soon discover that they have a natural right to a maritime outlet, so that, whatever may be the fate of Monterey and the more southerly ports, San Francisco will, to a moral certainty, sooner or later fall into the possession of Americans—the only possible mode of preventing such a result being the previous occupation of the port on the part of Great Britain. English, in some sense or other of the word, the richest portions of California must become. Either Great Britain will introduce her well-regulated freedom of all classes and colors, or the people of the United States will inundate the country with their own peculiar mixture of helpless bondage and lawless insubordination. Between two such alternatives, the Californians themselves have little room for choice, and even if there were ground for hesitation, they would, I am convinced, find in their actual experience sufficient reason for deciding in favor of the British, for they especially and emphatically complain that the Americans, in their mercantile dealings, are too wide awake for such drowsy customers as would rather be cheated at once than protect themselves by any unusual expenditure of vigilance and caution. So much as to Captain Sutter's history and prospects.

EDWIN BRYANT
1846

——>•●•<——

About the same time Sir George Simpson was visiting Yerba Buena, the first California-bound wagon train to cross the Sierra arrived after a grueling six-month trek. The sixty-nine-member team had followed the Oregon Trail to present-day Idaho and split up, half going on to the Oregon territory and half—led by John Bidwell and John Bartelson—following the Humboldt River into California. Oregon was the more appealing destination and attracted the majority of settlers in the early 1840s because it featured unlimited land and no bothersome Mexican government. But glowing descriptions from Bidwell and other pioneer-cum-publicists like John Marsh and Lansford W. Hastings convinced more and more emigrants to choose California. Two hundred and fifty made the trip in 1845, and more than 500 came the following year. Like the mountain men who had forged their trails, most overland emigrants resisted integration into Spanish-speaking communities. Bringing their families and neighbors with them, these Americans created their own farm colonies segregated from Californio culture. In 1841 fewer than 400 foreigners from the U.S. and Europe lived in California; over the next seven years that number would steadily rise to about 7,000, outnumbering the Californio population.

The Californian who played the largest role in promoting westward migration was Johann August Sutter, a self-aggrandizing fugitive who abandoned a wife, five children, and massive debts in Switzerland in 1834. He arrived in Monterey in 1839 and, calling himself Captain John Sutter of "the Royal Swiss Guard of France," managed to secure a gigantic, 48,000-acre grant of land in the Sacramento Valley. At the confluence of the Sacramento and American rivers he established a large fort, cattle ranch, and farm he dubbed New Helvetia, maintained by Hawaiian and Indian servants. "The Indians I did not marry or bury, I was everything [to]: patriarch, priest, father & judge," he boasted. Beginning with Bidwell in 1841, Sutter employed a growing number of American emigrants, as well as dispatched supplies to help wagon trains in trouble in the Sierra and sold land to new settlers once they arrived.

Another central figure in the ongoing Americanization of California was John Charles Frémont. Though of illegitimate birth, his charm and dashing good looks helped him secure a commission with the Army Corps of Topographical Engineers. At age twenty-seven he won the hand of sixteen-year-old Jessie Benton, the daughter of influential Senator Thomas Hart Benton. The senator helped Frémont gain authorization for a series of western exploring expeditions (including two to California) in the early 1840s. Frémont's reports of the expeditions—written with help from his young wife—were astonishingly popular with East Coast readers and catapulted the couple to national fame.

As egotistical and ambitious as Sutter, Frémont returned to California in early 1846 with sixty armed men, intending to test Governor José Castro's resolve. Frémont's timing was not accidental; he knew that there was a growing resentment among newly emigrated Americans toward the Mexican government and hoped to encourage a revolt. Castro expelled Frémont and his battalion to Oregon, setting off rumors (encouraged by Frémont) that Mexico was about to evict all foreign settlers. In June a group of disgruntled American squatters stole 170 horses from Castro's soldiers.

Emboldened by their success, they decided to capture Mariano Vallejo's home in Sonoma (an ironic choice because Vallejo, a well-respected retired military colonel, actually supported U.S. annexation of California).

Later that day the would-be revolutionaries fashioned a crude flag with a bear and star and declared the Bear Flag Republic of Independent California, telling the residents of Sonoma, "As enemies we will kill and destroy you! But as friends we will share with you all the blessings of liberty." They imprisoned Vallejo and a few others in Sutter's Fort while planning their next move. Frémont reappeared, christened the group his "California Battalion," and led their raid on the San Francisco *presidio* (by now little more than a muddy, ungarrisoned ruin). At this point, news reached them that President Polk, citing grievances but clearly coveting annexation of California, had officially declared war on Mexico two months earlier. The ridiculous Bear Flag Revolt, only a month old, promptly ended; Frémont volunteered to help U.S. Commodore Robert F. Stockton fight the Mexicans.

Both Sutter and Frémont would figure into the life of Edwin Bryant. Born near Amherst, Massachusetts, in 1805, Bryant had an unhappy childhood. His parents, Ichabod and Silence Bryant, were first cousins, and his father was frequently in prison, leaving Edwin to be raised by various relatives. Bryant left Massachusetts at age twenty-five for Kentucky, where he found work as a newspaper writer and editor. Stridently pro-Whig, Bryant became friends with Kentucky Senator Henry Clay and his family. The stresses of journalism took their toll on Bryant's health, and in 1846 he decided to accompany a wagon train to California and write a book about the experience. If expecting a vacation, he would soon learn better.

He left Louisville on April 18 and took a steamer to Independence, Missouri, origin of the Oregon and Santa Fe trails. Independence was a bustling outfitting center with a population of about 1,000; Bryant wrote that "the small town seemed to be literally overflowing with strangers of every grade of character and condition of life, collected from all parts of the continents of America and Europe, civilized and uncivilized." By May, Bryant's emigrant train (led by William H. Russell) had joined dozens of others on the Oregon Trail. As they traveled west, a rumor circulated from wagon to wagon that war had broken out with Mexico. "We read it as a good joke in which even the ladies and children participate," scoffed Russell. On June 19 Bryant and ten other men separated from Russell's group in order to travel faster. West of Fort Bridger, Wyoming, a plethora of routes were available; Bryant chose "Hastings' Cut-off," a trail that wound south around Great Salt Lake and along the Humboldt River. A few days later, the Donner Party—unlike Bryant, burdened with wagons, oxen, and children—followed a slightly more southern path with famously disastrous results.

Bryant—weak, lean, and weather-beaten from his 3,000-mile journey—crossed into California on August 30 and rested for a few days at William Johnson's ranch on the Bear River. Johnson had on hand a copy of the first newspaper printed in California, the *Californian*, which described the ongoing Mexican War. "This seemed and sounded very odd," wrote Bryant. "We had been traveling in as straight a line as we could, crossing rivers, mountains, and deserts, nearly four months beyond the bounds of civilization, and for the greater distance beyond the boundaries of territory claimed by our government; but here, on the remotest confines of the world as it were, where we expected to visit and explore a foreign country, we found ourselves under American authority, and about to be 'annexed' to the American Union." From there Bryant went on to visit Sutter, who impressed him with his genteel, European manners and obvious wealth. He reached Yerba Buena on September 21, 1846, and learned that a U.S. flag had flown over the small port for more than two months.

A few weeks later Bryant volunteered to join charismatic Frémont in battle against Mexican army captain José María Flores in southern California, one of the final campaigns of the Mexican War. The fighting proved to be short-lived. With help from General

Stephen Kearny and hundreds of settlers like Bryant, the Americans quickly overwhelmed the Mexican forces, who were weakened by a chronic lack of gunpowder, dissension among its military leaders, and widespread hopelessness among its soldiers. Flores and Governor Pío Pico surrendered on January 13, 1847. Although official annexation would not occur until the drafting of the Treaty of Guadalupe Hidalgo a year later, for all intents and purposes the U.S. conquest of California was now complete.

Bryant was back in Yerba Buena by February 13. General Kearney, replacing Mexican officials with American ones, asked him to become the town's *alcalde*. Bryant served there for a year before returning overland to Louisville to finish *What I Saw in California*, published in 1848 to immense popularity. His straightforward newspaperman's style and thorough notations of time, landscape, and weather would be studied by the thousands of gold-seekers who followed Bryant's overland path in subsequent years. On his return trip to San Francisco in 1849, the other forty-niners treated him like a celebrity.

In middle-age Bryant retired to rural Kentucky and lived off book royalties and lecture fees. He made a last, ill-fated revisit to California in 1869, this time by train. The long trip left him bedridden from exhaustion, and he committed suicide in December 1869 by throwing himself out of a Louisville bedroom window to escape his pain. Given his lifelong ill-health, it is remarkable the amount of land Bryant managed to cover in his sixty-four years. *What I Saw in California* went through countless printings during and after the gold rush; today it provides a dependable, firsthand account of an intensely turbulent period in California history. This excerpt from his account begins on September 3, 1846, outside Sutter's Fort.

EDWIN BRYANT

from *What I Saw in California*

September 3. We remained encamped near Sutter's Fort, or Fort Sacramento, as subsequently it has been named. This morning we were visited by numerous Indians from the neighboring *rancherías*, who brought with them watermelons, muskmelons, and strings of pan-fish, taken from a small pond about half a mile distant, with a sort of hand trap. The Indians wade into the pond with their traps in hand and take with them the fish, sometimes by dozens at a haul. These they wished to trade for such small articles as we possessed and the cast-off clothing of the members of our party. Some of these Indians were partially clothed, others were entirely naked, and a portion of them spoke the Spanish language. They exhibited considerable sharpness in making a bargain, holding their wares at a high valuation, and although their desire to trade appeared to be strong, they would make no sacrifices to obtain the articles offered in exchange for them. But such was the desire of our men to obtain vegetables, of which they had been for so long a time deprived, that there was scarcely any article that they possessed which they would refuse to barter for them.

The Indians generally are well made and of good stature, varying from five feet four inches to five feet ten and eleven inches in height, with strong muscular developments. Their hair is long, black, and coarse, and their skin is a shade lighter than that of a mulatto. They appear to be indolent and averse from labor of every kind, unless combined with their sports and amusements, when they are as reckless of fatigue and danger as any class of men I have seen.

Sutter's Fort, 1849, by Joseph Warren Revere, a naval officer who came to California to fight in the Mexican War. *Courtesy of the California Historical Society, Templeton Crocker Collection, FN-30530.*

By invitation of Captain Sutter, addressed to myself and Mr. Jacob, we visited and dined at the fort. The fort is situated near the confluence of the Río de los Americanos and the Río Sacramento. The valley of the Sacramento is here of great width, and consequently the fort is surrounded by an extensive plain, bounded by distant mountains on the east and on the west. This plain exhibits every evidence of a most fertile soil. The grasses, although they are now brown and crisp from the periodical drought, still stand with their ripened seeds upon them, showing their natural luxuriance. Groves or parks of the evergreen oak relieve the monotony of the landscape and dot the level plain as far as the eye can reach.

Captain Sutter received us with manifestations of cordial hospitality. He is a gentleman between forty-five and fifty years of age, and in manners, dress, and general deportment, he approaches so near what we call the "old school gentleman," as to present a gulfy contrast from the rude society by which he is surrounded. Captain Sutter is a native of Switzerland and was at one time an officer in

265

John Augustus Sutter (1803–1880). *Courtesy of The Bancroft Library.*

the French army. He emigrated to the United States and was naturalized. From thence, after a series of most extraordinary and romantic incidents, to relate which would furnish matter for a volume,
he planted himself on the spot where his fort now stands—then a
savage wilderness and in the midst of numerous and hostile tribes

of Indians. With the small party of men that he originally brought with him, he succeeded in defending himself against the Indians, until he constructed his first defensive building. He told me that several times, being hemmed in by his assailants, he had subsisted for many days upon grass alone. There is a grass in this valley that the Indians eat that is pleasant to the taste and nutritious. He succeeded by degrees in reducing the Indians to obedience, and by means of their labor, erected the spacious fortification, which now belongs to him.

The fort is a parallelogram, about 500 feet in length and 150 in breadth. The walls are constructed of *adobes*, or sun-dried bricks. The main building, or residence, stands near the center of the area, or court, enclosed by the walls. A row of shops, storerooms, and barracks are enclosed within and line the walls on every side. Bastions project from the angles, the ordnance mounted in which sweep the walls. The principal gates on the east and the south are also defended by heavy artillery, through portholes pierced in the walls. At this time the fort is manned by about fifty well-disciplined Indians and ten or twelve white men, all under the pay of the United States. These Indians are well-clothed and fed. The garrison is under the command of Mr. Kern, the artist of Captain [John C.] Frémont's exploring expedition.

The number of laboring Indians employed by Captain Sutter during the seasons of sowing and harvest is from two to three hundred. Some of these are clothed in shirts and blankets, but a large portion of them are entirely naked. They are paid so much per day for their labor, in such articles of merchandise as they may select from the store. Cotton cloth and handkerchiefs are what they most freely purchase. Common brown cotton cloth sells at one dollar per yard. A tin coin issued by Captain Sutter circulates among them, upon which is stamped the number of days that the holder has labored. These stamps indicate the value in merchandise to which the laborer or holder is entitled....

The laboring or field Indians about the fort are fed upon the offal of slaughtered animals and upon the bran sifted from the ground wheat. This is boiled in large iron kettles. It is then placed in wooden troughs standing in the court, around which the several messes seat themselves and scoop out with their hands this poor fodder. Bad as it is, they eat it with an apparent high relish; and no doubt it is more palatable and more healthy than the acorn mush, or *atole*, which constitutes the principal food of these Indians in their wild state.

The wheat crop of Captain Sutter, the present year (1846), is about 8,000 bushels. The season has not been a favorable one. The average yield to the acre Captain S. estimates at twenty-five bushels. In favorable seasons this yield is doubled; and if we can believe the statements often made upon respectable authority, it is sometimes quadrupled. There is no doubt that in favorable seasons—that is when the rains fall abundantly during the winter—the yield of wheat and all small grains in California is much greater per acre of land than in any part of the United States. The wheat fields of Captain S. are secured against the cattle and horses by ditches. Agriculture, among the native Californians, is in a very primitive state, and although Captain S. has introduced some American implements, still his ground is but imperfectly cultivated. With good cultivation the crops would be more certain and much more abundant. The crop from the same ground the second and third years, without sowing, is frequently very good.

Wheat is selling at the fort at two dollars and fifty cents per *fanega,* rather more than two bushels English measure. It brings the same price when delivered at San Francisco, near the mouth of the bay of San Francisco. It is transported from the Sacramento valley to a market in launches of about fifty tons burden. Unbolted flour sells at eight dollars per 100 pounds. The reason for this high price is the scarcity of flouring mills in the country. The mills that are now going up in various places will reduce the price of flour, and probably they will soon be able to grind all the wheat raised in the country. The streams of California afford excellent water power, but the flour consumed by Captain Sutter is ground by a very ordinary horse mill.

I saw near the fort a small patch of hemp, which had been sown as an experiment, in the spring, and had not been irrigated. I never saw a ranker growth of hemp in Kentucky. Vegetables of several kinds appeared to be abundant and in perfection, but I shall speak more particularly of the agricultural productions of California in another place, when my knowledge of the country and its resources becomes, from observation, more general and perfect.

Captain Sutter's dining room and his table furniture do not present a very luxurious appearance. The room is unfurnished, with the exception of a common deal table standing in the center, and some benches, which are substitutes for chairs. The table, when spread, presented a correspondingly primitive simplicity of aspect and of viands. The first course consisted of good soup, served to each guest in a china bowl with silver spoons. The bowls, after they had been used for this purpose, were taken away and cleansed by the Indian servant, and were afterwards used as tumblers or goblets, from which we drank our water. The next course consisted of two dishes of meat, one roasted and one fried, and both highly seasoned with onions. Bread, cheese, butter, and melons constituted the dessert. I am thus particular because I wish to convey as accurately as I can the style and mode of living in California of intelligent gentlemen of foreign birth, who have been accustomed to all the luxuries of the most refined civilization.

It is not for the purpose of criticizing, but to show how destitute the people of this naturally favored country have been of many of the most common comforts of domestic life, owing to the wretched system of government which has heretofore existed. Such has been the extortion of the government in the way of impost duties, that few supplies that are included among even the most ordinary elegancies of life have ever reached the inhabitants, and for these they have been compelled to pay prices that would be astonishing to a citizen of the United States or of Europe, and such as have impoverished the population. As a general fact, they cannot be obtained at any price, and hence those who have the ability to purchase are compelled to forego their use from necessity.

With our appetites, however, we enjoyed the dinner as much as if it had been served up in the most sumptuously-furnished dining saloon, with all the table appurtenances of polished silver, sparkling crystal, and snow-like porcelain. By our long journey we had learned to estimate the value of a thing for its actual utility and the amount of enjoyment it confers. The day is not distant when American enterprise and American ingenuity will furnish those adjuncts of civilization, of which California is now so destitute, and render a residence in this country one of the most luxurious upon the globe. The conversation at dinner turned upon the events that have recently occurred in the country, and that I shall narrate in another place.

From the 3rd to the 7th of September we remained encamped. Our camp is near an Indian *ranchería*. These *rancherías* consist of a number of huts constructed of a rib-work or frame of small poles or saplings in a conical shape, covered with straw, grass, or tule, a species of rush, which grows to the height of five or six feet. The huts are sometimes fifteen feet in diameter at their bases, and the number of them grouped together vary according to the number of the tribe which inhabits them. A different language in many respects is spoken at the different *rancherías*. In this remark I refer to the gentile Indians, as they are here called, and not to the christianized, the last of whom speak the Spanish. There was a large gathering at the *ranchería* on the night of the 6th to celebrate some event. Dancing, singing, loud shouting, and howling were continued without intermission the whole night. One of their orgies consisted in fixing a scalp upon a pole and dancing around it, accompanying the dance with, at first, a low, melancholy howl, then with loud shrieks and groans, until the performers appeared to become frantic with excitement of some kind, it would be difficult to tell what. The noise made by them was such as to prevent sleep, although a quarter of a mile distant from our camp.

The Sacramento River, at this point, is a stream nearly half a mile in width. The tide rises and falls some two or three feet. The water is perfectly limpid and fresh. The river is said to be navigable for craft of 100 tons burden, at all seasons, a hundred miles above this place. In the season of high waters, from January to July, it is navigable a much greater distance. The Sacramento rises above latitude 42° north and runs from north to south nearly parallel with the coast of the Pacific, until it empties into the bay of San Francisco by several mouths in latitude 38 1/2° north. It is fringed with timber, chiefly oak and sycamore. Grapevines and a variety of shrubbery ornament its banks and give a most charming effect when sailing upon its placid and limpid current. I never saw a more beautiful stream. In the rainy season, and in the spring, when the snows on the mountains are melting, it overflows its banks in many places. It abounds in fish, the most valuable of which is the salmon. These salmon are the largest and the fattest I have ever seen. I have seen salmon taken from the Sacramento five feet in length. All of its tributaries are equally rich in the finny tribe. American enterprise will soon develop the wealth contained in these streams, which hitherto has been entirely neglected.

The site of the town of Nueva Helvetia, which has been laid out by Captain Sutter, is about a mile and a half from the Sacramento. It is on an elevation of the plain and not subject to overflow when the waters of the river are at their highest known point. There are now but three or four small houses in this town, but I have little doubt that it will soon become a place of importance.

Near the *embarcadero* of New Helvetia is a large Indian "sweat house," or *temescál,* an appendage of most of the *rancherías.* The "sweat house" is the most important medical agent employed by these Indians. It has, I do not doubt, the effect of consigning many of them to their graves, long before their appointed time. A "sweat house" is an excavation in the earth, to the depth of six or eight feet, arched over with slabs split from logs. There is a single small aperture or skylight in the roof. These slabs are covered to the depth of several feet with earth. There is a narrow entrance, with steps leading down and into this subterraneous apartment. Rude shelves are erected around the walls, upon which the invalids repose their bodies. The door is closed and no air is admitted except from the small aperture in the roof, through which escapes the smoke of a fire kindled in the center of the dungeon. This fire heats the apartment until the perspiration rolls from the naked bodies of the invalids in streams. I incautiously entered one of these caverns during the operation above described and was in a few moments so nearly suffocated with the heat, smoke, and impure air that I found it difficult to make my way out.

In the afternoon of the 7th we received a note from Captain Sutter, stating that he had succeeded in obtaining a room in the fort for our accommodation and inviting us to accept of it. He sent two servants to assist in packing our baggage; and accepting the invitation, we took up our lodgings in the fort. By this change we were relieved from the annoyance of mosquitoes, which have troubled us much during the night at our encampment. But with this exception, so long have we been accustomed to sleeping in the open air, with no shelter but our blankets and the canopy of the heavens, that our encampment was preferable to our quarters within the confined walls of the fort.

It is scarcely possible to imagine a more delightful temperature or a climate which is more agreeable and uniform. The sky is cloudless, without the slightest film of vapor apparent in all the vast azure vault. In the middle of the day the sun shines with great power, but in the shade it is nowhere uncomfortable. At night so pure is the atmosphere that the moon gives a light sufficiently powerful for the purposes of the reader or student who has good eyesight. There is no necessity of burning the "midnight oil." Nature here lights the candle for the bookworm.

On the 9th, we commenced preparations for leaving the fort for San Francisco, a journey by land of about 200 miles. Our intention was to leave early the next morning. While thus engaged, some couriers arrived from the settlements on the Sacramento, about 100 miles north, with the startling information that 1,000 Walla-Walla Indians, from Oregon, had made their appearance in the valley for hostile purposes. The couriers, who were themselves settlers, appeared to be in great alarm and stated that they had seen the advance party of the Walla-Wallas, and that their object was to assault the fort for a murder, which they alleged had been committed one or two years since, by an American upon a chief of their tribe, and for some indebtedness of Captain Sutter to them, in cattle, etc. In the event of a failure in their assault upon the fort, then they intended to drive off all the cattle belonging to the settlers in the valley. This was the substance of their information. It was so alarming that we postponed at once our departure for San Francisco and volunteered such assistance as we could render in defending the fort against this formidable invasion.

The Walla-Wallas are a powerful and warlike tribe of Indians, inhabiting a district of country on the Columbia River. They are reported to be good marksmen and fight with great bravery and desperation. Their warriors are armed with good rifles and an abundance of ammunition, which they procure from the Hudson's Bay Company. They are rapidly advancing in civilization, and many of them have good farms under cultivation, with numerous herds of cattle and horses.

Couriers were immediately dispatched in every direction to apprise the settlers in the valley of the invasion, and to the nearest military posts for such assistance as they could render under the circumstances. The twelve pieces of artillery by which the fort is defended were put in order, and all inside were busily employed in preparing for the expected combat. Indian spies were also dispatched to reconnoiter and discover the position and actual number of the invaders.

The spies returned to the fort on the 11th without having seen the Walla-Walla invaders. A small party of some forty or fifty only are supposed to be about twenty-five or thirty miles distant, on the opposite side of the Sacramento. On the 12th, Lieutenant Revere[1] of the Navy, with a party of twenty-five men, arrived at the fort from Sonoma to reinforce the garrison; and on the morning of the 13th, it having been pretty well ascertained that the reported 1,000 hostile Walla-Wallas were a small party only of men, women, and children, whose disposition was entirely pacific, we determined to proceed immediately on our journey to San Francisco....

September 13. We commenced today our journey from New Helvetia to San Francisco. Our party consisted, including myself, of Colonel Russell, Dr. McKee of Monterey, Mr. Pickett, a traveler in the country, recently from Oregon, and an Indian servant, who

---

[1] Joseph Warren Revere (1812–1880), grandson of Paul Revere, came to California in 1845 onboard the *Portsmouth*. He raised the U.S. flag at Sonoma and went on to serve as a brigadier general for the Union in the Civil War.

had been furnished us by Captain Sutter. Starting about three o'clock p.m., we traveled in a south course over a flat plain until sunset and encamped near a small lake on the *rancho* of Mr. [Martin] Murphy, near the Cosçumne [Cosumnes] River, a tributary of the Sacramento, which heads near the foot of the Sierra Nevada. The stream is small, but the bottom lands are extensive and rich. Mr. Murphy has been settled in California about two years and, with his wife and several children, has resided at this place sixteen months, during which time he has erected a comfortable dwelling-house and other necessary buildings and conveniences. His wheat crop was abundant this year, and he presented us with as much milk and fresh butter as we desired. The grass on the upland plain over which we have traveled is brown and crisp from the annual drought. In the low bottom, it is still green. Distance: eighteen miles.

September 14. We crossed the Cosçumne River about a mile from our camp and traveled over a level plain covered with luxuriant grass and timbered with the evergreen oak, until three o'clock, when we crossed the Mickelemes [Mokelumne] River, another tributary of the Sacramento, and encamped on its southern bank in a beautiful grove of live-oaks. The Mickelemes, where we crossed it, is considerably larger than the Cosçumne. The soil of the bottom appears to be very rich and produces the finest qualities of grasses. The grass on the upland is also abundant, but at this time it is brown and dead. We passed through large tracts of wild oats during the day; the stalks are generally from three to five feet in length.

Our Indian servant, or *vaquero,* feigned sickness this morning, and we discharged him. As soon as he obtained his discharge, he was entirely relieved from the excruciating agonies under which he had affected to be suffering for several hours. Eating his breakfast and mounting his horse, he galloped off in the direction of the fort. We overtook this afternoon an English sailor named Jack, who was traveling towards Monterey, and we employed him as cook and hostler for the remainder of the journey.

A variety of autumnal flowers, generally of a brilliant yellow, are in bloom along the beautiful and romantic banks of the rivulet. Distance: twenty-five miles.

September 15. Our horses were frightened last night by bears, and this morning, with the exception of those that were picketed, had strayed so far that we did not recover them until ten o'clock. Our route has continued over a flat plain, generally covered with luxuriant grass, wild oats, and a variety of sparkling flowers. The soil is composed of a rich argillaceous loam. Large tracts of the land are evidently subject to annual inundations. About noon we reached a small lake surrounded by tule. There being no trail for our guidance, we experienced some difficulty in shaping our course so as to strike the San Joaquín River at the usual fording place. Our man Jack, by some neglect or mistake of his own, lost sight of us, and we were compelled to proceed without him. This afternoon we saw several large droves of antelope and deer. Game of all kinds appears to be very abundant in this rich valley. Passing through large tracts of tule, we reached the San Joaquín River at dark and encamped on the eastern bank. Here we immediately made large fires and discharged pistols as signals to our man Jack, but he did not come into camp. Distance: thirty-five miles.

September 16. Jack came into camp while we were breakfasting, leading his tired horse. He had bivouacked on the plain, and fearful that his horse would break loose if he tied him, he held the animal by the bridle all night.

The ford of the San Joaquín is about forty or fifty miles from its mouth. At this season the water is at its lowest stage. The stream at the ford is probably 100 yards in breadth, and our animals crossed it without much difficulty, the water reaching about mid-way of their bodies. Oak and small willows are the principal growth of wood skirting the river. Soon after we crossed the San Joaquín this morning, we met two men—couriers—bearing dispatches from Commodore Stockton,[2] the governor and commander-in-chief in California, to Sutter's Fort. Entering upon the broad plain, we passed, in about three miles, a small lake, the water of which was so much impregnated with alkali as to be undrinkable. The grass is brown and crisp, but the seed upon it is evidence that it had fully matured before the drought affected it. The plain is furrowed with numerous deep trails, made by the droves of wild horses, elk, deer, and antelope, which roam over and graze upon it. The hunting sportsman can here enjoy his favorite pleasure to its fullest extent.

Having determined to deviate from our direct course, in order to visit the *rancho* of Dr. Marsh,[3] we parted from Messrs. McRee and Pickett about noon. We passed during the afternoon several tule marshes, with which the plain of the San Joaquín is dotted. At a distance, the tule of these marshes presents the appearance of immense fields of ripened corn. The marshes are now nearly dry, and to shorten our journey we crossed several of them without difficulty. A month earlier, this would not have been practicable. I have but little doubt that these marshes would make fine rice plantations, and perhaps, if properly drained, they might produce the sugarcane.

While pursuing our journey we frequently saw large droves of wild horses and elk grazing quietly upon the plain. No spectacle of

---

[2] Commodore Robert F. Stockton (1795–1866) was the self-declared military governor of California from July 1846 to January 1847.

[3] John Marsh (1799–1856), former Harvard graduate, Indian agent, and amateur physician, arrived in California in 1836. Using his Harvard degree as a license to practice medicine, he opened California's first doctor's office in Los Angeles, accepting hides and cattle as payment. Famously cantankerous and miserly, Marsh bought a *rancho* near Mount Diablo (worked by local Indians) and was a tireless promoter of California's charms. Three of his Indian *vaqueros,* upset after years of maltreatment and low wages, murdered him in 1856.

moving life can present a more animated and beautiful appearance than a herd of wild horses. They were divided into droves of some one or two hundred. When they noticed us, attracted by curiosity to discover what we were, they would start and run almost with the fleetness of the wind in the direction toward us. But arriving within a distance of 200 yards, they would suddenly halt, and after bowing their necks into graceful curves and looking steadily at us a few moments, with loud snortings they would wheel about and bound away with the same lightning speed. These evolutions they would repeat several times, until having satisfied their curiosity, they would bid us a final adieu and disappear behind the undulations of the plain.

The herds of elk were much more numerous. Some of them numbered at least 2,000, and with their immense antlers, presented, when running, a very singular and picturesque appearance. We approached some of these herds within fifty yards before they took the alarm. Beef in California is so abundant, and of so fine a quality, that game is but little hunted and not much prized. Hence the elk, deer, and even antelope are comparatively very tame and rarely run from the traveler, unless he rides very near them. Some of these elk are as large as a medium-sized Mexican mule.

We arrived at the *rancho* of Dr. Marsh about five o'clock p.m., greatly fatigued with the day's ride. The residence of Dr. M. is romantically situated near the foot of one of the most elevated mountains in the range separating the valley of the San Joaquín from the plain surrounding the bay of San Francisco. It is called Mount Diablo and may be seen in clear weather a great distance. The dwelling of Dr. M. is a small, one-story house, rudely constructed of *adobes* and divided into two or three apartments. The flooring is of earth, like the walls. A table or two, and some benches and a bed, are all the furniture it contains. Such are the privations to which those who settle in new countries must submit. Dr. M. is a native of New England, a graduate of Harvard University, and a gentleman of fine natural abilities and extensive scientific and literary acquirements. He emigrated to California some seven or eight years since, after having traveled through most of the Mexican states. He speaks the Spanish language fluently and correctly, and his accurate knowledge of Mexican institutions, laws, and customs was fully displayed in his conversation in regard to them. He obtained the grant of land upon which he now resides—some ten or twelve miles square—four or five years ago; and although he has been constantly harassed by the wild Indians, who have several times stolen all his horses and sometimes numbers of his cattle, he has succeeded in permanently establishing himself. The present number of cattle on his *rancho* is about 2,000, and the increase of the present year he estimates at 500.

I noticed near the house a vegetable garden, with the usual variety of vegetables. In another enclosure was the commencement of an extensive vineyard, the fruit of which (now ripe) exceeds in delicacy of flavor any grapes that I have ever tasted. This grape is not indigenous but was introduced by the *padres* when they first established themselves in the country. The soil and climate of California have probably improved it. Many of the clusters are eight and ten inches in length and weigh several pounds. The fruit is of medium size, and in color a dark purple. The rind is very thin, and when broken, the pulp dissolves in the mouth immediately. Although Dr. M. has just commenced his vineyard, he has made several casks of wine this year, which is now in a state of fermentation. I tasted here, for the first time, *aguardiente,* or brandy distilled from the Californian grape. Its flavor is not unpleasant, and age, I do not doubt, would render it equal to the brandies of France. Large quantities of wine and *aguardiente* are made from the extensive vineyards farther south. Dr. M. informed me that his lands had produced a hundredfold of wheat without irrigation. This yield seems almost incredible; but if we can believe the statements of men

of unimpeached veracity, there have been numerous instances of reproduction of wheat in California equaling and even exceeding this.

Some time in July, a vessel [the *Brooklyn*] arrived at San Francisco from New York, which had been chartered and freighted principally by a party of Mormon emigrants, numbering between two
and three hundred, women and children included. These Mormons
are about making a settlement for agricultural purposes on the San
Joaquín River, above the *rancho* of Dr. Marsh. Two of the women
and one of the men are now here, waiting for the return of the main
party, which has gone up the river to explore and select a suitable
site for the settlement. The women are young, neatly dressed, and
one of them may be called good-looking. Captain Gant—formerly
of the U.S. Army—in very bad health, is also residing here. He has
crossed the Rocky Mountains eight times, and, in various trapping
excursions, has explored nearly every river between the settlements
of the United States and the Pacific Ocean.

The house of Dr. Marsh being fully occupied, we made our
beds in a shed a short distance from it. Suspended from one of the
poles forming the frame of this shed was a portion of the carcass of
a recently slaughtered beef. The meat was very fat, the muscular
portions of it presenting that marbled appearance produced by a
mixture of the fat and lean, so agreeable to the sight and palate of
the epicure. The horned cattle of California that I have thus far seen
are the largest and the handsomest in shape that I ever saw. There
is certainly no breed in the United States equaling them in size. They,
as well as the horses, subsist entirely upon the indigenous grasses
at all seasons of the year; and such are the nutritious qualities of the
herbage, that the former are always in condition for slaughtering,
and the latter have as much flesh upon them as is desirable, unless
(which is often the case) they are kept up at hard work and denied
the privilege of eating, or are broken down by hard riding. The varieties of grass are very numerous, and nearly all of them are heavily

seeded when ripe and are equal if not superior, as food for animals, to corn and oats. The horses are not as large as the breeds of the United States, but in point of symmetrical proportions and in capacity for endurance, they are fully equal to our best breeds. The distance we have traveled today I estimate at thirty-five miles.

September 17. The temperature of the mornings is most agreeable, and every other phenomenon accompanying it is correspondingly delightful to the senses. Our breakfast consisted of warm bread, made of unbolted flour; stewed beef, seasoned with *chile colorado,* a species of red pepper; and *frijoles,* a dark colored bean; with coffee. After breakfast I walked with Dr. Marsh to the summit of a conical hill, about a mile distant from his house, from which the view of the plain on the north, south, and east, and the more broken and mountainous country on the west is very extensive and highly picturesque. The hills and the plain are ornamented with the evergreen oak, sometimes in clumps or groves, at others standing solitary. On the summits and in the gorges of the mountains, the cedar, pine, and fir display their tall, symmetrical shapes; and the San Joaquín, at a distance of about ten miles, is belted by a dense forest of oak, sycamore, and smaller timber and shrubbery. The herds of cattle are scattered over the plain—some of them grazing upon the brown but nutritious grass; others sheltering themselves from the sun, under the wide-spreading branches of the oaks. The *toute ensemble* of the landscape is charming.

Leaving Dr. Marsh's about three o'clock p.m., we traveled fifteen miles over a rolling and well-watered country, covered generally with wild oats, and arrived at the residence of Mr. Robert Livermore[4] just before dark. We were most kindly and hospitably

---

[4] Robert Livermore (1799–1858) was an English sailor who abandoned his ship in California in 1822, married Josefa Higuera, and established a large *rancho* in present-day Livermore Valley.

received and entertained by Mr. L. and his interesting family. After our mules and baggage had been cared for, we were introduced to the principal room in the house, which consisted of a number of small *adobe* buildings, erected apparently at different times and connected together. Here we found chairs and, for the first time in California, saw a sideboard set out with glass tumblers and chinaware. A decanter of *aguardiente*, a bowl of loaf-sugar, and a pitcher of cold water from the spring were set before us; and being duly honored, had a most reviving influence upon our spirits as well as our corporeal energies. Suspended from the walls of the room were numerous coarse engravings—highly-colored with green, blue, and crimson paints—representing the Virgin Mary and many of the saints. These engravings are held in great veneration by the devout Catholics of this country. In the corners of the room were two comfortable-looking beds with clean white sheets and pillowcases, a sight with which my eyes have not been greeted for many months.

The table was soon set out and covered with a linen cloth of snowy whiteness, upon which were placed dishes of stewed beef—seasoned with *chile colorado*—*frijoles,* and a plentiful supply of *tortillas*, with an excellent cup of tea, to the merits of which we did ample justice. Never were men blessed with better appetites than we are at the present time.

Mr. Livermore has been a resident of California nearly thirty years; and having married into one of the wealthy families of the country, is the proprietor of some of the best lands for tillage and grazing. An *arroyo,* or small rivulet fed by springs, runs through his *rancho* in such a course that, if expedient, he could, without much expense, irrigate one or two thousand acres. Irrigation in this part of California, however, seems to be entirely unnecessary for the production of wheat or any of the small grains. To produce maize, potatoes, and garden vegetables, irrigation is indispensable. Mr.

Livermore has on his *rancho* about 3,500 head of cattle. His horses, during the late disturbances, have nearly all been driven off or stolen by the Indians. I saw in his *corral* a flock of sheep numbering several hundred. They are of good size, and the mutton is said to be of an excellent quality, but the wool is coarse. It is, however, well adapted to the only manufacture of wool that is carried on in the country—coarse blankets and *serapes*. But little attention is paid to hogs here, although the breeds are as fine as I have ever seen elsewhere. Beef being so abundant and of a quality so superior, pork is not prized by the native Californians.

The Señora L. is the first Hispano-American lady I have seen since arriving in the country. She was dressed in a white cambric robe, loosely banded round the waist, and without ornament of any kind, except several rings on her small, delicate fingers. Her complexion is that of a dark brunette, but lighter and more clear than the skin of most Californian women. The dark, lustrous eye; the long black and glossy hair; the natural ease, grace, and vivacity of manners and conversation—characteristic of Spanish ladies—were fully displayed by her from the moment of our introduction. The children, especially two or three little *señoritas*, were very beautiful and manifested a remarkable degree of sprightliness and intelligence. One of them presented me with a small basket wrought from a species of tough grass and ornamented with the plumage of birds of a variety of brilliant colors. It was a beautiful specimen of Indian ingenuity.

Retiring to bed about ten o'clock, I enjoyed, the first time for four months, the luxury of clean sheets with a mattress and a soft pillow. My enjoyment, however, was not unmixed with regret, for I noticed that several members of the family, to accommodate us with lodgings in the house, slept in the piazza outside. To have objected to sleeping in the house, however, would have been considered discourteous and offensive.

September 18. Early this morning a bullock was brought up and slaughtered in front of the house. The process of slaughtering a beef is as follows: a *vaquero,* mounted on a trained horse, and provided with a *lasso,* proceeds to the place where the herd is grazing. Selecting an animal, he soon secures it by throwing the noose of the *lasso* over the horns and fastening the other end around the pommel of the saddle. During the first struggles of the animal for liberty, which usually are very violent, the *vaquero* sits firmly in his seat and keeps his horse in such a position that the fury and strength of the beast are wasted without producing any other result than his own exhaustion. The animal, soon ascertaining that he cannot release himself from the rope, submits to be pulled along to the place of execution. Arriving here, the *vaquero* winds the *lasso* around the legs of the doomed beast and throws him to the ground, where he lies perfectly helpless and motionless. Dismounting from his horse, he then takes from his leggin the butcher knife that he always carries with him and sticks the animal in the throat. He soon bleeds to death, when, in an incredibly short space of time for such a performance, the carcass is flayed and quartered, and the meat is either roasting before the fire or simmering in the stewpan. The lassoing and slaughter of a bullock is one of the most exciting sports of the Californians; and the daring horsemanship and dexterous use of the lariat usually displayed on these occasions are worthy of admiration. I could not but notice the Golgotha-like aspect of the grounds surrounding the house. The bones of cattle were thickly strewn in all directions, showing a terrible slaughter of the four-footed tribe and a prodigious consumption of flesh.

A *carretada* of fossil oyster shells was shown me by Mr. Livermore, which had been hauled for the purpose of being manufactured into lime. Some of these shells were eight inches in length and of corresponding breadth and thickness. They were dug from a hill two or three miles distant, which is composed almost entirely of this fossil. Several bones belonging to the skeleton of a whale, discovered by Mr. L. on the summit of one of the highest elevations in the vicinity of his residence, were shown to me. The skeleton when discovered was nearly perfect and entirely exposed, and its elevation above the level of the sea between one and two thousand feet. How the huge aquatic monster, of which this skeleton is the remains, managed to make his dry bed on the summit of an elevated mountain, more experienced geologists than myself will hereafter determine. I have an opinion on the subject, however, but it is so contrary in some respects to the received geological theories that I will not now hazard it.

Leaving Mr. Livermore's about nine o'clock a.m., we traveled three or four miles over a level plain, upon which immense herds of cattle were grazing. When we approached they fled from us, with as much alarm as herds of deer and elk. From this plain we entered a hilly country, covered to the summits of the elevations with wild oats and tufts or bunches of a species of [perennial bunch] grass, which remains green through the whole season. Cattle were scattered through these hills, and more sumptuous grazing they could not desire. Small streams of water, fed by springs, flow through the hollows and ravines, which, as well as the hillsides, are timbered with the evergreen oak and a variety of smaller trees. About two o'clock p.m., we crossed an *arroyo* that runs through a narrow gorge of the hills and struck an artificial wagon road, excavated and embanked so as to afford a passage for wheeled vehicles along the steep hillside. A little farther on we crossed a very rudely constructed bridge. These are the first signs of road-making I have seen in the country. Emerging from the hills, the southern arm of the bay of San Francisco came in view, separated from us by a broad and fertile plain some ten or twelve miles in width, sloping gradually down to the shore of the bay and watered by several small creeks and estuaries.

We soon entered through a narrow street the Mission of San José, or St. Joseph. Passing the squares of one-story *adobe* buildings, once inhabited by thousands of busy Indians, but now deserted, roofless, and crumbling into ruins, we reached the *plaza* in front of the church and the massive two-story edifices occupied by the *padres* during the flourishing epoch of the establishment. These were in good repair, but the doors and windows with the exception of one were closed, and nothing of moving life was visible except a donkey or two, standing near a fountain that gushed its waters into a capacious stone trough. Dismounting from our mules, we entered the open door, and here we found two Frenchmen dressed in sailor costume, with a quantity of coarse shirts, pantaloons, stockings, and other small articles, together with *aguardiente,* which they designed retailing to such of the natives in the vicinity as chose to become their customers. They were itinerant merchants—or peddlers—and had opened their wares here for a day or two only, or so long as they could find purchasers.

Having determined to remain here the residue of the day and the night, we inquired of the Frenchmen if there was any family in the place that could furnish us with food. They directed us to a house on the opposite side of the *plaza,* to which we immediately repaired. The *señora,* a dark-skinned and rather shriveled and filthy specimen of the fair sex—but with a black, sparkling, and intelligent eye—met us at the door of the miserable hovel and invited us in. In one corner of this wretched and foul abode was a pile of raw hides, and in another, a heap of wheat. The only furniture it contained were two small benches, or stools, one of which, being higher than the other, appeared to have been constructed for a table. We informed the *señora* that we were travelers and wished refreshment and lodgings for the night. *"Está bueno, señores, está bueno,"* was her reply; and she immediately left us, and opening the door of the kitchen, commenced the preparation of our dinner. The interior of the kitchen, of which I had a good view through the door, was more revolting in its filthiness than the room in which we were seated. In a short time, so industrious was our hostess, our dinner—consisting of two plates of jerked beef (stewed and seasoned with *chile colorado*), a plate of *tortillas*, and a bowl of coffee—was set out upon the most elevated stool. There were no knives, forks, or spoons on the table. Our amiable landlady apologized for this deficiency of table furniture, saying that she was *"muy pobre"* (very poor) and possessed none of these table implements. "Fingers were made before forks," and in our recent travels we had learned to use them as substitutes, so that we found no difficulty in conveying the meat from the plates to our mouths.

Belonging to the mission are two gardens, enclosed by high *adobe* walls. After dinner we visited one of these. The area of the enclosure contains fifteen or twenty acres of ground, the whole of which is planted with fruit trees and grapevines. There are about 600 pear trees and a large number of apple and peach trees, all bearing fruit in great abundance and in full perfection. The quality of the pears is excellent, but the apples and peaches are indifferent. The grapes have been gathered, as I suppose, for I saw none upon the vines, which appeared healthy and vigorous. The gardens are irrigated with very little trouble from large springs that flow from the hills a short distance above them. Numerous aqueducts, formerly conveying and distributing water over an extensive tract of land surrounding the mission, are still visible, but as the land is not now cultivated, they at present contain no water.

The mission buildings cover fifty acres of ground, perhaps more, and are all constructed of *adobes* with tile roofs. Those houses or barracks that were occupied by the Indian families are built in compact squares, one story in height. They are generally partitioned into two rooms, one fronting on the street, the other upon a court or *corral* in the rear. The main buildings of the mission are two stories in height, with wide corridors in front and rear. The walls are massive and, if protected from the winter rains, will stand for ages. But if exposed to the storms by the decay of the projecting roofs or by leaks in the main roof, they will soon crumble or sink into shapeless heaps of mud. I passed through extensive warehouses and immense rooms, once occupied for the manufacture of woolen blankets and other articles, with the rude machinery still standing in them, but unemployed. Filth and desolation have taken the place of cleanliness and busy life. The granary was very capacious, and its dimensions were an evidence of the exuberant fertility of the soil, when properly cultivated under the superintendence of the *padres*. The calaboose is a miserable dark room of two apartments, one with a small loophole in the wall, the other a dungeon without light or ventilation. The stocks, and several other inventions for the punishment of offenders, are still standing in this prison. I requested permission to examine the interior of the church, but it was locked up, and no person in the mission was in possession of the key. Its length I should suppose is from 100 to 120 feet, and its breadth between thirty and forty, with small exterior pretensions to architectural ornament or symmetry of proportions.

Returning from our rambles about the mission, we found that our landlady had been reinforced by an elderly woman, whom she introduced as *"mí madre,"* and two or three Indian *muchachas,* or girls, clad in a costume not differing much from that of our mother Eve. The latter were obese in their figures, and the mingled perspiration and filth standing upon their skins were anything but agreeable to the eye. The two *señoras*, with these handmaids near them, were sitting in front of the house, busily engaged in executing some needlework.

Supper being prepared and discussed, our landlady informed us that she had a husband, who was absent but would return in the course of the night, and if he found strange men in the house, he would be much offended with her. She had therefore directed her *muchachas* to sweep out one of the deserted and half-ruined rooms on the opposite square, to which we could remove our baggage and in which we could lodge during the night; and as soon as the necessary preparations were made, we retired to our dismal apartment. The "compound of villainous smells" that saluted our nostrils when we entered our dormitory for the night augured unfavorably for repose. The place had evidently been the abode of horses, cattle, pigs, and foul vermin of every description. But with the aid of a dark-colored tallow candle, which gave just light enough to display the murkiness and filth surrounding us, we spread our beds in the cleanest places and laid down to rest. Distance traveled: eighteen miles.

September 19. Several Californians came into the mission during the night or early this morning; among them the husband of our hostess, who was very kind and cordial in his greetings. While our man Jack was saddling and packing the mules, they gathered around us to the number of a dozen or more and were desirous of trading their horses for articles of clothing; articles which many of them appeared to stand greatly in need of, but which we had not to part from. Their pertinacity exceeded the bounds of civility, as I thought; but I was not in a good humor, for the fleas, bugs, and other vermin, which infested our miserable lodgings, had caused me a sleepless night by goring my body until the blood oozed from the skin in countless places. These ruinous missions are prolific generators and the nurseries of vermin of all kinds, as the hapless traveler who tarries in them a few hours will learn to his sorrow. When these bloodthirsty assailants once make a lodgment in the clothing or bedding of the unfortunate victim of their attacks, such are their courage and perseverance that they never capitulate. "Blood or death" is their motto—the war against them, to be successful, must be a war of extermination.

Poor as our hostess was, she nevertheless was reluctant to receive any compensation for her hospitality. We, however, insisted upon her receiving a dollar from each of us *(dos pesos),* which she finally accepted; and after shaking us cordially by the hand she bade us an affectionate *adiós,* and we proceeded on our journey.

From the mission of San José to the *pueblo* of San José the distance is fifteen miles, for the most part over a level and highly fertile plain, producing a variety of indigenous grasses, among which I noticed several species of clover and mustard, large tracts of which we rode through, the stalks varying from six to ten feet in height. The plain is watered by several *arroyos,* skirted with timber, generally the evergreen oak.

We met this morning a Californian *carreta,* or traveling cart, freighted with women and children, bound on a pleasure excursion. The *carreta* is the rudest specimen of the wheeled vehicle I have seen. The wheels are transverse sections of a log, and are usually about two-and-a-half feet in diameter, and varying in thickness from the center to the rim. These wheels are coupled together by an axletree, into which a tongue is inserted. On the axletree and tongue rests a frame, constructed of square pieces of timber, six or eight feet in length, and four or five in breadth, into which are inserted a number of stakes about four feet in length. This framework being covered and floored with raw hides, the carriage is complete. The *carreta* that we met was drawn by two yokes of oxen, driven by an Indian *vaquero,* mounted on a horse. In the rear were two *caballeros,* riding fine spirited horses, with gaudy trappings. They were dressed in steeple-crowned, glazed *sombreros, serapes* of fiery colors, velvet (cotton) *calzoneros,* white cambric *calzoncillos,* and leggins and shoes of undressed leather. Their spurs were of immense size.

The party halted as soon as we met them, the men touching their heavy *sombreros* and uttering the usual salutation of the morning, *"Buenos días, señores,"* and shaking hands with us very cordially. The same salutation was repeated by all the *señoras* and *señoritas* in the *carreta*. In dress and personal appearance the women of this party were much inferior to the men. Their skins were dark, sallow, and shriveled, and their costume, a loose gown and reboso, were made of very common materials. The children, however, were all handsome, with sparkling eyes and ruddy complexions. Women and children were seated, *à la Turque,* on the bottom of the *carreta,* there being no raised seats in the vehicle.

We arrived at the *pueblo* de San José about twelve o'clock. There being no hotels in California, we were much at loss where to apply for refreshments and lodgings for the night. Soon, however, we were met by Captain Fisher, a native of Massachusetts, but a resident of this country for twenty years or more, who invited us to his house. We were most civilly received by Señora F., who, although she did not speak English, seemed to understand it very well. She is a native of the southern Pacific coast of Mexico, and a lady of fine manners and personal appearance. Her eldest daughter, about thirteen years of age, is very beautiful. An excellent dinner was soon set out, with a variety of the native wines of California and other liquors. We could not have felt ourselves more happy and more at home, even at our own firesides and in the midst of our own families.

The *pueblo* de San José is a village containing some six or eight hundred inhabitants. It is situated in what is called the *pueblo* valley, about fifteen miles south of the southern shore of the bay of San Francisco. Through a navigable creek, vessels of considerable burden can approach the town within a distance of five or six miles. The *embarcadero,* or landing, I think, is six miles from the *pueblo*. The fertile plain between this and the town, at certain seasons of the

year, is sometimes inundated. The *pueblo* valley, which is eighty or
100 miles in length, varying from ten to twenty in breadth, is well
watered by the Río Santa Clara and numerous *arroyos,* and is one
of the most fertile and picturesque plains in California. For pastoral charms, fertility of soil, variety of productions, and delicious
voluptuousness of climate and scenery, it cannot be surpassed. This
valley, if properly cultivated, would alone produce breadstuffs
enough to supply millions of population. The buildings of the
pueblo, with few exceptions, are constructed of *adobes,* and none
of them have even the smallest pretensions to architectural taste or
beauty. The church, which is situated near the center of the town,
exteriorly resembles a huge Dutch barn. The streets are irregular,
every man having erected his house in a position most convenient
to him. Aqueducts convey water from the Santa Clara river to all
parts of the town. In the main *plaza,* hundreds—perhaps thousands—of squirrels, whose abodes are underground, have their residences. They are of a brownish color and about the size of our common gray squirrel. Emerging from their subterraneous abodes, they
skip and leap about over the *plaza* without the least concern, no one
molesting them.

The population of the place is composed chiefly of native Californian land proprietors. Their *ranchos* are in the valley, but their
residences and gardens are in the town. We visited this afternoon
the garden of Señor Don Antonio Suñol.[5] He received us with much
politeness and conducted us through his garden. Apples, pears,
peaches, figs, oranges, and grapes, with other fruits that I do not
now recollect, were growing and ripening. The grapevines were
bowed to the ground with the luxuriance and weight of the yield;
and more delicious fruit I never tasted. From the garden we crossed

---

[5] Spanish-born Antonio María Suñol (1800–1865) came to California in 1818 while
serving in the French navy. He jumped ship in Monterey, married into the prominent
Bernal family, and worked a *rancho* near the present-day city of Fremont.

over to a flouring mill recently erected by a son-in-law of Don Antonio, a Frenchman by birth. The mill is a creditable enterprise to the proprietor, and he will coin money from its operations.

The *pueblo* de San José is one of the oldest settlements in Alta California. Captain Fisher pointed out to me a house built of *adobes*, which has been standing between eighty and ninety years, and no house in the place appeared to be more substantial or in better repair. A garrison, composed of marines from the United States ships and volunteers enlisted from the American settlers in the country, is now stationed here. The post is under the command of Purser Watmough, of the United States sloop-of-war *Portsmouth,* commanded by Captain [John] Montgomery. During the evening I visited several public places (bar-rooms) where I saw men and women engaged promiscuously at the game of monte. Gambling is a universal vice in California. All classes and both sexes participate in its excitements to some extent. The games, however, while I was present, were conducted with great propriety and decorum so far as the native Californians were concerned. The loud swearing and other turbulent demonstrations generally proceeded from the unsuccessful foreigners. I could not but observe the contrast between the two races in this respect. The one bore their losses with stoical composure and indifference; the other announced each unsuccessful bet with profane imprecations and maledictions. Excitement prompted the hazards of the former, avarice the latter.

September 20. The morning was cloudy and cool; but the clouds broke away about nine o'clock, and the sun shone from a vaporless sky, as usual. We met, at the *pueblo,* Mr. Grove Cook, a native of Gerrard County, Kentucky, but for many years a resident of California. He is the proprietor of a *rancho* in the vicinity. We determined to leave our mules in charge of Mr. Cook's *vaquero* and proceed to San Francisco on hired horses. The distance from the *pueblo* de San José to San Francisco is called sixty miles. The time occupied in performing the journey—on Californian horses at Californian speed—is generally six or seven hours. Procuring horses for the journey and leaving our baggage, with the exception of a change of clothing, we left the *pueblo* about eleven o'clock a.m.

The Mission of Santa Clara is situated about two-and-a-half miles from the town. A broad *alameda*, shaded by stately trees (elms and willows) planted by the *padres*, extends nearly the entire distance, forming a most beautiful drive or walk for equestrians or pedestrians. The motive of the *padres* in planting this avenue was to afford the devout *señoras* and *señoritas* a shade from the sun when walking from the *pueblo* to the church at the mission to attend Mass. A few minutes over the smooth, level road, at the rapid speed of our fresh Californian horses, brought us to the mission, where we halted to make our observations. This mission is not so extensive in its buildings as that of San José, but the houses are generally in better repair. They are constructed of *adobes*. The church was open, and entering the interior, I found the walls hung with coarse paintings and engravings of the saints, etc. The chancel is decorated with numerous images and symbolical ornaments used by the priests in their worship. Gold paper and tinsel, in barbaric taste, are plastered without stint upon nearly every object that meets the eye, so that when on festive occasions the church is lighted, it must present a very glittering appearance.

The rich lands surrounding the mission are entirely neglected. I did not notice a foot of ground under cultivation, except the garden enclosure, which contained a variety of fruits and plants of the temperate and tropical climates. From want of care these are fast decaying. Some excellent pears were furnished us by Mrs. Bennett, an American lady of amazonian proportions, who, with her family of sons, has taken up her residence in one of the buildings of the mission. The picture of decay and ruin presented by this once flourishing establishment, surrounded by a country so fertile and scenery so enchanting, is a most melancholy spectacle to the passing traveler and speaks a language of loud condemnation against the government.

Proceeding on our journey, we traveled fifteen miles over a flat plain, timbered with groves and parks of evergreen oaks, and covered with a great variety of grasses, wild oats, and mustard. So rank is the growth of mustard in many places that it is with difficulty that a horse can penetrate through it. Numerous birds flitted from tree to tree, making the groves musical with their harmonious notes. The black-tailed deer bounded frequently across our path, and the lurking and stealthy *coyotes* were continually in view. We halted at a small cabin, with a *corral* near it, in order to breathe our horses and refresh ourselves. Captain Fisher had kindly filled a small sack with bread, cheese, roasted beef, and a small jug of excellent schiedam. Entering the cabin, the interior of which was cleanly, we found a solitary woman—young, neatly dressed, and displaying many personal charms. With the characteristic ease and grace of a Spanish woman, she gave the usual salutation for the hour of the day, *"Buenas tardes, señores caballeros,"* to which we responded by a suitable salutation. We requested of our hostess some water, which she furnished us immediately in an earthen bowl. Opening our sack of provisions, we spread them upon the table and invited the *señora* to partake of them with us, which invitation she accepted without the slightest hesitation and with much good nature, vivacity, and even thankfulness for our politeness. There are no women in the world for whose manners nature has done so much, and for whom art and education, in this respect, have done so little, as these Hispano-American females on the coast of the Pacific. In their deportment towards strangers they are queens, when, in costume, they are peasants. None of them, according to our tastes, can be called beautiful; but what they want in complexion and regularity of feature is fully supplied by their kindliness, the soul and sympathy which beams from their dark eyes, and their grace and warmth of manners and expression.

While enjoying the picnic with our agreeable hostess, a *caballada* was driven into the *corral* by two *vaqueros,* and two gentlemen soon after came into the house. They were Messrs. Lightson and Murphy, from the *pueblo*, bound for San Francisco, and had stopped to change their horses. We immediately made ready to accompany them and were soon on the road again, traveling at racehorse speed— these gentlemen having furnished us with a change of horses, in order that we might be able to keep up with them.

To account for the fast traveling in California on horseback, it is necessary to explain the mode by which it is accomplished. A gentleman who starts upon a journey of 100 miles and wishes to perform the trip in a day will take with him ten fresh horses and a *vaquero*. The eight loose horses are placed under the charge of the *vaquero,* and are driven in front, at the rate of ten or twelve miles an hour, according to the speed that is required for the journey. At the end of twenty miles, the horses that have been rode are discharged and turned into the *caballada,* and horses that have not been rode, but driven along without weight, are saddled and mounted and rode at the same speed, and so on to the end of the journey. If a horse gives out from inability to proceed at this gait, he is left on the road. The owner's brand is on him, and if of any value, he can be recovered without difficulty. But in California, no one thinks of stopping on the road on account of the loss of a horse or his inability to travel at the rate of ten or twelve miles an hour. Horseflesh is cheap, and the animal must go as long as he can, and when he cannot travel longer he is left, and another horse is substituted.

Twenty-five miles, at a rapid gait over a level and fertile plain, brought us to the *rancho* of Don Francisco Sanchez, where we halted to change horses. Breathing our animals a short time, we resumed our journey and reached the Mission of San Francisco Dolores, three miles from the town of San Francisco, just after sunset. Between the mission and the town the road is very sandy, and we determined to remain here for the night, corralling the loose animals and picketing those we rode. It was some time, however, before we could find a house to lodge in. The foreign occupants of the mission buildings, to whom we applied for accommodations for the night, gave us no satisfaction. After several applications, we were at last accommodated by an old and very poor Californian Spaniard, who inhabited a small house in one of the ruinous squares, formerly occupied by the operative Indians. All that he had (and it was but little) was at our disposal. A more miserable supper I never sat down to; but the spirit of genuine hospitality in which it was given imparted to the poor viands a flavor that rendered the entertainment almost sumptuous—in my imagination. A cup of water cheerfully given to the weary and thirsty traveler, by him who has no more to part with, is worth a cask of wine grudgingly bestowed by the stingy or the ostentatious churl. Notwithstanding we preferred sleeping on our own blankets, these poor people would not suffer us to do it, but spread their own pallets on the earth floor of their miserable hut, and insisted so strongly upon our occupying them that we could not refuse.

September 21. We rose at daylight. The morning was clear, and our horses were shivering with the cold. The Mission of San Francisco is situated at the northern terminus of the fertile plain over which we traveled yesterday, and at the foot, on the eastern side, of the coast range of mountains. These mountains are of considerable elevation. The shore of the bay of San Francisco is about two miles distant from the mission. An *arroyo* waters the mission lands and empties into the bay. The church of the mission and the main buildings contiguous are in tolerable repair. In the latter, several Mormon families, who arrived in the ship *Brooklyn* from New York, are quartered. As in the other missions I have passed through, the Indian quarters are crumbling into shapeless heaps of mud.

Our aged host, notwithstanding he is a pious Catholic and considers us as heretics and heathens, gave us his benediction in a very impressive manner when we were about to start. Mounting our horses at sunrise, we traveled three miles over low ridges of sand hills, with sufficient soil, however, to produce a thick growth of scrubby evergreen oak, and brambles of hawthorn, wild currant and gooseberry bushes, rosebushes, briers, etc. We reached the residence of Wm. A. Leidesdorff,[6] Esquire, late American vice-consul at San Francisco, when the sun was about an hour high. The morning was calm and beautiful. Not a ripple disturbed the placid and glassy surface of the magnificent bay and harbor, upon which rested at anchor thirty large vessels consisting of whalemen, merchantmen, and the U.S. sloop-of-war *Portsmouth*, Captain Montgomery. Besides these, there were numerous small craft, giving to the harbor a commercial air, of which some of the large cities on the Atlantic coast would feel vain. The bay, from the town of San Francisco due east, is about twelve miles in breadth. An elevated range of hills bounds the view on the opposite side. These slope gradually down, and between them and the shore there is a broad and fertile plain, which is called the Contra Costa. There are several small islands in the bay, but they do not present a fertile appearance to the eye.

We were received with every mark of respectful attention and cordial hospitality by Mr. Leidesdorff. Mr. L. is a native of Denmark, was for some years a resident of the United States, but subsequently the captain of a merchant vessel, and has been established

---

[6] William Alexander Leidesdorff (1810–1848), born in the Virgin Islands, was the son of a Danish planter and a woman of African descent. After making a small fortune as a New Orleans cotton broker, Leidesdorff moved to Yerba Buena in 1841 and constructed the City Hotel. He died of typhus in 1848.

at this place as a merchant some five or six years. The house in which he resides, now under the process of completion, is the largest private building in the town. Being shown to a well-furnished room, we changed our travel soiled clothing for a more civilized costume, by which time breakfast was announced, and we were ushered into a large dining hall. In the center stood a table, upon which was spread a substantial breakfast of stewed and fried beef, fried onions and potatoes, bread, butter, and coffee. Our appetites were very sharp, and we did full justice to the merits of the fare before us. The servants waiting upon the table were an Indian *muchachito* and *muchachita,* about ten or twelve years of age. They had not been long from their wild *rancherías* and knew but little of civilized life. Our host, however, who speaks, I believe, nearly every living language—whether of Christian, barbarian, or savage nations—seemed determined to impress upon their dull intellects the forms and customs of civilization. He scolded them with great vivacity, sometimes in their own tongue, sometimes in French, Spanish, Portuguese, Danish, German, and English, in accordance with the language in which he was thinking at the moment. It seemed to me that the little fat Indians were more confused than enlightened by his emphatic instructions. At the table, besides ourselves and host, was Lieutenant W.A. Bartlett,[7] of the U.S. sloop-of-war *Portsmouth,* now acting as *alcalde* of the town and district of San Francisco.

The *Portsmouth,* Commander Montgomery, is the only United States vessel of war now lying in the harbor. She is regarded as the finest vessel of her class belonging to our Navy. By invitation of Lieutenant Bartlett, I went on board of her between ten and eleven o'clock. The crew and officers were assembled on deck to

[7] Washington Allon Bartlett (ca.1820–1871) came to California onboard the *Portsmouth* and—because he could speak Spanish—was named Yerba Buena's first American *alcalde*. In January 1847 he renamed the town San Francisco.

"View of the Place of Anchorage at Yerba Buena in St. Francisco," ca. 1847, by F. Swinton. *Courtesy of the California Historical Society, FN-31312.*

attend Divine service. They were all dressed with great neatness and seemed to listen with deep attention to the Episcopal service and a sermon, which were read by Commander Montgomery, who is a member of the church.

In the afternoon I walked to the summit of one of the elevated hills in the vicinity of the town, from which I had a view of the entrance to the bay of San Francisco, and of the Pacific Ocean. A thick fog hung over the ocean outside of the bay. The deep roar of the eternally restless waves, as they broke one after another upon the beach, or dashed against the rock-bound shore, could be heard with great distinctness, although some five or six miles distant. The entrance from the ocean into the bay is about a mile-and-a-half in breadth. The waters of the bay appear to have forced a passage through the elevated ridge of hills next to the shore of the Pacific. These rise abruptly on either side of the entrance. The water at the entrance and inside is of sufficient depth to admit the largest ship

that was ever constructed; and so completely land-locked and protected from the winds is the harbor, that vessels can ride at anchor
in perfect safety in all kinds of weather. The capacity of the harbor
is sufficient for the accommodation of all the navies of the world.

The town of San Francisco is situated on the south side of the
entrance, fronting on the bay, and about six miles from the ocean.
The flow and ebb of the tide are sufficient to bring a vessel to the
anchorage in front of the town and to carry it outside, without the
aid of wind, or even against an unfavorable wind. A more approach-
able harbor, or one of greater security, is unknown to navigators.
The permanent population of the town is at this time between 100
and 200,[8] and is composed almost exclusively of foreigners. There
are but two or three native Californian families in the place. The
transient population, and at present it is quite numerous, consists
of the garrison of marines stationed here, and the officers and crews
attached to the merchant and whale ships lying in the harbor. The
houses, with a few exceptions, are small *adobes* and frames, constructed without regard to architectural taste, convenience, or comfort. Very few of them have either chimneys or fireplaces. The inhabitants contrive to live the year round without fires, except for
cooking. The position of San Francisco for commerce is, without
doubt, superior to any other port on the Pacific coast of North
America. The country contiguous and tributary to it cannot be surpassed in fertility, healthfulness of climate, and beauty of scenery.
It is capable of producing whatever is necessary to the sustenance
of man, and many of the luxuries of tropical climates, not taking
into the account the mineral wealth of the surrounding hills and
mountains, which there is reason to believe is very great. This
place is, doubtless, destined to become one of the largest and most

---

[8] Bryant's footnote: "This was September 1846. In June 1847, when I left San Francisco
on my return to the United States, the population had increased to about 1,200, and
houses were rising in all directions."

opulent commercial cities in the world, and under American authority it will rise with astonishing rapidity. The principal merchants now established here are Messrs. Leidesdorff, Grimes & Davis, and Frank Ward, a young gentleman recently from New York. These houses carry on an extensive and profitable commerce with the interior, the Sandwich Islands, Oregon, and the southern coast of the Pacific. The produce of Oregon for exportation is flour, lumber, salmon, and cheese; of the Sandwich Islands, sugar, coffee, and preserved tropical fruits.

California, until recently, has had no commerce in the broad signification of the term. A few commercial houses of Boston and New York have monopolized all the trade on this coast for a number of years. These houses have sent out ships freighted with cargoes of dry goods and a variety of knick-knacks saleable in the country. The ships are fitted up for the retail sale of these articles, and trade from port to port, vending their wares on board to the *rancheros* at prices that would be astonishing at home. For instance, the price of common brown cotton cloth is one dollar per yard, and other articles in this and even greater proportion of advance upon home prices. They receive in payment for their wares, hides and tallow. The price of a dry hide is ordinarily one dollar and fifty cents. The price of tallow I do not know. When the ship has disposed of her cargo, she is loaded with hides and returns to Boston, where the hides bring about four or five dollars, according to the fluctuations of the market. Immense fortunes have been made by this trade; and between the government of Mexico and the traders on the coast, California has been literally skinned, annually, for the last thirty years. Of natural wealth the population of California possesses a superabundance and are immensely rich; still, such have been the extortionate prices that they have been compelled to pay for their commonest artificial luxuries and wearing apparel, that generally they are but indifferently provided with the ordinary necessaries of civilized life. For a suit of clothes, which in New York or Boston would cost seventy-five dollars, the Californian has been compelled to pay five times that sum in hides at one dollar and fifty cents; so that a *caballero,* to clothe himself genteelly, has been obliged, as often as he renewed his dress, to sacrifice about 200 of the cattle on his *rancho.* No people, whether males or females, are more fond of display; no people have paid more dearly to gratify this vanity; and yet no civilized people I have seen are so deficient in what they most covet....

On the 21st, by invitation of Captain Montgomery, I dined on board of the sloop-of-war *Portsmouth.* The party, including myself, consisted of Colonel Russell, Mr. Jacob, Lieutenant Bartlett, and a son of Captain M. There are few if any officers in our Navy more highly and universally esteemed for their moral qualities and professional merits than Captain M. He is a sincere Christian, a brave officer, and an accomplished gentleman. Under the orders of Commodore [John Drake] Sloat, he first raised the American flag in San Francisco. We spent the afternoon most agreeably, and the refined hospitality, courteous manners, and intelligent and interesting conversation of our host made us regret the rapidly fleeting moments. The wines on the table were the produce of the vine of California, and having attained age, were of an excellent quality in substance and flavor.

I attended a supper party given this evening by Mr. Frank Ward. The party was composed of citizens of the town and officers of the Navy and the merchant and whale ships in the harbor. In such a company as was here assembled, it was very difficult for me to realize that I was many thousand miles from home, in a strange and foreign country. All the faces about me were American, and there was nothing in scene or sentiment to remind the guests of their remoteness from their native shores. Indeed, it seems to be a settled opinion that California is henceforth to compose a part of the

United States, and every American who is now here considers himself as treading upon his own soil, as much as if he were in one of the old thirteen revolutionary states.

Edward Kemble
1847–48

⟹⟸

The months following the Mexican War brought many changes to Spanish-speaking Californians' way of life. Soldiers returned to their homes to discover their livestock stolen, fences destroyed, and crops trampled. In Sonoma, Mariano Vallejo estimated the Americans had inflicted more than $100,000 in damages to his *rancho* and half that to his brother's. Ex-governor Alvarado had to sell his *rancho* in present-day Mariposa County to Frémont to pay off war debts. For the most part, Californios gamely tried to resume life as it had been under Mexico's ambivalent watch. Vallejo went so far as to shave off his beard, Yankee-style, and march in a victory parade at Portsmouth Square in Yerba Buena (recently renamed San Francisco).

San Francisco grew by leaps and bounds after the American conquest, soon replacing Monterey as the coast's main port. (It helped that ships could now unload their cargoes directly onto a dock instead of having to ferry goods by rowboat onto shore.) Real estate sold briskly, and hotels, houses, and businesses were erected at a rapid rate. "The little village…is fast becoming a town of importance," remarked Bryant when he returned in February 1847. "There is a prevailing air of activity, enterprise, and energy; and the men, in view of the advantageous position of the town for commerce, are making large calculations upon the future; calculations I believe will be fully realized."

The population of the town had unexpectedly tripled the previous summer when Samuel Brannan arrived with 238 Mormons onboard the *Brooklyn*. Brannan, born in Maine, had converted to the Church of Jesus Christ of Latter-Day Saints in his early twenties and edited a New York City Mormon newspaper. To escape persecution, Mormon leader Brigham Young decided to move the church headquarters from Illinois to Utah in 1845, envisioning a Mormon nation in the west. Brannan was selected to lead a party of East Coast Mormons around Cape Horn to establish a colony in California. Much to his dismay, when the *Brooklyn* arrived at San Francisco Bay on July 31, 1846, it anchored alongside the U.S.S. *Portsmouth*. The U.S. Navy had beaten them there.

An opportunistic risk-taker and—despite religious proscription—a heavy drinker, Brannan began using Mormon tithes to launch a variety of personal business investments, including opening a general store at Sutter's Fort, buying up huge tracts of real estate, and founding California's first flour mill and San Francisco's first newspaper. The Mormon Church charged him with embezzlement in one of the first jury trials in California, but disagreements among the jurors gave Brannan his freedom. He continued to improperly collect and use Mormon funds until the church excommunicated him.

Edward Cleveland Kemble was one of the few non-Mormons to sail with Brannan on the *Brooklyn*. He was born in Troy, New York, in 1828, the son of John Kemble, editor and owner of the *Troy Northern Budget*, and Mary Ann Whipple, whose grandfather William fought with George Washington and signed the Declaration of Independence. As a teenager Edward worked as an apprentice in the print shop of Sam Brannan's newspaper, *The Prophet*. He was awed by Brannan, only ten years older, who ran his own newspaper, corresponded with Brigham Young, and preached every Sunday to captivated New York audiences. When Kemble was nineteen, Brannan invited him to come along to California. Kemble, who had gobbled up western literature by Dana, Hastings, and Frémont, jumped at the chance to see the frontier for himself.

Once in California, Kemble—like Byant—volunteered to fight with the U.S. Army. After participating in the Battle of Natividad in San José, he got a chance to meet his hero Frémont and ride with him into battle in southern California. After the war, Kemble returned to San Francisco and was placed in charge of Brannan's newly founded weekly paper, the *California Star*. Under his editorship, the *Star* merged with *The Californian* and eventually became the *Alta California*, San Francisco's first daily paper.

On January 24, 1848, an American carpenter named James Marshall noticed some glittering particles in a tailrace of a sawmill he was constructing for John Sutter on the south fork of the American River. Curious, he rode down to New Helvetia and showed the particles to Sutter, who cracked open his copy of *Encyclopedia Americana* to the entry on gold. He tested Marshall's samples and declared them to be "gold of the finest quality, at least twenty-three carats." Afraid the discovery would delay the construction of his sawmill, Sutter swore everyone in the room to secrecy, but word still spread. Sutter himself not only told governor Richard B. Mason the news but sent along six ounces of gold to substantiate it. Rumors spread to San Francisco, and Kemble traveled to Sutter's Mill to investigate, hoping for a small article for the next edition of the *California Star*. When he arrived he took one look at the rustic mill and its "churlish and inhospitable" crew before scrawling a disbelieving "humbug!" across his notepad.

But the rumors persisted. Sutter's workers began buying liquor with gold dust at Brannan's general store, and the Mormon, sensing an opportunity, quietly stocked his store with picks, pans, shovels, and other equipment likely to soon be in high demand. On May 22 Brannan marched through downtown San Francisco waving his hat in one hand and a bottle of gold dust in the other, hollering, "Gold! Gold! Gold from the American River!" Within a month every town in California was virtually deserted, and a worldwide rush for California gold had begun.

Even skeptical Kemble felt the grip of gold fever. He suspended publication of the *California Star* on June 14 and headed for the gold fields. Like virtually every other miner, Kemble found that gold mining was a dirty, back-breaking business with little reward and quit soon enough. He went on to become one of the most prominent newspapermen in California, writing for several papers in San Francisco and Sacramento. He compiled an extensive "History of California Newspapers" in 1858, an invaluable record of early California journalism. In March 1873, thirteen years before his death, Kemble assembled a series of articles for the *Sacramento Daily Union* outlining his experiences in early California. Written with the wisdom of hindsight, to be sure, they furnish a vivid picture of California on the eve of the gold rush—by now a thoroughly American land.

EDWARD KEMBLE

Reminiscences of early San Francisco

The population of San Francisco, at the period of which we write [spring 1847], was a little less than 500 natives (or Californians proper) and "foreigners," as Americans, Englishmen, Kanakas, and other outsiders were called.

The war for the acquisition of California by the dominant party of these foreigners was over [January 13, 1847], and our flag was flung from Sutter's Fort to San Diego. Fremont's battalion had been disbanded at Los Angeles, and the settlers, hunters, newly-arrived emigrants, runaway sailors, Mormons, and Indians, who had composed the Pathfinder's army, were on their way to their several homes in the north. Among them was the writer of these sketches, a long-haired youth, clad in uniform of the battalion—a sailor's shirt with a star in each corner of the broad collar, fringed buckskin trousers, Mexican *sombrero* (without the glazed covering), and buckskin moccasins. He had sold in Los Angeles, for 75 cents on the dollar, the scrip in which he had been paid for his five months service [thirty-five dollars, plus six dollars allowance, per month]; bought four good horses at five dollars to eight dollars each; and in company with three other members of the battalion, leisurely retraced the late wearisome line of march, not now through desolate, rainy regions, but under the matchless skies of an early California spring, fetlock-deep in tender grass and brilliant flowers. Riding gaily along by day and camping wherever the night overtook them, feasting high on flour slapjacks and boiled jerked-beef, they

Edward Cleveland Kemble (1828–1886), left, with his *Alta California* co-editor, Edward C. Gilbert. *Courtesy of the California Historical Society, FN-16641.*

forgot the miseries of their late fruitless marches and in a week re-joined their friends in the new San Francisco.

I shall not easily forget the changed aspect of the place under the stimulus which the occupation of California by American forces had imparted. Stevenson's Regiment[1] had arrived, and one company was quartered in the old *adobe* custom-house on Portsmouth Square, where I had last seen the marines of the *Portsmouth* sloop-of-war, the original garrison which hoisted the flag on the pole in front of the house. It was early evening as we entered the town by the old mission road—a three-mile stretch of deep sand. Lights gleamed on shore and shipboard, fifty for one that we had been accustomed to see when martial law was first proclaimed in the little quiet *pueblo* the summer before. Drinking-houses were in full blast; the sounds of a fiddle and the unmistakable strains of the "Arkansaw Traveler" came from a saloon situated near the road; the Leidesdorff House, or City Hotel, was brilliantly lighted and thronged with strangers and officers in strange uniforms; and above the hum of voices and loud laughter, as we rode by the long porch, arose the clink of glasses and the click of the billiard balls....The clearly recognizable voice of a New York short-boy bawled out to us—"Hey! Two-forty on the Bloomingdale Road! Where yer goin' with them crabs—sa-ay?"

It was a novel sensation to sleep under a roof that night, and a grand exhilaration the next morning to climb to the top of Telegraph Hill and look down upon this great city of half a thousand inhabitants with its 150 *adobe* and frame houses, its two hotels and

---

[1] The First Regiment of New York Volunteers, commanded by Jonathan D. Stevenson, was a motley group of 917 New York City farmers, mechanics, artisans, and petty criminals. These self-proclaimed adventurers agreed to fight Mexicans in exchange for free passage to California, but by the time they arrived in the spring of 1847, the war was over. During the gold rush, several men from Stevenson's Regiment formed the Regulators (commonly called the Hounds), a brutal vigilante group who "hounded" Hispanic San Franciscans out of town. Other members of Stevenson's Regiment went on to become prominent Californians, including John B. Frisbie (secretary of the Constitutional Convention of 1849), Rev. Thaddeus Leavenworth (*alcalde* of San Francisco in 1848 and 1849), Dr. Felix Wierzbicki (author of the first English-language book published in California), and San Francisco newspapermen Edward G. Buffum and Edward C. Gilbert.

five or six stores, and its busy waterfront (Montgomery Street), which was then, as for years afterward, the combined Broadway, Wall, and Water Street of San Francisco. I remember scanning the crescent-shaped shore, from the north side of the hill on which I stood to Rincon Point, and wondering if the time would ever come when this indentation would be filled in by the city's growth and the line of the city front extended straight across from Telegraph Hill to Rincon Point.

The great event of that spring was the sale of the beach and water lots, great chiefly as the forerunner of great things and the dispenser of great fortunes to a favored few. To a large majority of the townspeople, it was an occasion of no special interest; to a few (it was whispered at the time, a secret conclave, or, as it would be termed now, a ring) the sale afforded the opportunity for a grand speculation. The property was sold by order of General [Stephen Watts] Kearny at a public auction. The *alcalde* of the town[2] was a young purser's clerk, or other civilian employed in the Navy, who had recently been appointed to the important office of Chief Magistrate, and who seems at the outset to have fallen into the hands of a worse company than ever infested the road to Jericho in the days when the good Samaritan went traveling that way....

The beach and water lots were sold at an auction on the 20th day of June—knocked off by a sprightly little fellow whom the *alcalde* had appointed sheriff—and the knot of buyers, twenty or thirty in number, was made up of merchants, Army and Navy officers (buying, of course, by proxy), and speculators who had just come out. For a few hundred dollars men bought real estate on which they realized two or three years afterwards as many hundreds of thousands of dollars. The terms of sale (only half complied with

---

[2] In the spring of 1847, San Francisco's *alcalde* was Philadelphia-born lawyer George Hyde (1819–1890).

as to the cash payments) was one-fourth of the money at day of sale and balance in six, twelve, and eighteen months....

In the month of August of this year, Edward Gilbert, then a lieutenant in Stevenson's regiment, took the first "census" of San Francisco. The actual population of the place was reported to be 459—of this number 273 could read and write. The number of tenements of all descriptions composing the town was 157, an increase of 100 percent in five months.

San Francisco was at this time a city without churches or religious institutions of any kind except a Sunday school commenced in the spring by some pious members of Stevenson's regiment. There was, of course, the regular service of the Roman Catholic Church at Mission Dolores and an occasional visit from one of the chaplains of the men of war on the coast; but even the Mormons who came around in the ship *Brooklyn* yielded to the sense of separation and complete isolation from religious influences that infected the entire community, and seemed to forget when Sunday came about. The first effort to plant a Protestant church was made in the interests of the Episcopal body by a man who afterwards proved to be a sheep of a particularly dark fleece. This fellow [Thaddeus Leavenworth] subsequently became *alcalde* and protracted the reign of injustice and corruption in that office far into the succeeding year. As an illustration of the ungodliness of the times, it may be mentioned that the anniversary of our national independence, occurring this year on Sunday, was celebrated by dinners, speeches, and balls on the Christian Sabbath, and, most remarkable of all, no one seemed to think such an observance of the day at all questionable....

The ships of war, departing from the harbor at the approach of winter, withdrew the sailor element of the population, which occasionally disturbed the quiet of the place, but at the same time deprived society of some of its leaders and ornaments in the persons of the gay, young officers. While the war vessels lay in port, dinners

"San Francisco in 1847," 1847, by William Rich Hutton. *Courtesy of The Huntington Library, San Marino, California.*

and balls, on ship and on shore, supplied a lively round of pleasure. In their absence the Spanish *fandangos* were revived and became the chief amusement of the town. An occasional horse race varied the sport. Excursions and horseback rides to different parts of the peninsula on which San Francisco stands were frequent. Little trips by sailing vessels (launches) to attractive points on the bay or up the Sacramento gave change of life and scene to the town-wearied. The ranches dotting the valleys lateral to the bay, and still in the hands of their original California owners, were always open and abounding in hospitality. Picnics to Fort Point, mussel-roasting on the shores of the bay, strawberry parties on the cliffs beyond the *presidio*, and visits to the sea lions made up the daily life of the pleasure-seeker in San Francisco in the spring and fall of 1847.

The overland immigration of that year added half a dozen families to the population, and a few pleasant people found their way over from the Sandwich Islands and China. A notable event was the arrival of a shipload of goods selected in New York City with reference to the improved state of the California market (now

314

largely influenced by American tastes and customs) and the open-ing of a "New York store." Two or three other mercantile houses were set up this fall. The two weekly newspapers varied their con-tents with accounts of General [Winfield] Scott's battles in Mexico—ninety days old—and late and important intelligence from the States—four to five months on its way. The staple fare of the newspapers, however, was the local broils, *alcalde* battles, editorial personalities, and arrivals and departures of shipping.

The rainy season set in early, but the storms were not severe. The war for the conquest of California was at an end, and peace and good order reigned throughout the length and breadth of the Ter-ritory. Frémont was on his way to the States, under arrest by Gen-eral Kearny for disobedience of orders.[3] The disbanded volunteers were either settled upon farms or looking out for speculative open-ings, such as new town and mill sites afforded. Throughout the northern valleys, thinly settled as they were, we heard of prepara-tions for farming on a scale never before attempted in California. A considerable emigration came through from Oregon and took up claims. The hope of the country lay in the direction of agriculture, and every encouragement was given by merchants and through the country press to plant largely. American plows were breaking the virgin soil in all the choice farming localities about the bay and along the rivers. Few thought of harvests in connection with the hard and dry soil of the open plains through which our two chief rivers coursed. Wheat along the alluvial bottoms and wheat in the little garden spots up the rich valleys north of San Francisco was the limit of our first venture of agricultural faith. Fruit—except the Mission

---

[3] Hero though he was, Charles C. Frémont overstepped his authority in the waning months of the Mexican War, and General Kearny ordered him back to Washington, D.C., for trial. In January 1848 Frémont was found guilty of disobedience of orders, but he proudly returned to California, where he was elected one of the state's first two senators.

grapes and pears—and vegetables—except beans, peas, and a few potatoes—it had not entered into the mind of the California farmer to attempt to cultivate. I remember an Army officer of high standing in San Francisco, a gentleman of rare intelligence and ripe judgment, gave me a paragraph about peaches, clipped from a New Jersey paper, to which he had appended some remarks. The item showed the profits that the Reybolds had realized from the sale of their large crop of peaches. The comment of the officer was: "Similar paragraphs will someday be written of the productiveness of California in this fruit." I am not aware that a peach had ever been raised in the country up to that time.

The new year, which was danced in with *fandangos* and wet with libations of crusty old port of native manufacture (our later vintage has not produced the port wines of such acceptable flavor as the cellars of old "Don Luís" of Los Angeles[4] held in store at that day), beheld new and more startling changes in the aspect of affairs throughout the northern region than any we have yet described.... The air was full of rumors of rich mineral deposits having been found in different parts of the country. Prospecting parties were out in every direction, and claims were being "denounced for quicksilver" in a dozen different places. No one as yet talked of gold. Silver was the limit of conjecture and speculation. Iron and copper were suspected, and tin and black lead reported. As early as January, the mineral quest began.

I remember visiting the redwoods near Bodega with a party of wood choppers, most of them Mormons from the *Brooklyn* colony, and sitting by the evening campfire when all the conversation was about the chances of precious metals being found in the hills. One of the party had brought into camp a small boulder to which bits

---

[4]Juan Luís Vignes (ca.1779–1862)—born Jean Louis in his native Bordeaux, France—emigrated to California in the early 1830s and utilized his training as a wine maker to establish a famous vineyard in southern California.

of shining mica adhered. He said that down in Georgia, where he once lived, they would have "allowed" that such a rock was a sign of gold. Another said it was more like a lead sign, or what they used to call "galena" out West. The editor of the *Star,* who made a trip up the Sonoma and Napa valleys, returned with a pocket full of specimens of minerals…which furnished matter for profoundly stupid editorials for several weeks. Men traveled through the country with hammers in their pockets with which to break off fragments of boulders and suspicious-looking stones. Riding along the road up the American forks in company with an old Californian friend, he was continually leaving my side to try his hammer and his metallurgic tests on the wayside rocks. The country was going mineral-mad without any apparent cause. No valuable mines had been discovered except those at New Almaden.[5] But everybody believed in the existence of great wealth; no one could say of what. Silver and quicksilver were prognosticated; gold was written in no man's prophesyings.

Late in February a special publication was prepared at the *Star* office, to send overland to meet the spring emigration of that year from the East, and for circulation in the States. It was such a sheet as was made up in aftertimes at all the California newspaper offices, and called the "Steamer Papers," filled with mining intelligence and murders, for the edification of our Eastern friends and the depreciation of California morals in the markets of the old world. The *Star*'s special [April 1, 1848] set a good example, which was unworthily followed. It was filled to overflowing—four pages and a supplement—with interesting and generally correct accounts of California, her "resources and prospects." Her agricultural advantages

---

[5] Miners had been harvesting mercury from the mines at New Almaden (located south of San José) since 1845. Mercury, useful for separating gold flakes from dirt, became extraordinarily valuable during the gold rush, and New Almaden produced about $1 million worth annually.

formed the chief theme; her grazing and sheep-raising and wine-making opportunities were next presented; her manufacturing facilities were stated; and lastly her mineral attractions were modestly set forth. Several thousand copies of this publication were sent over the mountains by special courier.

I was standing in Howard & Mellus' store, on Montgomery Street, near what is now Commercial Street, one day in March of this year, watching Sutter's launch, *Sacramento,* with its crew of Kanakas and Digger Indians, maneuver against an ebb tide to make her landing off the foot of Clay Street, about a stone's throw from the beach at Montgomery Street, and wondering if the two or three anxious-looking passengers in the stern were acquaintances, when the clerk of the store, who had been also watching the little schooner-rigged vessel, quietly remarked, "I suppose we shall hear if that story is true about the gold mine up the American."

I have already said that the upper country had "turned loose" this spring to hunt for silver, quicksilver, coal, iron, copper, sulfur, saltpeter, salt, black lead, and in short, everything but gold (not excepting diamonds, which were reported to have been discovered in the Sonoma Valley), and that paragraphs in the two local papers about new mineral developments were beginning to grow stale and unprofitable. I was hoping for an item from the *Sacramento* to vary this monotony, and in the mind's eye of a printer had measured the chances for about a "stick-full of matter" needed to fill up the closing column and send the weekly *Star* to press. There had been woven into the dull gossip of the town that week a tiny thread of gold, caught from a rumor that floated like a gossamer down from the upper country, but it was too thin and insubstantial to make any sort of figure in the pattern, and had been rejected from the news material with which the *Star* looms with lofty discrimination supplied the market. Some native Californian, it was said, one of those hard riders who were continually posting about the country on their fast horses, had ridden across from Sutter's *embarcadero*, through the "tule cut-off," to the ranches back of Benicia, and thence, crossing Carquinez Straits, had come through Livermore's Pass to San José and San Francisco—all in two days from the point of starting (opposite the present site of Sacramento)—and he had brought a report that some of Captain Sutter's men had found gold on the American Fork.

So, when Howard & Mellus' clerk suggested that the launch *Sacramento* might bring further tidings about the gold mine up the American, the editor of the *Star* hoped it might bring an item about the number of acres Captain Sutter would sow in wheat this spring, and thus foreshadow a more certain golden harvest in the fall.

The passengers by the *Sacramento*—only four days from Sutter's Fort—were strangers, and when they stepped ashore one of them asked where Captain Vioget[6] lived, and being shown made haste in that direction, leaving the *Star* reporter to interview the others. They didn't know anything of Captain Sutter's sowing, or how many hides he would send down, or whether any parties were rendezvousing at the fort for a start across the plains, or whether the prospects of an emigration from Oregon of the dissatisfied last year's comers was as reported, or what was what, or which was which, for any practical purpose that the *Star* editor plied his questions. The chances of the "stick-full of matter" began to diminish to a bare possibility of a line or two, when one of them said if we would "come up to the store" he would show us something.

And back to the store we all went. It is the strangest thing that I cannot remember this man's name. He had been in the employ of Captain Sutter, but had come down on business of his own. He was

---

[6] Jean Jacques Vioget (1799–1855), a Swiss-born soldier, engineer, and artist who served in Napoleon's army, came to California in 1837. He made one of the earliest surveys of Yerba Buena and also mapped New Helvetia for Sutter.

black-eyed, bushy-bearded, lank and nervous, and chewed tobacco as a schoolgirl chews gum—as though the lower jaw was run by clockwork. Standing at the counter, he took out a greasy purse and out of that produced a little rag, which he carefully opened, disclosing a few thin flakes of a dull yellow metal. "That there," said he in an undertone, "is gold, and I know it, and know where it comes from, and there's a plenty more in the same place, certain and sure!"

Too thin! What would have been the modern criticism on the specimens and on the stranger's profession of faith in them? He was not in the least excited, and we set him down as acting a part. Other townspeople came into the store, and the little rag, with its lusterless bits of metal, was handed around. One said it was mica, and another that it was "fool's gold"—he had "seen plenty of it in Oregon." By and by the exhibitor was joined by his companion, who had inquired the way to "old Vioget's." I afterwards learned that he had gone there to submit some specimens to the captain for "a test," as he was reputed to have some skill in the analysis of minerals. Vioget's opinion, if given at all, was not revealed. The party at the store separated without any very lively impression having been made on the lookers-on, and, if I remember aright, the *Star* went to press that night without an item concerning the gold mines....

In October 1847, the first steamboat was launched into the bay in the hold of a Russian bark, consigned to Captain Leidesdorff, the American vice-consul. The little stranger came hitherward from the Russian settlements on the Amoor River and was originally destined for the inland waters of Alaska. Leidesdorff, though a foreigner, was imbued with the spirit of Yankee enterprise and foresaw the greatness of California long in advance of his American brother merchants. He had the little steamboat put together and endeavored to freight merchandise to different points on the bay. The *Sitka,* as she was called, actually made the first trip to the present site of Sacramento and was the pioneer of steam navigation on these waters. It would detract from her fame to place on record the time of her first trip. Let the waters of the bay, in which she foundered a cable's length from shore, be as the gentle wave of oblivion upon that page of her history. Her engine was too feeble and her hull too frail to wrestle with the northers that visited the bay that winter. She was resurrected in the spring, and her machinery having been taken out, the little craft was fitted up as a schooner and called the *Rainbow*. Having made one or two successful trips to Sonoma and San José, she was dispatched to New Helvetia (Sacramento) in April. The first gold prospecting party that left San Francisco for the mines were passengers on that trip, and their adventures will be subsequently related.

The mercantile firms doing business in San Francisco at this time were Mellus & Howard, already mentioned, who advertised "cloths, cassimeres, pantaloon stuffs of various kinds, prints, brown and white cottons, tickings, tea, coffee, sugar, molasses, Columbia River flour, gin, *aguardiente,* ale, hollow ware, iron and steel, which they offer low for cash or hides," etc. Shelly & Norris (corner of Clay and Kearny streets), Ward & Smith, Dickson & Hay, and W. H. Davis & Co. dealt in a similar line of goods. Robert A. Parker, at the "Adobe Store" on the hill back of Portsmouth Square, and Gelston & Co. ("New York store") at the foot of Washington Street, were the latest comers—the former from Boston—and offered fresh and assorted stocks, introducing "novelties" in dry goods and fancy articles, such as had never been seen before in this market, and only 120 days from the States. The business of these mercantile houses cannot be said to have been extensive, although the local paper congratulates its readers on the brisk business done in April, the month in which the first ripple of excitement consequent on the discovery of gold was noticed. The editor says (April 22, 1848)—"The amount of sales by our merchants this week has exceeded twenty thousand dollars."

The inland commerce of California was carried on by means of launches, or sloops and schooners of fifteen or twenty tons burthen, used chiefly for hide droghing purposes. The coast trade was confined to half a dozen brigs and schooners, running between San Francisco and the Columbia River, or the southern ports of Santa Cruz, Monterey, San Pedro, and a Mexican port or two. There was a monthly arrival from the Sandwich Islands and an occasional visitor from China. An eastern arrival was an event to make merry over. During December 1847 and the three first months of 1848, there were fourteen arrivals of all kinds, two of which were from China and South American ports, the Sandwich Islands and coastwise traders. In the fall of the year (about September), the whalers of the North Pacific dropped in to water and recruit supplies. Our merchants were ever casting hungry eyes in the direction of this whaling fleet and fishing assiduously for these fishermen.

The historian of these times will find a barren page when he carries his search into the local annals after religious educational items. The billiard-rooms of the two hotels provided the chief mental and moral pasturage of the average San Franciscan of those times for the entire seven days of the week. It is proper to state, however, that there was very little drunkenness and rarely a case of disorder. The town was governed almost without the aid of a constable. Gambling of course there was, as in every unreformed Mexican *pueblo*. The Town Council of 1848 made an effort to abolish it, but, some of its own members having been caught trying their hand in secret places at monte, the attempt was abandoned. The first schoolhouse was erected during the fall of 1847. It stood on the southwest corner of Portsmouth Square, occupying a part of the *plaza* itself. It was a little one-story frame building and passed subsequently through a variety of uses. In the winter of 1847–48 it was used for religious purposes. The first regularly organized Protestant congregation in San Francisco held its services there.

We didn't believe in it; we didn't profess to believe in it! The first party to the gold mines was not a party to any such miserable fraud as we believed the pretended gold discoveries to be. They would have told you—and it was true—that they were not going to look for gold; they had not lost any gold—and if Captain Sutter's mill hands on the American Fork had found gold, they ought to be allowed to keep it....

The first party that left San Francisco to go to the gold mines consisted of Major Pierson B. Reading, George McKinstry, Jr., and the editor [Kemble] of the little paper already mentioned; time of year, the last week in March or the first in April [1848]; conveyance, Leidesdorff's "launch" or schooner, the *Rainbow*. Major Reading, the accomplished gentleman, the adventurous pioneer, the amateur trapper and hunter, and the gallant soldier, will be remembered by all the old Californians. McKinstry was a pleasant writer and companion and was employed at Sutter's Fort in keeping the hospitable captain's books and accounts. The editor of the *Star* was a youth, not out of his teens, a printer and pioneer, who had served in the campaign in the south under Frémont....

This was the party, and the vessel in which they embarked was admirably suited to the occasion—full of the suggestions of failure. The *Rainbow* was one of those morning illuminations at which "sailors take warning"; it had not bright promise to be fulfilled. It was the hull of the little *Sitka,* the pioneer steamboat on the bay, from which the boiler and engine had been removed—the shell of the grub from which the butterfly had departed. Keats, the poet, says of a maiden divested of her crinoline and drawing the drapery of her couch about her to lie down to pleasant dreams, that it was— "As though a rose would shut and be a bud again."

This, in the language of high art, was the *Rainbow*. Her captain and supercargo was Glidden, a young clerk in the employ of

Leidesdorff. The party embarked in the best of spirits, although it was the first trip of the vessel, in her schooner-rig, up the Sacramento, and sailors pronounced her too crank for the stiff winds of the bay. Departing on the "last of the ebb, to meet the flood at Angel's Island" (the sailing directions of all launches in those times), the day was so beautiful, the bay and landscape so bright—spread around them in such unbroken quiet and repose—that they were inspired to raise song and chorus, suggested no doubt by the captain's name:

"'Twas there I met ole Johnny Glidden, long time ago!"

One trip up the Sacramento in those weary days and nights of schooner navigation—of flapping sails and "ashen breezes" by day, and flapjacks and ashcakes and embattled hosts of mosquitoes along the banks at night—was so much like another, and either one or the other so uninviting of repetition that even the reproduction of the incidents of such a one as I am narrating seems undesirable. The party were from five to seven days on the journey. At "old Schwartz'," on the river, a few miles below the *embarcadero* of Sutter's Fort (present site of Sacramento) they stopped to have a feast of salmon....

The *Rainbow* made her landing in fine style, all ill omens having failed on the trip, and Major Reading's little Indian body servant, who had accompanied him from San Francisco, ran up to the fort to apprise Captain Sutter of the arrival. Soon there were saddle horses led by an Indian *vaquero* galloping through the trees to be placed at the disposal of the major for the conveyance of the party to the fort. The setting sun was throwing a flood of mellow light beneath the arching branches, brightening the silver shafts of the cottonwood and turning to molten gold the miniature lakes spread out on every side....

The next morning after their arrival, the gold hunters (still disclaiming such a title, however) resumed their journey. During the

evening spent with Captain Sutter they had not been specially enlightened in regard to the discoveries. If Captain Sutter was a be-
liever in their importance, he managed to hide it from his friends
more successfully than the artless old gentleman concealed anything
before or since. [James] Marshall's enthusiasm appeared rather to
amuse than convince him, though he was troubled at the shape
matters had taken at the mill. Work had been suspended on account
of high water, and the men did not even appear disposed to engage
in logging while the mill lay idle. Out of his anxiety for the fate of
the mill, rather than interest in the new discoveries, Captain Sutter
consented to take one of the party to the gold mines. He had been
there once before, in the previous month, when Marshall, wild with
excitement, had dragged him thither to behold the future scene of
the world's wonder—a few grains of dull-looking metal stopped in
the quill of some mountain bird was the first remittance of gold
made from the mines of California.

There was, then, Captain Sutter, Major Reading, McKinstry,
and the editor aforesaid—with two Indian "boys," Antonio and
José, favorites of the captain, to look after the horses and make
camp—and the party started at an early hour, because it was not
expected to reach the mill before the next day. Captain Sutter, singular as it may seem, is a very poor horseman. Rarely in those days
did he ever venture on the back of a horse, riding a mule in prefer-
ence. On this occasion he was mounted on a favorite mule called
Katy. Frequently that morning, in crossing marshy places or ascending slippery paths, the captain would fall to the rear and be heard
in low tones of earnest expostulation with his mule: "Now, den,
Katy—de oder foot! God bless me, Katy—de oder foot, child!"

Little of interest occurred during the day's ride, except that
Major Reading, carrying a small hammer, frequently rode out from
the trail to break off bits of rock, and once or twice he thought he
had found traces of silver....

Straight before them, seeming so very near in the transparent atmosphere of that early morning, rose in solemn majesty the hoary heads of the Sierras. How reverend their aspect, how fixed and immutable their mien! A wild, wild group of mountains intervened, and then the beautiful vale of Coloma, nestling at their feet, cleft by the cold, rushing waters of the American. The hills that stand around it are clad with dense forests of evergreen. From the nearest summits, the pine and redwood rear high their sturdy crests motionless and without a murmur, or the song of a bird from their branches. The course of the river is lost to the eye in the dense growth of forest—we can scarcely catch at this distance the sound of its white, flashing waters. Only one sign of life, and that is a thin, blue column of smoke ascending dreamily from the depths of the vale, marking the locality of the lumbermen's camp.

Down the hill we rode, single file, with jingling Spanish spurs and bridle-bit, shaping our course for the camp without regard to the meanderings of the trail. The sun was well up in the heavens, but the eastern slopes of the mountains lay buried in the shadows. The major, on his iron-gray steed, led the way, glancing right and left from under his broad-brimmed hat for silver signs, while the captain, on his mule, brought up the rear, picking his steps with anxious care, grasping the pummel of the saddle and dropping a word of earnest expostulation now and then to Katy. The chill air of the valley steals around us, and the roar of the rapids rises upon our ears. On a beach of land near the base of the long hill that we are descending, under majestic, spreading trees, we spy the camp of Marshall and his companions. It is a rude bivouac in the open air, with blankets, smoke-blackened kettles and tins, and provender sacks and boxes strewed all around, as though the men were on a march. The morning meal had been consumed, and the lumbering crew (they would have passed for a "lumbering" set most anywhere) were sitting or sprawling on the ground about the smolder-

Sutter's Mill as it appeared in 1848, from *The Annals of San Francisco, 1855. Courtesy of the California Historical Society, North Baker Research Library, FN-31311.*

ing fire. They hardly returned our greeting as we rode up. It was apparent from the first moment we came in sight, we were unwelcome guests. We had not been slow to perceive in the words and looks that were exchanged before we came within hearing that the object of our visit was well understood and would receive no aid or encouragement from Marshall and his friends.

We unsaddled our beasts, and while Captain Sutter and Marshall started off by themselves, the major and the rest of the party endeavored to gain a little information respecting the gold discovery from the other lumbermen. Opening oysters with a wooden toothpick would have been an easy task compared to that

job. One of the fellows "allowed" he didn't "go much on its being gold, anyway." Another guessed Marshall was a "little mite
cracked" on the subject. In answer to the direct question where the
gold was found, the reply was, "Oh, anywhere along the race or
down by the river, where you've a mind to try for it." Which was
true enough, as it afterwards appeared, but intended to be a very
smart and evasive answer. Marshall, when afterwards asked to des-
ignate the precise locality where he first discovered the gold, took
a large chip and, without speaking, made two scratches upon it with
the point of a knife with which he had been moodily whittling, and
then struck the blade in where the lines intersected, jerking out only
the word "thar," and going on with his whittling without deigning
any further explanation. No wonder men said Marshall was crazy.
But he was not crazy; he was only eccentric, and just now he was
acting a part.

Whew! It was getting warm as the sun began to send his rays
vertically into the valley. There was not a breath of air. The major
proposed that we should try our luck gold mining "along the race
or the river or anywhere." So, borrowing an Indian basket, one of
those handsome, water-tight utensils, woven of grass and ornamented with the gay plumage of the scarlet-winged chenate—a
household vessel very common in those days—we walked down to
the nearest point of the mill race. The major filled the basket with
earth and commenced the laborious process of washing for gold
after the fashion of the placer miners in southern California. It was
a new operation to the lookers on—probably Reading himself had
never tried his hand at it before. It was very slow—we looked in vain
for a sign of gold when the black sand was reached. "Try again,"
said the major, cheerily, proceeding to refill the basket. Higher rose
the sun and hotter fell his beams on boulder and stream. The mill
stood idle and deserted a few hundred yards below us. We began
to look around for a shade. The major bent his back to his work.

Slowly, we walked down to the mill. Everything appeared unfinished or finished in haste, and a mechanic would have called it a bad job the moment his eye fell on the work. The dam was overflowed; the water had backed up into the race and nearly surrounded the mill. We saw no traces of gold-digging, nor could we find where men had washed their gold. Some Indians appeared on the other side. They were on their way up to the camp to talk with their friend, Captain Sutter, whose arrival in the valley they seem to have ascertained by a sort of instinct.

We left the river and wandered back into the woods, leaving the major twirling and dipping his basket while we slowly directed our steps by a shaded path to the camp. The churlish and inhospitable crew of lumbermen had gone out to make a feint of logging, or some other labor, for Captain Sutter's satisfaction. Our Indian boys prepared a lunch, and soon the Indians dropped in, one by one, and after a friendly salutation, sat down and eyed us in silence. Sutter came up and there was a grand handshaking, and now from another quarter, "remote, unfriended, melancholy, slow," approaches the sole representative of the mining interest in our party. He is greeted with a quiet "what success, major?" and replies, "not enough to buy a drink," which would be literally less than the value of a Spanish real in gold. There could be no reality in such gold discoveries as these. So we dropped the subject for the time being, and the editor of the *Star* noted in his memorandum book, as a subject for his next week's paper, the practical result of a test made of the gold-producing qualities of the soil at the alleged gold mines, and wrote overall, in emphatic character, "humbug."

That evening, when the cold dews began to descend, we heaped up the lumbermen's fire with logs and turned to our Indian visitors, each of whom had been provided with his supper and a present, and asked them what they knew about gold in these mountains. They replied that they knew much about it—that it was very bad. As this seemed to confirm the editor of the *Star* in his opinion, he was naturally desirous to know more. So Captain Sutter, through one of his boys acting as interpreter and turning it into Spanish, elicited the surprising fact that the existence of the gold had been known to the Indians for many generations, and that it was considered by them as owned and guarded by evil spirits. There was a lake, said the chief speaker, not far from here, where there is plenty of this bad medicine, but it is guarded by a fearful animal. The Indian described him as a species of dragon, which had an unpleasant appetite for human flesh and would devour all who came into his domains for gold.

The Indians appeared to know nothing of the value of the yellow metal, and the conclusion we reached after hearing their statement was that the early mission *padres* had obtained a knowledge of the gold mines and had warned their Indian proselytes not to tamper with them, intending to develop these mines with Indian labor someday. Such a knowledge certainly existed among the Franciscans who founded the California missions, and it may be that gold mining was carried on by them in a small way by means of Indians. The first mining regularly attempted after the discoveries of 1848 was prosecuted mainly by the aid of Indians. Until the dastardly outrage committed on a party of unoffending Indians by drunken Oregon desperados in the spring of this year, there was no difficulty in getting labor from these humble people. The shooting of half a dozen in cold blood, after they had been lured into camp on a pretense of friendship, drove the tribes into the mountains and provoked retaliations, which cost the lives of several innocent white men. This was the beginning of troubles between the red race and our own people in California. As usual, the whites were the cruel aggressors.

The first party to the gold mines from San Francisco in 1848 returned as empty-handed as it had started, so far as the mere acquisition of gold was concerned. In the acquisition of knowledge it was more successful. The editor of the *California Star,* for example, had derived, as he believed, facts which justified him in proclaiming the gold discoveries to be a delusion and a snare. Accordingly, the next issue of the paper after his arrival denounced the whole theory and alleged success as an arrant cheat and imposture. The *Stars* in their courses fought against the gold mines.[7]

---

[7] Two weeks later, on May 12, 1848, Brannan shouted, "Gold! Gold! Gold from the American River!" in downtown San Francisco. By May 15, the town's population plummeted as almost every resident clamored to reach Sutter's Mill. By the middle of June, even Kemble had caught gold fever. His *Star* ceased publication with the final line: "We have done. Let our word of parting be, *Hasta Luego.*"

Timeline

CA. 8,000 B.C. — First undisputed archaeological evidence of humans in California

CA. 3,000 B.C. — First evidence of advanced (mortar and pestle) acorn processing in California

CA. 1 A.D. — First evidence of bow-and-arrow hunting in California

1510 — The name "California" first appears in *Las Sergas de Esplandián*, a Spanish novel by Garcí Ordóñez de Montalvo about a mythical island rich with gold

1521 — Spanish *conquistador* Hernán Cortés conquers the Aztec capital of Tenochtitlán and establishes colony of New Spain

1533 — Spanish sailors make first European sighting of Baja California

1542 — Sea expedition led by Juan Rodríguez Cabrillo "discovers" Alta California, claims San Diego Bay for Spain, and sails as far north as southern Oregon

1579 — Sir Francis Drake makes an emergency landing in northern California during first British circumnavigation of the globe

1587 — Pedro de Unamuno, commander of a Manila galleon on its way to Acapulco, explores the central California coastline for a possible port

1588 — Britain's Royal Navy improbably defeats the "invincible" Spanish Armada, opening the New World to English trade and colonization

1602 — Sebastián Vizcaíno visits and names San Diego and Monterey bays

1606 — Spanish royal order prohibits further exploration of Alta California

1607 — First permanent English settlement in North America founded at Jamestown, Virginia

1620 — British Pilgrims onboard the *Mayflower* land at Plymouth, Massachusetts

1697 — Jesuits found first of twenty missions in Baja California

1747 — Spanish King Ferdinand VI decrees "California is not an island," officially ending a myth that had persisted in European imaginations for more than two centuries

1763 — Treaty of Paris ends Europe's Seven Years' War; France returns Cuba and the Philippines to Spain and cedes Canada to Britain

1765 — Visitador-General José de Gálvez arrives in New Spain charged with shoring up Spanish sovereignty in North America

1767 — Spanish King Charles III expels all Jesuits from the New World for plotting against the crown

1769 — Looking for Monterey, the "sacred expedition"—led by Gaspar de Portolá—stumbles onto San Francisco Bay

  — Junípero Serra founds first mission in Alta California (Mission San Diego de Alcalá)

1770 — Serra founds second mission in Alta Calfornia (Mission San Carlos Borromeo)

  — Pedro Fages explores the San Francisco Bay Area and catches first glimpse of the Golden Gate

1772 — Fages and Juan Crespí explore in the East Bay

1775 — The *San Carlos,* commanded by Juan de Ayala, becomes the first non-Indian vessel to sail into San Francisco Bay

1776 — Juan Bautista de Anza leads thirty-four Spanish families from Sonora to a settlement at San Francisco Bay; Francisco Palóu founds Mission San Francisco de Asís nearby

  — In Philadelphia, American rebels sign the Declaration of Independence

1777 — California's new governor Felipe de Neve oversees the founding of Mission Santa Clara de Asís and Alta Calfornia's first *pueblo*, San José

1778 — British explorer James Cook "discovers" the Hawaiian Islands and charts the Pacific coast of North America northward from Oregon, laying the basis for future British claims to the region

1781 — Neve founds Los Angeles, Alta California's second *pueblo*

  — Yuma Indians destroy two missions along the Colorado River and kill thirty-four Spaniards

1784 — Publication of Cook's journal—with its descriptions of abundant Pacific Northwest furs—stirs European imaginations

  — Serra dies at Mission San Carlos

1785 — Fermín Francisco de Lasuén succeeds Serra as father-president

1786 — French navigator Jean François de La Pérouse sojourns at Monterey

1790 — Spain and England agree on the Nootka Sound Convention, opening the North Pacific to entrepreneurs of both nations

  — California's non-Indian population reaches 1,000

1791 — Alejandro Malaspina, leader of a Spanish round-the-world expedition, visits Monterey

1792–94 — George Vancouver visits San Francisco and Monterey bays onboard the *Discovery*

1796 — The *Otter*, first American ship to visit California, anchors at Monterey

1797 — Lasuén oversees the founding of four new missions, including Mission San José de Guadalupe

1799 — Russian-American Fur Company establishes a permanent base (Sitka) on Baranof Island in southeast Alaska

1800 — California's non-Indian population reaches 1,800

1803 — United States purchases the Louisiana Territory from France, extending its western border to the Rocky Mountains

1805 — Lewis and Clark expedition reaches the Pacific Ocean

1806 — Russian Count Nikolai Petrovich Rezanov, accompanied by Georg von Langsdorff, visits San Francisco Bay to secure supplies for impoverished Sitka

1808 — French troops commanded by Napoleon Bonaparte invade and conquer Spain

1810 — Rebels led by Father Miguel Hidalgo begin a decade of revolution in Mexico

1812 — Russians establish two colonies in northern California—Bodega Bay and Fort Ross

1816 — The *Rurik,* a Russian-sponsored exploring expedition, visits San Francisco Bay

1817 — San Rafael Arcángel becomes Alta California's twentieth mission

1820 — California's non-Indian population reaches 3,200

1821 — Mexico declares its independence from Spain and claims New Mexico, Texas, and California

1822 — American merchant William A. Gale opens a Bryant and Sturgis hide shop in Monterey

1823 — San Francisco Solano de Sonoma becomes Alta California's twenty-first and final mission

1825 — José María Echeandía becomes first governor of California appointed by the Federal Republic of Mexico

1826 — Frederick William Beechey, exploring in the North Pacific onboard the *Blossom,* completes the first detailed map of San Francisco Bay

— Fur-trapper Jedediah Strong Smith leads first trans-Sierra party into California

1829 — Former neophyte Estanislao leads a large war band of Miwok Indians against more than 100 Mexican troops near the Stanislaus River

1834 — California governor José Figueroa begins secularization of the missions

1835 — British merchant William A. Richardson founds town of Yerba Buena

— President Andrew Jackson unsuccessfully offers Mexico $3.5 million for lands including Texas and northern California

1835–36 — Richard Henry Dana, Jr. sails the California coast onboard the hide-and-tallow ship *Pilgrim*

1836 — American rebels in Texas declare independence from Mexico

1839 — Swiss émigré John Sutter arrives in California and constructs barony of New Helvetia in the Sacramento Valley

1841 — British Hudson's Bay Company establishes store and warehouse at Yerba Buena

— John Bidwell and John Bartelson lead first wagon train into California

1841–42 — Sir George Simpson visits Yerba Buena, Sonoma, Monterey, and Los Angeles on behalf of the Hudson's Bay Company

1842 — U.S. Commodore Thomas ap Catesby Jones, erroneously believing war had been declared with Mexico, occupies Monterey for one day

— American settlement of Oregon Territory begins with the opening of the Oregon Trail

1845 — President James Polk unsuccessfully offers Mexico $40 million for New Mexico and northern California

— John C. Frémont publishes *Report of the Exploring Expedition to Oregon and North California* to widespread acclaim

1846 — President Polk declares war on Mexico (May 13)

— Disgruntled American Bear Flaggers declare California an independent republic (June 14)

— The *Brooklyn,* carrying Samuel Brannan, Edward Kemble, and more than 200 Mormons, arrives in Yerba Buena from Boston (July 31)

— American newspaperman Edwin Bryant arrives in Yerba Buena (September 21)

1847 — Mexican general Andrés Pico surrenders to Frémont at Cahuenga (January 13)

- Yerba Buena renamed San Francisco (January 30)
- The last of the forty-seven survivors of the Donner Party arrive in California (April)

1848 — American carpenter James Marshall discovers gold in a tailrace of the American River (January 24)

- Treaty of Guadalupe Hidalgo sets the Río Grande as Mexico's northern border and cedes California, Nevada, Utah, New Mexico, Arizona, and Texas to the U.S. (Feb. 10)
- Brannan shouts "Gold! Gold! Gold from the American River!" in downtown San Francisco, setting off the California gold rush (May 12)
- California's non-Indian population reaches 13,000

GLOSSARY OF SPANISH TERMS

adiós good-bye; farewell
administrador administrator
adobe sun-dried clay brick
aguardiente brandy
alameda grove
alcalde chief administrator and judicial officer; mayor
alcatraz pelican
alférez lieutenant
alguaziles sheriffs
amigo friend
arroba weight of twenty-five pounds; Spanish liquid measure
arroyo stream; brook
atole gruel, usually made from acorn
balsa raft or boat made of reeds
barrego Spanish regional dance

berrendo prong-horned antelope
bestia beast, animal
bota leather bag
buenas tardes good afternoon; good evening
buenos días good morning
buey liquid measure
burro donkey
caballada herd of horses
caballero horseman; gentleman
calabozo prison
calzoncillos underpants
calzoneros trousers buttoned on both sides of the legs
camino road
carreta wagon; cart
carretada cartload; wagonload

chile colorado pepper-like spice
cicerone guide
ciervo stag
comandante commanding officer
conquistador conquerer
corral yard; enclosure
cortes representative assembly
coyote prairie wolf
cuarta unit of measurement
diseño hand-drawn map defining the boundaries of a rancho
don title of respect prefixed to a male Christian name
doña title of respect prefixed to a female Christian name
dos two
embarcadero pier
enramada arbor; grove
está bueno it is good
fandango Spanish regional dance
fanega measure of wheat
farallones small, rocky islands
fiesta party; festival
fraile friar; monk; priest
frijoles beans
gente de razón people of reason
gentile pagan
gobernador governor
hasta luego see you soon
inválido retiree; invalid
isla island
lasso rope; lariat
madre mother
mariposa butterfly
matanza slaughtering season (of animals)
mesa table; plateau
misión mission
misionero missionary
misiones missions
mostacho mustache
muchachita little girl
muchachito little boy
muchacho boy
muchacha girl

muy very
neófito neophyte; novice
nueva new
olla pot
pacificación pacification; peace
padre father; priest
peso Spanish silver coin
piastre coin, usually silver
pinole meal made of ground corn or wheat and mesquite beans
plaza town square
pobre poor
polilla moth larva
práctico ship captain
presidio military fort; garrison
provincia province
pueblo town; village
puerto port; harbor; haven
ranchería collection of huts; settlement; camp
ranchero rancher
rancho ranch; farm
real unit of Latin American currency; royal
reboso shawl
religioso monk; priest
río river
señor Mr.; sir; gentleman
señora Mrs.; madam; lady
señorita Miss; young lady
serape blanket; shawl
sí yes
siesta nap
sombrero hat
tamale dish made of cornmeal, meat, and chili wrapped in a corn husk
temescál sweat house
temporal period of stormy weather
tortilla thin, unleavened cornmeal pancake
vaquero cowboy
vara measure of length
venado deer; stag
visitador-general officer appointed by Spain to oversee a province
yerba buena good herb

FURTHER READING

The narratives contained in this anthology are only a few of the many firsthand accounts written by visitors to early California. Interested readers would do well to consult the following notable primary sources:

Bandini, José. *A Description of California in 1828*. Translated by Doris Marion Wright. Berkeley: Friends of the Bancroft Library, 1951.

Bidwell, John. *Echoes of the Past*. Chico, CA: *The Chico Advertiser*, 1914.

Colton, Walter. *Three Years in California*. New York: A. S. Barnes & Co., 1852.

Davis, William Heath. *Sixty Years in California: A History of Events and Life in California*. San Francisco: A. J. Leary, 1889.

Duhaut-Cilly, Auguste. *A Voyage to California, the Sandwich Islands, & Around the World in the Years 1826–1829*. Translated and edited by August Frugé and Neal Harlow. San Francisco: The Book Club of California, 1997.

Frémont, John Charles. *Narrative of the Exploring Expedition to the Rocky Mountains in the Year 1842*. London: Wiley and Putnam, 1846.

Malaspina, Alejandro. *Malaspina in California*. Edited by Donald C. Cutter. San Francisco: John Howell, 1960.

La Pérouse, Jean François de. *Life in a California Mission: Monterey in 1786*. Introduction and commentary by Malcolm Margolin. Berkeley: Heyday Books, 1989.

Petit-Thouars, Abel Du. *Voyage of the Venus: Sojourn in California*. Translated by Charles N. Rudkin. Los Angeles: Glen Dawson, 1956.

Pierce, Richard A. and John H. Winslow, eds., *H.M.S. Sulphur at California, 1837 and 1839*. San Francisco: Book Club of California, 1969.

Robinson, Alfred. *Life in California*. Edited by Doyce B. Nunis, Jr. New York: DaCapo Press, 1969.

Thomes, William H. *On Land and Sea: Or, California in the Years 1843, '44, and '45*. Boston: DeWolfe, Fiske, 1884.

Wilkes, Charles. *Narrative of the United States Exploring Expedition during the Years 1838, 1839, 1840, 1841, 1842*. Vol. 5. Philadelphia: Lea and Blanchard, 1845.

PERMISSIONS

Beechey, Frederick William. From *Narrative of a Voyage to the Pacific and Beering's Strait to Cooperate with the Polar Expeditions, 1825–1828.* London: 1831.

Bryant, Edwin. From *What I Saw in California.* New York: D. Appleton, 1848.

Chamisso, Adelbert von. From *A Voyage Around the World with the Romanzov Exploring Expedition in the Years 1805–1808.* Translated by Henry Kratz. Honolulu: University of Hawaii Press, 1986. Reprinted by permission of Henry Kratz.

Crespí, Juan. From *Who Discovered the Golden Gate?* Edited by Frank M. Stanger and Alan K. Brown. San Mateo, CA: San Mateo Historical Society, 1969. Reprinted by permission of the San Mateo Historical Association.

Dana, Richard Henry Jr. From *Two Years Before the Mast.* Boston: Fields, Osgood & Co., 1869.

Kemble, Edward. From *Sacramento Daily Union.* March and April, 1873.

Langsdorff, Georg von. From *Langsdorff's Narrative of the Rezanov Voyage.* San Francisco: Thomas C. Russell, 1927.

Palóu, Francisco. "The Founding of the Presidio and Mission of Our Father Saint Francis." Translated by George Ezra Dane. *California Historical Society Quarterly* 14, no. 2 (June 1935), p. 102–108. Reprinted by permission of the California Historical Society.

Rezanov, Nikolai Petrovich. From *The Rezanov Voyage to Nueva California in 1806.* San Francisco: Thomas C. Russell, 1926.

Santa María, Vicente. From *The First Spanish Entry into San Francisco Bay.* Edited by John Galvin. San Francisco: J. Howell, 1971.

Simpson, George. From *An Overland Journey Around the World, During the Years 1841 and 1842.* London: H. Colburn, 1847.

Vancouver, George. From *Vancouver in California: 1792–1794.* Vol. 1. Edited and annotated by Marguerite Eyer Wilbur. Los Angeles: Glen Dawson, 1953.

INDEX

About the Editor

Joshua Paddison is a freelance writer and research historian who lives in San Francisco. He has worked for a variety of historical institutions and publications, including the Southern Oregon Historical Society, the California Council for the Humanities, and *California History* journal. He served as chief researcher for *Gold Rush: A Literary Exploration* (Heyday Books, 1997) and worked on *Gold Fever: The Lure and Legacy of the California Gold Rush* and *A Golden State: Mining and Economic Development in Gold Rush California* (both University of California Press, 1999). He is currently a graduate student in U.S. history at San Francisco State University.